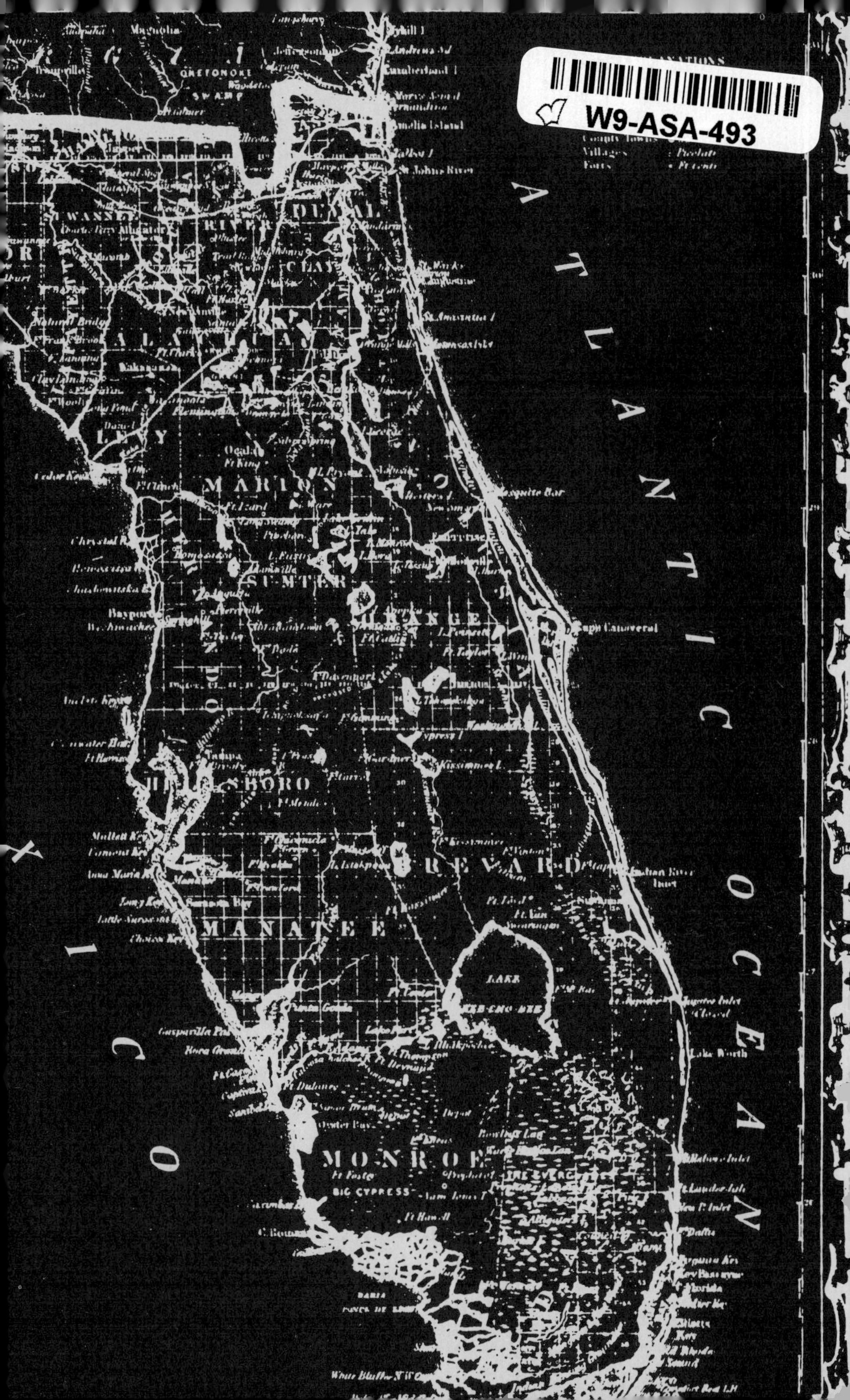
ATLANTIC
OCEAN
X I C O
DUVAL
CLAY
MARION
SUMTER
ORANGE
BREVARD
MANATEE
MONROE
BIG CYPRESS
Cape Canaveral
Mosquito Bar
Indian River Inlet
Jupiter Inlet
Lake Worth
Charlotte Harbour
Gasparilla Pass
Boca Grande
Captiva
Sanibel
Punta Gorda
Chrystal R.
Chassahowitska R.
Cedar Keys
Magnolia
Campbelton
Jefferson
Cumberland I.
Amelia Island
St. Johns River
St. Augustine
Matanzas Inlet
Natural Bridge
Ocala
Ft. King
Tampa
Bayport
Ft. Dulaney
Oyster Bay
Ft. Lauderdale
New R. Inlet
Ft. Harrell
Ft. Poinsett
Ft. Taylor
Tohopekaliga L.
Kissimmee L.
LAKE
OKEE-CHO-BEE
Villages
Forts
County Towns
EXPLANATIONS

FLORIDA DURING THE CIVIL WAR

FLORIDA DURING THE CIVIL WAR

By John E. Johns

university of florida press
gainesville, florida 1963

A UNIVERSITY OF FLORIDA PRESS BOOK

Library of Congress
Catalogue Card No. 63-17302

Printed by The Miller Press
Jacksonville, Florida

DEDICATED TO

MARTHA, JOHN, Jr., AND STEVEN

PREFACE

THIS IS THE STORY of Florida during the Civil War. Floridians seceded from the United States, joined the Confederate States, and faced the future with confidence. Secession to most Floridians was legal, logical, and justified. The majority of them hailed the creation of the Confederacy as a permanent respite from the sectional controversies which had plagued the people of the United States prior to 1860. When somber reflection replaced the early elation over secession, Floridians at first maintained their faith in the ultimate triumph of the Confederate cause. However, civilian morale rapidly deteriorated as governmental services became dislocated, casualty lists increased in length, and the effect of the blockade became more severe, thus contributing to the total collapse of the Confederacy.

My interest in this subject began as a graduate student in Professor Fletcher M. Green's course on the Old South at the University of North Carolina. This interest in southern history resulted in my doctoral dissertation, "Florida in the Confederacy," which I submitted to the University of North Carolina in 1959. The present volume includes much new material found within Florida in recent years and is a complete revision of my original dissertation.

The publication of this work has been made possible by the financial support of the Florida Civil War Centennial Committee and the state of Florida. The committee chairman, Mr. Adam G. Adams, has been most helpful in suggesting the location of source material and in serving as liaison with the Governor of Florida on publication problems.

I am particularly grateful to Professor Samuel Proctor of the University of Florida, who has assisted me in the gathering of material and illustrations and in reading the manuscript. My debt to the staff of the P. K. Yonge Library of Florida History is especially great for it was in the magnificent collections of that library that most of my sources were found. The librarians of the Florida Historical Society Library and the officials of the Florida State Library were also most helpful. The staff of the University of North Carolina Library, the Southern Historical Collection, Duke University Library, the Library of Congress, the National Archives, and the New York Public Library have likewise contributed much toward the completion of this work.

Finally, I am grateful to my wife, Martha Mauney Johns, whose strong forbearance as the wife of a graduate student and college professor has made the hours of research for this book possible.

John E. Johns
Stetson University
DeLand, Florida

CONTENTS

I

THE GATES OF HELL

ON JANUARY 10, 1861, Florida seceded from the United States. The next day, following the signing of the Ordinance of Secession, ex-Governor Richard Keith Call, a former Whig and a Unionist, was accosted by a number of jubilant Secessionists.

"Well, Governor," they shouted, "we have done it!"

"And what have you done?" asked the old man, waving his walking cane over his head. "You have opened the gates of Hell, from which shall flow the curses of the damned to sink you to perdition."[1*]

The success of the secession movement which had brought forth this ominous prediction from the old Unionist was the result of events within the nation and within Florida between 1850 and 1860. Florida had shared with the rest of the nation the economic prosperity of the 1850's. The leaders of the state devoted their energies to the problem of economic development, particularly to the construction of railroads and the effort to secure federal and state aid for the construction of railroads and other means of transportation. Political leaders like Edward Carrington Cabell and David Levy Yulee became railroad presidents. These men, and others of their class, did not devote all their energies to railroad development, but also built up plantations and slaveholdings. The number and size of the cotton plantations increased rapidly. The size of the slaveholdings was increased so that the new lands could be adequately planted and harvested. Roads were blazed out, sawmills were built, and towns grew in size and importance.[2] The value of real and personal property rose from $22,862,270 in 1850 to $82,592,641 in 1860.[3]

*Notes to Chapter I begin on page 216.

The decade of the 1850's was marked by an increase in the number of settlers coming to Florida. These settlers not only aided in the state's economic development but were to affect greatly its politics as most of them were from Georgia and South Carolina. In 1850 there had been 11,316 persons of Georgia origin and 4,470 persons of South Carolina origin in Florida; by 1860 the number of Georgia-born residents of Florida had increased to 17,550 and those from South Carolina to 8,284.[4] The effect of this large influx can be seen when a town in the rapidly expanding plantation area is studied. Gainesville, in Alachua County, had a population in 1860 of 223 white inhabitants. Ninety-seven of these had been born in South Carolina. Of the forty-five native-born Floridians in the town in 1860, over half were the children of parents born in South Carolina. All the other citizens of Gainesville, except sixteen foreign-born, were of southern birth.[5] These new settlers brought their traditions and their state-rights philosophy with them. Most of them were Democrats and remained loyal to the party and concepts of their patron saint, John C. Calhoun. It was evident by 1860 that because of the heavy infiltration of South Carolinians "the cancerous fibers of secession had already extended through the state."[6]

The rise to power of a radical South Carolina group in Florida can be partially explained by the leading position which South Carolina had taken under Calhoun and his successors in the defense of the rights of the South. The South Carolina radicals among the Florida Democrats offered a definite program and followed an aggressive policy, thereby attracting a following which grew in size and importance as crisis followed crisis in the relationship between North and South.[7]

Another factor in the triumph of the radical Democrats was the death of the Whig party. Whiggery had been a potent force in Florida politics prior to 1852. In that year Florida Democrats were careful to tone down the radicalism which had lost them the elections of 1850 and 1851, and a discreet silence was maintained on the Compromise of 1850 during the campaign. In fact, the Democratic convention passed a resolution deprecating further agitation arising from the institution of slavery, and Augustus Emmett Maxwell of the moderate wing of the party was nominated for Congress; however, James E. Broome, leader of the growing "South Carolina" radical wing of the party, succeeded in getting the nomination as the party's gubernatorial candidate.[8] Broome, a native of South Carolina, was thoroughly indoctrinated with the ideas of Calhoun. He was opposed to the Compromise and was characterized by the Whigs as a rampant fire-eater and Secessionist.[9]

The state elections in October and the general elections in November resulted in complete victory for the Democrats. However, Maxwell defeated his Whig opponent, Edward Carrington Cabell, by the slender margin of 22 votes, 4,590 to 4,568.[10] Broome was elected governor, defeating George T. Ward by a majority of 292 votes, 4,628 to 4,336. The Democrats increased their majorities in both houses of the General Assembly.[11]

The defeat in 1852 marked the end of the Whig party. Split asunder over the slavery question, the party never again was strong enough to contest a national election.[12] Many who had voted the Whig ticket went over to the Democrats and those die-hard Whigs who could not bring themselves to do this aligned themselves with such parties as the Americans and the Constitutional Unionists.[13]

The Know-Nothing or American party originated in the North as a secret society called the Supreme Order of the Star-Spangled Banner. It had as its principal program the protection of native American institutions and the Protestant faith by checking the influx of foreigners into the country and combating Catholicism. Conservatives in the South saw in the movement an organization which might be used to replace the dying Whig party. The antiforeign principles of the party appealed to the slaveholders who believed that the ranks of the abolitionists and the political power of the North were being swelled by the influx of foreigners. The emphasis on the unAmerican character of the Catholic church and its subversive influence was seen by many as an emotional issue which might divert attention from the even more explosively emotional issue of slavery.[14]

The American party was well advanced in Florida by the spring of 1855. During the first week of April, a state convention was held and secrecy abandoned. The name *American* was adopted and committees were formed to direct the party at state and local levels. In the nominations for the 1856 state election, David S. Walker was named for governor and James M. Baker for representative in Congress.[15]

The Democratic State Convention of 1856 met at Madison. Controlled by the radical wing of the party, it nominated radicals for the major offices. Madison Starke Perry, an Alachua County planter of South Carolina origin, became the party's gubernatorial candidate. George Sidney Hawkins, a West Florida lawyer, became the congressional candidate.[16]

The American party in Florida made its major effort in the simultaneous state and national race in 1856. In the final month before balloting, local issues began to dominate the electioneering. Both gubernatorial candidates were trustees of the state Internal Improvement Fund, which controlled large amounts of land that were being sold to settlers and speculators. Walker, the American party candidate, had voted against a proposal to increase the price of the lands which the Internal Improvement Fund was selling. Perry, the Democratic candidate, had voted for the increase. The Democrats charged that Walker was speculating in these lands and desired to keep the price and the resulting profit to the state low. Walker's friends charged that Perry wanted the increase so that the small farmer would be removed from competition and the large land speculators could have unopposed access to the land. Walker, as a result, emerged as the champion of the small-farmer class while Perry became the candidate of the planter and speculator.[17]

The election was hard fought. Many small farmers were lured into the fold of the American party by the advocacy of its candidate for cheap land. The defection was not large enough, however, to swing the election to the Americans. All Democratic candidates defeated their opponents by small margins. Perry won over Walker in the gubernatorial contest by a vote of 6,214 to 5,894, and Hawkins won the congressional race by a vote of 6,392 to 5,649. The Democrats also retained safe majorities in both houses of the General Assembly. In the general election of November, 1856, the Democratic candidate for President, James Buchanan, defeated Millard Fillmore by a greater majority than the party's gubernatorial and congressional candidates had received. No Florida votes were recorded for John Charles Frémont, the Republican candidate for President.[18]

There was no longer any question as to the political ascendency of the Democratic party in Florida. It had successfully welded together the growing entrepreneurial element in the state and the enlarged and increasingly influential planter group. The party had successfully withstood the small-farmer revolt and could now busy itself with the task of strengthening its position throughout the state. This was done two years later when Democratic candidates won their contests with ease, bringing the General Assembly under the control of the radical leaders.[19] As the nation entered the period of extreme sectional emotionalism generated by John Brown's raid at Harpers Ferry and the election of 1860, Florida was controlled by men who had their origins deep in the philosophy of state rights and who were outspoken in their support of southern rights.

The fight for political supremacy within the state had not dulled the interest of the people to happenings on the national scene. Floridians reacted as the rest of the nation was reacting to the issues which stirred sectional controversy. They remained loyal to their section. This loyalty was genuine, but the radical leaders were careful not to let it wane in its intensity. The press and patronage were used to keep radical concepts before the people of Florida. The opposition was effectively controlled as it could muster only three newspapers in the entire state and, of course, had no patronage. The Jacksonville *Florida Republican*, the Tallahassee *Florida Sentinel,* and the *Pensacola Gazette* were the only papers that opposed the radical Democrats.[20]

The formation of the Republican party was the primary cause for the vast popular support which aligned itself behind the Florida Democrats. As early as 1856, Republicanism was being denounced as a "fanatical organization," and threats of secession were made in case John C. Frémont, the Republican candidate, was elected President.[21] Governor James E. Broome cautioned Floridians, after the election, to remember that the election had been a contest between sections and that James Buchanan "does not go into the Presidential chair backed by the moral force of the country." "The time has come," he added, "that the South should let fanaticism know that she has made her last submission."[22]

Following John Brown's raid, in 1859, Governor Perry told the General Assembly that there was no doubt that the Republican party was responsible for the raid and that in "view of passing events" the state militia should be thoroughly organized, armed, and officered "to be able to render efficient service in cases of sudden and pressing emergency." He then called for an "eternal separation from those whose wickedness and fanaticism forbid us longer to live with them in peace and safety." Florida, Governor Perry felt, should be heard in "tones not loud but deep" and should prepare for the "emergency of the approaching Presidential election."[23]

The General Assembly, acting on these recommendations, reorganized the state militia and patrol systems.[24] The General Assembly also resolved that "in view of our national affairs the time for argument has passed, the time for action arrived." The governor was authorized to cooperate with other southern states in the protection of their rights in the event of the election of a Republican President. The governor could convene the General Assembly in extraordinary session if he should think it necessary.[25]

The people of Florida thought the time for action had come. In late 1859 and throughout 1860 voluntary military units were formed throughout the state. In 1859 the Jacksonville Light Infantry and the Pensacola Guards were organized. In early 1860 the Fernandina Rifles, the Gainesville Southern Guards, the Tampa Perry Guards, and companies at Quincy, Tallahassee, Micanopy, and Ocala, were organized. Later in the year there were extensive militia musters at which such organizations as the Jefferson Guards and the Jefferson Rifles were reviewed and presented with flags.[26]

Amid this rising martial spirit, Florida Democrats met in convention, April 9, 1860, to choose delegates for the national nominating convention at Charleston, South Carolina. Nineteen of the thirty-seven Florida counties were present or represented by proxy. The Tallahassee *Floridian and Journal* of April 14 considered this an excellent attendance because the only order of business was the selection of delegates. The convention selected six delegates, and six alternates, and passed resolutions which upheld state rights and condemned the theory of Stephen Arnold Douglas concerning the rights of slaveholders in the territories as set forth in the Freeport Doctrine. The convention did not officially express a preference for any candidate to head the national ticket; however, the individuals at the convention were free in their praise of Senator Robert Mercer Taliaferro Hunter of Virginia.[27]

When the Democratic National Convention met at Charleston the Freeport Doctrine became the focal point of discussion. Douglas' theory of slavery was bitterly opposed by the more extreme Southerners because he held that a territorial legislature might effectually exclude slavery by the simple device of failure to pass a slave code necessary to the existence of the institution. This was contrary to the theory held by Southerners and upheld by the Supreme Court in the Dred Scott decision; namely, that slave property rights had the protection of the federal Constitution and that slave property could be carried into any of the territories. The platform committee was composed of one man from each of the thirty-two states represented at the convention. After a bitter debate, the two Pacific Coast states, California and Oregon, joined with the fifteen southern states to present a majority report favoring the southern stand on the slavery issue. The fifteen northern states, however, succeeded in getting the convention to adopt their minority platform based on the Freeport Doctrine. As a result, the delegates from eight southern states, including the six from Florida, withdrew from the convention. The bolters scheduled a convention of their own for June 11 at Richmond, Virginia, to determine their program.[28]

The Florida delegates did not withdraw before they had placed a written protest before the convention. Many of the southern state delegations had foreseen the possibility of such action and had prepared written statements of withdrawal from the convention in advance of the crisis. The Florida delegation had not prepared one "and were compelled, amid the excitement, the noise, and the confusion of the hour, to give but a brief statement in justification of the proceedings they felt it their duty to adopt." It was as follows:

> The undersigned Democratic delegates from the State of Florida enter this their solemn protest against the action of the Convention in voting down the platform of the majority . . . we protest against receiving the Cincinnati Platform with the interpretation that it favors the Doctrine of Squatter Sovereignty in the territories, which doctrine, in the name of the people we represent, we repudiate.[29]

Upon their return to Florida, the delegates found that news of the momentous happenings had preceded them. Mass meetings had been held in several towns, and without exception the action of the delegates to the late Democratic convention was endorsed. Thomas Jefferson Eppes, one of the delegates, addressed a large crowd in Fernandina on his arrival from Charleston and was frequently interrupted by shouts of applause. When Eppes finished his speech, the crowd organized and adopted resolutions stating that the Florida delegation had taken the only course of action that could have saved the state from "disgraceful submission to injustice and inequality." The Putnam County Democratic Executive Committee denounced the Charleston convention as "an insult upon the South and the State of Florida," and the Alachua County Democrats, in convention assembled, condemned "the unconstitutional heresy of squatter sovereignty as insulting to the South."[30]

The Democratic State Convention reassembled at Quincy, June 4, 1860, and upheld the radical southern position. The action of the delegates at Charleston was heartily approved and delegates were chosen for the Richmond convention. John Milton, the planter from Jackson County who had been chairman of the delegation to the Charleston convention, was nominated as the party's candidate for governor. The unity that existed against the North did not carry over into state politics as Milton did not receive the nomination until the twenty-third ballot, and then only after a fierce contest.[31]

The Richmond meeting on June 11 was unsuccessful. Only South Carolina's delegates were officially accredited to it, and after two futile days the convention adjourned with all the delegates except South Carolina's going on to Baltimore where the adjourned Democratic convention reassembled on June 18. The animosity between the Charleston seceders and the Douglas men of the Northwest had not been allayed in the slightest degree, and the Democratic party remained a house divided against itself. A new walkout of southern delegates was led by Virginia. The remaining delegates nominated Stephen A. Douglas for President and Benjamin Fitzpatrick of Alabama for Vice-President. Herschel V. Johnson of Georgia accepted the nomination for Vice-President after Fitzpatrick declined it.

The Baltimore seceders, having been joined by all of the delegates to the Richmond convention except those of South Carolina, met in another hall. They adopted the southern platform and nominated John Cabell Breckinridge of Kentucky as the Presidential candidate and Joseph Lane of Oregon for Vice-President. This completed the division of the Democratic party into sectional parties. The party had been wrecked upon the rock of nonintervention with the institution of slavery in the territories.[32]

The Republican National Convention, in the meantime, had met at Chicago in May, 1860, and nominated Abraham Lincoln of Illinois as its candidate for President, and Hannibal Hamlin of Maine for Vice-President. The Republican platform demanded the exclusion of slavery from the territories but endorsed noninterference with the institution within the states. It also called for free homesteads for actual settlers and a program of protective tariffs and internal improvements. The platform was phrased so as to appeal both to the midwestern farmer and to the eastern industrialist. With the support of these groups and with the Democratic party split the Republicans could look to the elections of 1860 with great hope of victory.[33]

A fourth political party entered the elections in 1860. The Constitutional Union party, made up of old-line Whigs and Americans, met in convention at Chicago on May 9, 1860. The delegates were, for the most part, older politicians who had banded together in an effort to allay sectional animosities and in an attempt to save the Union. This platform ignored the slavery issue and appealed to "the Constitution of the Country, the union of States, and the enforcement of the laws." The Constitutional Unionists nominated John Bell of Tennessee as their candidate for President and Edward Everett of Massachusetts for Vice-President.[34]

In Florida, where the Whig party no longer existed, the Americans were branded as "Negro-worshippers," and the Independent Democrats discredited by a railroad scandal, the opposition to the Democrats rallied to the banner of the Constitutional Unionists. This opposition group declared itself "not less sensitive to the wrongs of the South as threatened and perpetrated by the Republican party, or less decided to oppose them to the uttermost, than those pseudochampions of the South, the Democrats."[35] The Constitutional Union party, the non-Democrats felt, was the only banner around which the conservative elements of the nation could rally.

The Constitutional Union State Convention met in Quincy on June 27, 1860, with delegates from twenty-seven counties present. The convention endorsed the party's national candidates and platform. Edward A. Hopkins of Duval County was nominated as candidate for governor, and Benjamin F. Allen of Leon County for Congress.[36] The Constitutional Unionists were prepared to wage an intensive political campaign in an effort to take political power from the radical Democrats.

The real political battle in Florida was between the Constitutional Union party, which represented a coalition of the old-line Whig, conservative anti-Secessionists, and the radicals, who controlled Florida Democrats. There was no state Republican party organization, and Stephen A. Douglas was so discredited within Florida that only a few voices in East Florida were raised in his defense.[37]

The Democrats did not underestimate their opposition. They carried on an intensive campaign which saw John Milton, the gubernatorial candidate, speak in almost every settlement in the state.[38] The Democrats also had a tremendous advantage because a great majority of the newspapers gave them their support. Eighteen of Florida's twenty-four newspapers gave Breckinridge and Lane their backing and actively supported the state ticket. Only one paper, the *Jacksonville Mirror*, supported Douglas. Five papers, the *Pensacola Gazette*, the Tallahassee *Florida Sentinel*, the *Milton Courier*, the *Marianna Enterprise*, and the Lake City *Independent Press*, supported the Constitutional Union ticket.[39] These latter journals had formerly been Whig papers and, with the exception of the *Independent Press*, were all in West Florida.

The radical Democrats used this overwhelming support of the press effectively. They characterized the Constitutional Union party as being composed "entirely of fossil Whigs" who were attempting to use the split in the Democratic party to regain power,[40] and ridiculed its platform as being cowardly, shirking all the issues of the day.[41] But the sectional controversy was used as the principal issue. Democratic editors used to good account the argument that any person who worked for the election of Douglas or Bell was actually antisouthern, since neither could be elected, and the only candidate to benefit from such activity would be Abraham Lincoln. The editor of the *Cedar Key Telegraph* phrased it this way: "the Douglas-Bell men of the South, like *Wendell Phillips*, have gone crazy—they have entered into a 'covenant with death and a league with hell,' and are doing all within their power to elect Mr. Lincoln."[42] Constitutional Union speakers were satirized as "Union-Shriekers" who should certainly see their folly in entering the election campaign as "true Southerners."[43]

The Democrats won the elections. In October they won a clear-cut victory in the state election. The Constitutional Unionists, however, received a surprisingly large vote considering the factors of the sectional strife and the vituperation and invective of the Democratic press. John Milton, the Democratic candidate for governor, defeated Edward Hopkins by a vote of 6,994 to 5,248. The Democrats won the other races with greater majorities and also maintained a safe majority in both houses of the General Assembly.[44] In the national election of November 7, 1860, the Breckinridge and Lane ticket carried the state by an even larger majority. Breckinridge received 8,543 votes, Bell 5,437, and Douglas only 367 votes. Abraham Lincoln polled no votes in Florida.[45]

Florida Democrats had little opportunity to rejoice over their victory. Word soon arrived that Abraham Lincoln had been elected President of the United States. The "Black Republicans" had won the White House. The crisis was now at hand.

The election of Lincoln did not come as a complete surprise to Floridians. The possibility of his election and the course that Florida and the South should take if he were elected had been fully discussed in the papers of the state. As early as August 23, 1860, the Fernandina *East Floridian* had stated that "if in consequence of Northern fanaticism the irrepressible conflict must come we are prepared to meet it." The degree of preparation of the state was questioned by Dr. Holmes Steele, mayor of Jacksonville. Dr. Steele, a physician, newspaper editor, and captain of the Jacksonville Light Infantry, felt that the "times . . . are ominous" and that Florida should "in peace prepare for war." The most immediate duty the state had, he declared, was to arm itself for the protection of its citizens against "fanaticism."[46]

"What shall Florida do?" asked the *St. Augustine Examiner* when discussing the likelihood of Lincoln's election. "Secede, of course!" was the immediate answer supplied to the question.[47] This opinion was shared by Governor Perry. On November 9, 1860, he wrote to Governor William H. Gist of South Carolina saying:

> I have industriously sought to learn the public mind in this State in the event of the election of Lincoln, and am proud to say Florida is ready to wheel into line with the gallant Palmetto State, or any other Cotton State or States in any course which she or they may . . . adopt. . . . Florida may be unwilling to subject herself to the charge of temerity or immodesty by leading off, but will most assuredly co-operate with or follow the lead of any single Cotton State which may secede.[48]

The people reacted as the radical leaders expected. Lincoln was burned in effigy, and in St. Augustine a "secession flag" was raised and "blue cockades" were worn by many of the citizens.[49] Vigilance committees were formed in many localities, often of the "most influential and responsible citizens," for the purpose of "keeping a strict watch upon the movements of strangers, and our slave population."[50] Demands for immediate secession began to appear in the press and one of the leading papers of the state ran a platform, "The secession of The State of Florida, The Dissolution of the Union, The Formation of a Southern Confederacy," on its editorial page for four consecutive issues.[51] Mass meetings of citizens were held in many towns to protest the election of Lincoln. In Alachua County, the home of radical Governor Perry, two such meetings demanded secession, the immediate arming of the state, cooperation with any and all southern states that seceded, and immediate withdrawal of the Florida delegation to Congress.[52]

Governor Perry did not have to call a special session of the General Assembly. It convened in regular session on November 26, 1860, and the next day the governor delivered his annual message. He informed the legislature that the long awaited crisis was now at hand and that "further forbearance . . . would justify the allegation that we are afraid to resist." The only hope left to the South, he said, was immediate secession. Any attempt to postpone it until some overt act had been committed against the South by Lincoln would be to court the fate of the inhabitants of Santo Domingo.

Governor Perry recommended that the General Assembly take immediate action to meet the crisis. He asked that it issue a call for a convention of the people of the state, revise the militia laws to make them more efficient, and appropriate $100,000 as a military fund "to be expended as fast as the public necessities may require."[53]

The General Assembly responded quickly. Bills were immediately introduced providing for a state convention on January 3, 1861, and for the revision of the state militia laws. The act calling for the state convention passed unanimously after the radical Democrats had defeated attempts to postpone the date until January 17 and to have any action taken by the convention submitted to the people for ratification.[54] The General Assembly also appropriated $100,000 for the purchase of arms and ammunition. Governor Perry left immediately after adjournment for South Carolina to arrange for the purchase of military supplies and to confer with secessionist leaders who had gathered there to observe the South Carolina secession convention.[55]

In Florida, amid the popular demonstrations and legislative action, the only blunt and outspoken opposition came from Richard Keith Call. The ex-governor and leader of the opposition to the radical Democrats published an *Address to the People of Florida* in which he denounced secession as "treason against our Constitutional government." He maintained that the election of Lincoln was not justification for secession, and asked, "Is it not a fact that the present disunion movement in Florida is not because of the election of Mr. Lincoln but from a long cherished hate of the Union by the leading politicians of the state?" Call maintained that the calling of a convention of the people at this time could only produce "the most fatal consequences." He appealed to the patriotism of the people and implored them to remain calm. Fervently he asserted, "I pray that in the hour of death, the Stars and Stripes may still wave over me, and wave forever over our whole united country." Call's words went unheeded.

The legislation providing for a convention was received by Governor Perry on November 30, 1860, and he immediately issued a proclamation calling for the election of delegates. The convention was held at Tallahassee on January 3, 1861. Under the provisions of the act, the election of delegates was to be held on Saturday, December 22, 1860, under the same rules as prescribed for election of members to the General Assembly. Each senatorial district was to elect a delegate, and each county was to elect as many delegates as it had members in the lower house of the General Assembly. The convention's task was to take "into consideration the dangers incident to the position of this State in the Federal Union . . . and to amend the Constitution of the State of Florida, so far as the same . . . may be necessary . . . to take care that . . . Florida shall suffer no detriment." A majority of the convention was to constitute a quorum.[56]

The great distances and poor transportation facilities within Florida presented a problem to the radical Democrats. They wanted to be certain that the radical counties of Dade and Monroe, at the southern tip of Florida, were legally represented at the convention. Many political leaders had expressed doubt that the returns from these two counties could be received, canvassed, the official results announced, and the duly elected delegates gotten to Tallahassee on time. Extraordinary measures were ordered by the General Assembly. The governor was required to have a special messenger at each precinct in the two counties. This messenger was to take the certified results from his precinct to the probate judge of Monroe County at Key West on December 26 before the time for the steamer to sail for St. Marks. The probate judge and three other citizens of good repute were to canvass the vote and issue certificates of election to the winners in time for the delegates to board the steamer. This certificate would allow them to take their seats in the convention.[57]

The issue in the campaign for the election of convention delegates was not that of secession against the preservation of the Union; it was immediate secession against cooperative secession. Because of economic and geographic ties with Georgia and Alabama, the "cooperativists" desired Florida to secede only after those states had seceded. There was also some scattered sentiment against secession at any time, but this pro-Union feeling was usually confined to the privacy of letters to intimates, or voiced publicly with so many qualifications and explanations that it was not an issue in the elections.[58] The one exception was Richard Keith Call.

As the election campaign progressed, it became obvious that those favoring immediate secession were gaining a distinct advantage over their opponents. The very pressure of events and the excitement of the time favored the more radical stand.[59] Radicalism was also aided by strong ecclesiastical support. Francis Huger Rutledge, Episcopal bishop of Florida, was a rabid Secessionist and offered a contribution of $500 toward defraying the expenses of the government when, by an ordinance of secession, Florida should become an independent republic.[60] The Florida Baptist State Convention, which met at Monticello in the early part of December, 1860, passed a resolution to the effect that the integrity of the South should be maintained even if it meant secession.[61]

Fear of war did not deter the radicals. Those who desired secession and feared war could conveniently convince themselves and others that there would be no war as a result of withdrawal from the Union.[62] Others openly stated that war would result if Florida seceded, but welcomed the prospect with elation. A young man of Fernandina wrote to his fiancée in Virginia, "We are anxious for a bout with the North . . . and are perfectly willing to fight."[63]

As the election date neared, the momentous issue to be decided began to invade even the homes of the people, dividing many families. Susan Bradford Eppes reported that her father, a rabid Secessionist, believed that secession could be accomplished peacefully while one of her brothers, Junius, a strong Union man, believed that war was inevitable. Her mother believed in gradual, compensated emancipation. Family division could be tolerated by the radicals but opposition from others was not. Employees were dismissed for disagreeing with the politics of their employers and at least one New England tutor was transported by "the carriage in which she had taken so many pleasant rides" to the station in time "to catch the first train out of Tallahassee" because she opposed secession.[64]

When the election was held on December 22, these elements plus the fact that all election machinery was in the hands of the Secessionists made the result a foregone conclusion. All that those opposing secession could hope for was that the "cooperative" Secessionists would win enough votes to postpone actual withdrawal from the Union. If the action was postponed, many hoped that the policy of President-elect Lincoln would be conciliatory enough to remove the feeling that secession was unavoidable.[65] This hope was doomed to failure, but it was to give the radicals many anxious moments.

The Convention of the People of Florida assembled at Tallahassee on January 3, 1861. The town was so crowded with politicians from neighboring states, as well as from Florida, that the two hotels could not accommodate everyone. The out-of-state visitors constituted a powerful lobby for immediate secession. Among them were Edmund Ruffin of Virginia, famous as an agricultural reformer and rabid Secessionist, and Edward C. Bullock of Alabama, and Leonidas W. Spratt of South Carolina, sent by their states as official commissioners to Florida.[66]

The convention assembled in the hall of the House of Representatives and John C. Pelot of Alachua County was selected as temporary chairman. On taking the chair, he addressed the convention upon the gravity of the situation and the reasons for convening it. He stressed that this was no ordinary occasion, for "Northern fanaticism has endangered our liberties and institutions," and the election of Abraham Lincoln, "a wild abolitionist," had destroyed all hope for the future. The purpose of the convention, he declared, was "to devise the best means for our security"; this was a grave responsibility which must be met with "calmness and deliberation." Rashness, he felt, might prove disastrous. Bishop Rutledge then invoked divine guidance upon the convention in order that it might "perceive the right path and steadfastly walk therein . . . and . . . aim supremely at the fulfillment of their solemn duty."[67]

The convention adjourned over January 4 to meet again on the fifth. There was a twofold reason for this action: first, President James Buchanan had set that day aside as one of fasting and prayer because of the impending political crisis; and second, the radicals were not certain of their convention strength and desired more time to rally their forces, some of whom had not yet arrived because of poor transportation facilities.[68]

When the convention reassembled on January 5, the process of permanent organization was immediately begun. John C. McGehee, a large slaveholder and resident of Madison County, was chosen president. His background and personality were typical of many delegates. He was a South Carolinian by birth and lived in a county settled largely by South Carolinians. He was a pious Christian who was convinced of the moral righteousness of slavery and the southern cause. For him this sentiment had found expression in radical political affiliations.[69] In his address to the convention, McGehee sounded a ringing call for immediate secession, and implored the delegates to keep "the faith" with the people who had elected them. This could best be done, he declared, by placing the people of Florida "in a position of safety above the power and beyond the reach of their enemies."[70]

After the presidential address the convention proceeded with its organization. A secretary, assistant secretaries, a sergeant-at-arms, and other officers were elected, and various standing committees were provided for. The president was to appoint the committee members, and each committee was to occupy itself with some contemplated constitutional change. The mere fact that these committees were appointed to busy themselves with such problems before the Ordinance of Secession was passed shows that the radicals knew that their majority was large enough to take any action which they desired. That action was, of course, immediate secession.

The convention also received official notification from Governor Perry that commissioners from the "sister states" of Alabama and South Carolina were in town and desired to "confer and consult with the people of Florida in Convention assembled." A committee was appointed to confer with the commissioners and learn their pleasure. It was desired that they would address the convention on Monday, January 7. A committee was also appointed to extend to Edmund Ruffin, who did not come in an official capacity, the privilege of the convention floor.

After the convention had organized and made arrangements to receive the visiting Secessionists, it turned to its main concern, the question of Florida's future relations with the national government. Actually the question was how best to sever relations with the national government because the convention had met for the purpose of removing Florida from the Union.

Two plans of secession were offered. The first, by George W. Parkhill, would refer any action of the convention regarding secession to the people in a popular referendum, the vote to be taken only after Alabama and Georgia had taken definite action on secession. This was the plan formulated by the conservative cooperationists and had as its chief purpose delay, but it was tabled by the convention. The other plan, offered by the radical federal judge, McQueen McIntosh, would have the convention declare secession a constitutional right, that "existing causes are such as to compel the state of Florida to . . . exercise that right," and that the convention had the power to act for the people of Florida. This was the radical plan and would most assuredly, if adopted, bind the convention to immediate secession. This plan was also tabled, but the convention ordered one hundred copies of it printed, so that it could be discussed the following Monday.

On Monday, January 7, before the discussion of the two secession plans, the convention heard addresses by Edward C. Bullock, commissioner from Alabama, Leonidas W. Spratt, commissioner from South Carolina, and Edmund Ruffin. There was scarcely standing room as these three Secessionists spoke. Spratt read the South Carolina secession ordinance to the members of the convention, and then read the address of the committee of the state of South Carolina, "On Relations of the Slave-holding States of North America." He concluded with an address of his own on the action and policy of South Carolina.[71] Spratt made a deep impression on his audience as he spoke out strongly for secession and his remarks aroused wild enthusiasm. The next day nearly every convention member wore a rosette of palmetto, as an indication of his determination to stand by South Carolina.[72]

On the afternoon following the speeches of the commissioners and of the distinguished guest, Edmund Ruffin, the convention returned to the debate on the resolutions of Judge McQueen McIntosh. These resolutions were adopted and Florida was officially committed to a concept of the Union consistent with the contemplated action of secession. Their adoption also meant that the radicals had won a signal victory for immediate secession, for the resolutions declared the right of the convention to act for the people of Florida. There would be no troublesome popular vote taken on the question of secession. Before adjourning the session, President McGehee appointed a select committee of thirteen to prepare ordinances, including an ordinance of secession, for the consideration of the convention. Eight members of this committee were immediate

Secessionists and five were cooperationists. The committee also included a fair geographic representation of all sections of the state.[73]

While the committee drafted its ordinances, the convention continued routine business. Tallahassee remained in a great state of excitement. The halls of the capitol were crowded day and night. Citizens, "even ladies," attended the various meetings held by committees and other working divisions of the convention. While the ordinances were being drafted, dispatches arrived reporting that Louisiana had called a convention and that Mississippi was about to pass an ordinance of secession. This aroused even greater excitement as many Floridians wanted the honor of being the second state to secede. "Make haste, make haste, or they will get ahead of us," became the cry of the Secessionists.[74]

On January 9, the select committee submitted its report on secession and the ordinance of secession which it had prepared. The report on secession set forth the compact theory of the national government as the basis of secession and declared that since Florida had been admitted to the Union "on an equal footing with the original states in all respects whatsoever" and was now being denied that equality, the committee felt that Florida should resume all the rights which she had delegated to the federal government and declare herself an independent nation.

The five cooperationist members of the committee did not sign the report; but they did not offer a resolution of their own. Hence, no debate occurred until after the reading of the ordinance of secession. The ordinance, as prepared by the committee, was too ambiguous to satisfy the convention. Without specifically mentioning secession, it simply provided that the "Constitution of the United States, the treaties and laws heretofore made in pursuance thereof . . . so far as the same can be applicable to a single State, shall remain and continue in full force in this State, until . . . altered or repealed."

The convention, in committee of the whole, refused to accept so indefinite an ordinance. Instead, the drafting was referred to the committee of the judiciary with instructions to report an ordinance within an hour. At the end of the given time, the following ordinance was reported:

We the people of the State of Florida in Convention assembled, do solemnly ordain, publish, and declare,

That the State of Florida hereby withdraws herself from the

Confederacy of States existing under the name of the United States of America, and from the existing Government of the said States; and that all political connection between her and the Government of the said States ought to be, and the same is hereby totally annulled, and said Union of States dissolved; and the State of Florida is hereby declared a Sovereign and Independent Nation; and that all ordinances heretofore adopted, in so far as they create or recognize said Union, are rescinded; and all laws or parts of laws in force in this State, in so far as they recognized or assented to said Union, be and they are hereby repealed.

When this ordinance was considered for passage, the cooperationists, led by George T. Ward of Leon County and Abraham K. Allison of Gadsden County, attempted to amend it so that the actual secession of the state would be delayed. Allison would have kept the ordinance from becoming effective until after Alabama and Georgia had seceded, or, if they did not secede, until it had been approved by the voters of the state. This effort was defeated by a convention vote of forty-two to twenty-seven. Ward offered an amendment which would have delayed secession until after Georgia and Alabama seceded, but which did not include the approval of the question by the people of Florida. This was defeated by the surprisingly close vote of thirty-nine to thirty. Three other amendments of similar content were offered but were defeated by slightly larger margins.[75] Seeing that their cause was hopeless, the cooperationists offered no more amendments.

A study of the votes on the amendments shows that twenty-one delegates voted for all five of the amendments. These delegates came largely from the old Whig counties of Middle and West Florida. The votes of Escambia, Walton, and Jackson counties in West Florida were cast solidly for the amendments. On the other hand, the delegates from Washington, Holmes, and Franklin counties of West Florida voted for immediate secession. The delegates from Wakulla and Gadsden counties in Middle Florida voted for delay as did four of the five delegates from Leon County, the largest slaveholding county in the state. The other votes for the delay of secession came from scattered sections of East and South Florida.[76] Thus it can be seen that the convention did not show any division as to sectionalism in the state or factionalism within the ranks of the planters, artisans, or small farmers. But opinion in the state, as expressed by the vote, shows that Florida east of the Suwannee River was more radical than Florida west of that river. It is also significant that radicalism was strongest in the more newly developed and frontier areas of the state where the number of slaves was not large. The radical in Florida feared abolition as much for its effect upon his social system as he feared the loss of slave property.

Every member of the convention was present on January 10, when the vote on the adoption of the ordinance was taken. Of the sixty-nine votes cast, sixty-two were for, and seven against, its adoption.[77] At twenty-two minutes past twelve the ordinance was declared adopted. When the vote was announced, "the applause was deafening—men whooped and women clapped their hands." Outside the hall men embraced each other or clasped hands. Many exclaimed, "My heart's wish is fulfilled—I am ready to die now."[78]

The Ordinance of Secession was then enrolled on parchment and bound with blue ribbon. The honor of embellishing the parchment which contained "The Declaration of Independence of The Sovereign State of Florida" went to Miss Elizabeth M. Eppes, a native of Florida and a lineal descendant of Thomas Jefferson. Miss Eppes accepted the honor "in behalf of the ladies . . . of Florida who," she assured the convention, "go heart and hand into the cause."[79] The convention adjourned until the next day, January 11, when the signing of the embellished ordinance would constitute the principal order of business.

An abortive effort to stay the rush to secession was held on the evening of January 10. A meeting called by Richard Keith Call was held at Lake Jackson Church for the purpose of rallying the people "around their allegiance" to the United States. Some three to four hundred people, "whose heart beat time to the music of the Union," attended. It was too late, however, for word of the passage of the Ordinance of Secession reached the group just before the assembly came to order. Thus the meeting, designed to invoke and encourage Union sentiment, turned into obsequies for that Union.

For those attending, it was a sad occasion. Twenty-three young girls "representing the sisterhood of the states" sang for the last time the songs "Hail Columbia" and "The Star-Spangled Banner." Several speeches were delivered, but having received word that the convention had adopted the secession ordinance, the people realized that "it was too late to threaten and there was nothing to promise, but there were solemn warnings in touching pathos." The ladies of Concordia had made a beautiful United States flag that was displayed. When the meeting adjourned, the flag was given to an elderly Mason to be placed with the "jewels" of the Concordia Masonic Lodge. Significant of the times was the fact that only three men had the courage to drive out from Tallahassee to attend the meeting.[80]

On January 11, convention members marched from the assembly hall to the east portico of the capitol. There, in the presence of the governor-elect, the General Assembly, the Supreme Court, the members of the governor's cabinet, and a large crowd of citizens, sixty-four of the sixty-nine members of the convention affixed their signatures to the Ordinance of Secession. The occasion was not without mixed emotions. When George T. Ward, later to fight and die as a Confederate soldier, signed the ordinance, he declared, "When I die I want it inscribed upon my tombstone that I was the last man to give up the ship." In contrast, the Reverend James B. Owens loudly stated while signing, "Unlike my friend Colonel Ward, I want it inscribed on my tombstone that I was the FIRST man to quit the old rotten hulk." As the last delegate signed, a great cheer went up from the crowd.

There were no cheers from Richard Keith Call, however. Amid the wild celebration he sat with his head bowed while tears streamed down his face.[81] To him the secession of Florida was no victory to be celebrated; rather it was an event which was to "open the gates of Hell."

Secession was celebrated in towns and villages throughout the state. In Tallahassee there were parades, salutes were fired, speeches were made, and there were other manifestations of popular jubilation over Florida's withdrawal from the Union.[82] In Madison, which had been settled by South Carolinians, the celebration lasted well into the night. Many prominent men publicly offered to drink "all the blood spilt in any struggle with the North."[83] Enthusiasm remained high for days and it became a common occurrence for passengers on a train to get off at a railroad station, listen to a fiery speech by some prominent passenger, resume their seats, and continue their journey.[84]

The Unionists did not recant following secession. They felt that they had been robbed of victory because the convention had refused to submit the Ordinance of Secession to popular vote; they believed that the people would have voted it down. Surly looks passed between Unionist and Secessionist, and little care was taken to conceal their mutually bitter feelings. The policy of the Unionists soon became one of cooperation, however, so that the radicals might carry out their plans "without a chance to blame us for the awful responsibility they have assumed."[85] This policy of cooperation remained after hostilities began, and many men of Union sentiment died upon the battlefield as Confederate soldiers.

The secession of Florida was now a reality. It had been the logical action for the state to take. Florida's rapid economic and social development during the fifteen years before 1860 had been along the traditional lines of a staple-crop economy with its accompanying social structure. Florida was linked to the South geographically, economically, and culturally. Therefore, her interests were with the South. The rise of the radical Secessionists in the state was but a manifestation of the realization of this fact by the population. Whether or not Florida would secede had actually been settled in the elections of 1856 with the triumph of the radical wing of the Democratic party. The election of Lincoln merely made secession easier and quicker by destroying the position of the moderates.

Floridians congratulated themselves on the fact that a great revolution had taken place with very little inconvenience to anyone. To them the future was bright. The struggle just finished would only serve to "brighten the beams of a glorious day."[86]

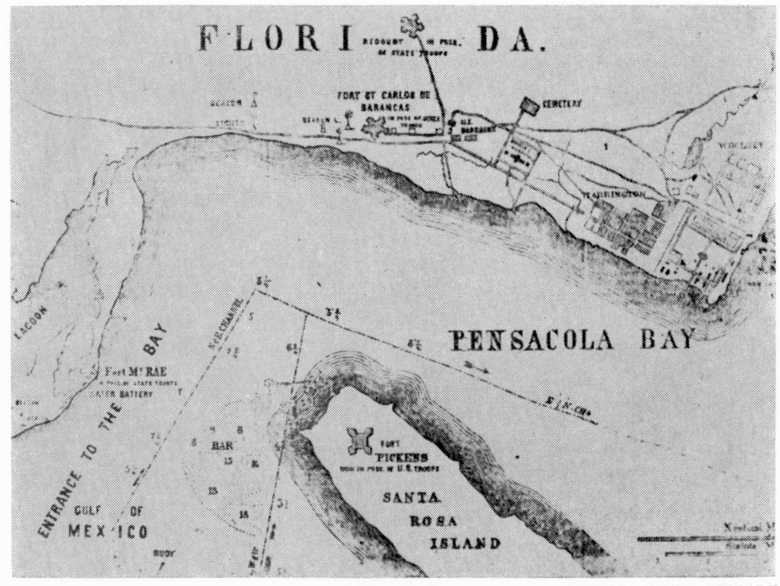

FLORIDA STATE LIBRARY

Pensacola Harbor and Fort Pickens

Fort Pickens, on Santa Rosa Island, in Pensacola Bay

FLORIDA STATE LIBRARY

MAJ.-GEN. W. W. LORING
BRIG.-GEN. T. W. BREVARD
MAJ.-GEN. J. P. ANDERSON
BRIG.-GEN. W. S. WALKER

BRIG.-GEN. ROBERT BULLOCK
BRIG.-GEN. JOS. FINEGAN
BRIG.-GEN. WM. MILLER
MAJ.-GEN. M. L. SMITH

BRIG.-GEN. W. G. M. DAVIS
BRIG.-GEN. J. J. FINLEY
BRIG.-GEN. FRANCIS A. SHOUP
BRIG.-GEN. E. A. PERRY

General Edmund Kirby Smith

Captain J. J. Dickison
(from *Dickison and His Men*)

THE NATIONAL ARCHIVES

CONFEDERATE SHORE BATTERY DEPLOYED AGAINST FORT PICKENS

THE FEDERAL ATTACK UPON SCHOONER *Judah* IN PENSACOLA HARBOR, SEPTEMBER 14, 1861, WAS THE FIRST BLOODSHED IN FLORIDA.

FLORIDA STATE LIBRARY

THE NATIONAL ARCHIVES

FEDERAL FORCES OCCUPYING JACKSONVILLE

FROM *The New York-Illustrated News,* 1862

NATIONAL TROOPS MARCHING THROUGH SECOND STREET, NEW FERNANDINA, FLORIDA, FROM A SKETCH BY "OUR OWN SPECIAL ARTIST."

FEDERAL PICKET BOAT ATTACKED NEAR FERNANDINA BY CONFEDERATE SHARPSHOOTERS STATIONED IN TREES

FROM WILSON, *The Black Phalanx*

Florida State University Library

Madison Starke Perry

Florida State University Library

Abraham Kyrkendal Allison

John Milton

Florida State University Library

Richard Keith Call

(*Florida Historical Quarterly*)

Stephen Russell Mallory
Secretary of the Navy of the Confederate States

(morris, *Florida Handbook*)

FROM *Dickison and His Men*

FIGHT AT NO. 4, NEAR CEDAR KEYS

BATTLE OF GAINESVILLE

FROM *Dickison and His Men*

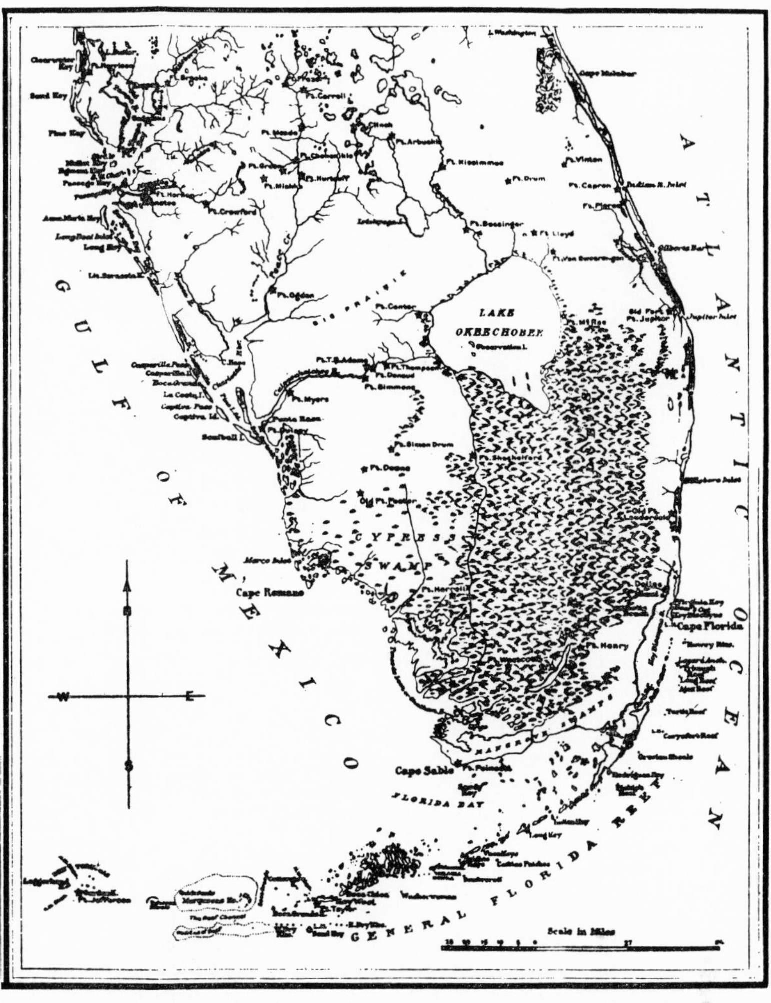

Area patrolled by Federal East Gulf Blockading Squadron

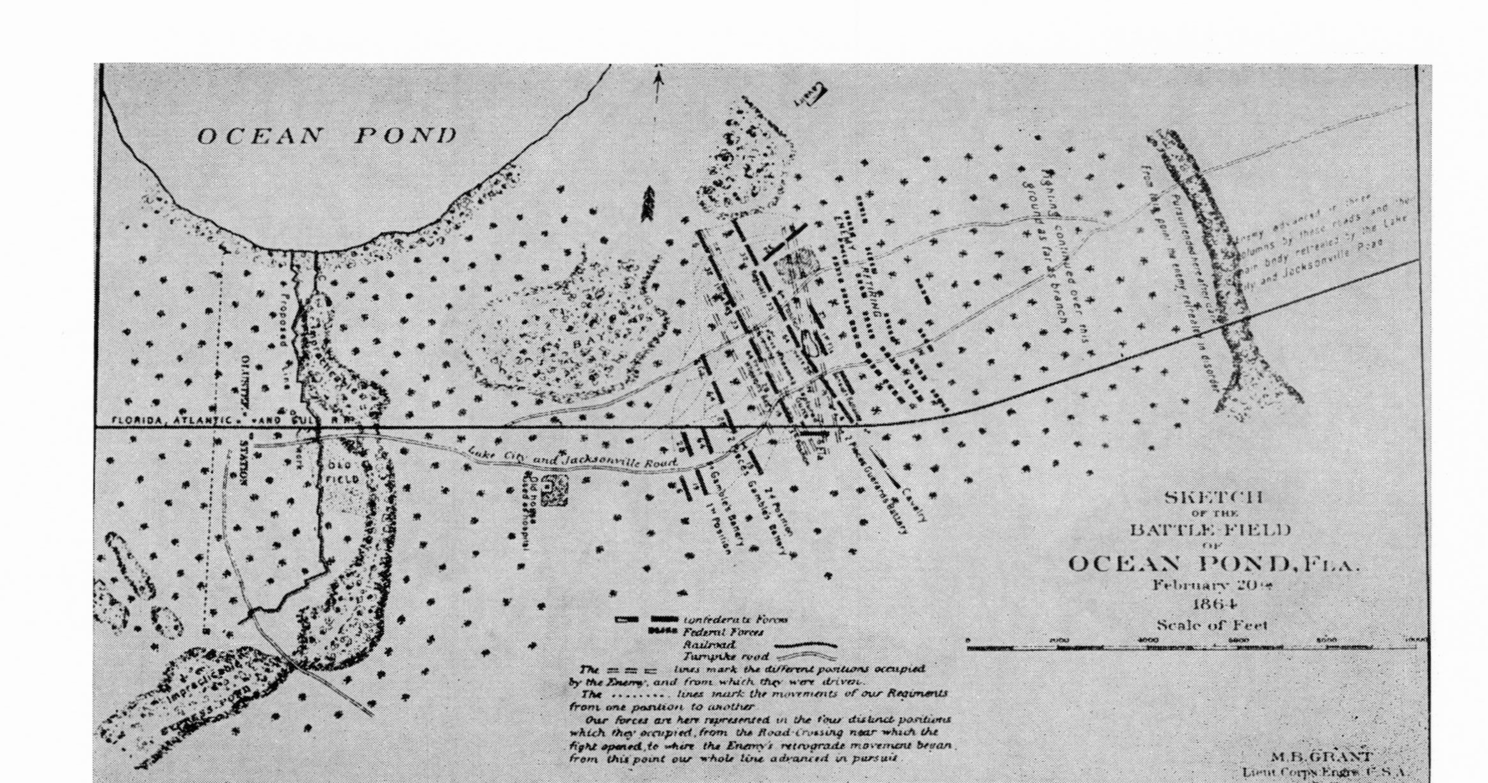

OCEAN POND
SKETCH OF THE BATTLE-FIELD OF OCEAN POND, FLA.
February 20th 1864
Scale of Feet
FLORIDA, ATLANTIC AND GULF R.R.
Lake City and Jacksonville Road
OLUSTEE STATION
Proposed Line
Impracticable
OLD FIELD
BAY
Old house used as hospital
Fighting continued over this ground as far as branch
Pursuit ended here after dark
From this point the enemy retreated in disorder
ENEMY RETIRING
Cavalry
Gamble's Battery 1st Position
2 Pieces Gamble's Battery 2d Position
2 Pieces Guerard's Battery
Confederate Forces
Federal Forces
Railroad
Turnpike road
The = = = lines mark the different positions occupied by the Enemy, and from which they were driven.
The .... lines mark the movements of our Regiments from one position to another.
Our forces are here represented in the four distinct positions which they occupied, from the Road-Crossing near which the fight opened, to where the Enemy's retrograde movement began, from this point our whole line advanced in pursuit.
M.B. GRANT
Lieut. Corps Engrs. C.S.A.
Del.

FROM *Dickison and His Men*

BATTLE OF OLUSTEE

POSITION OF CONFEDERATE AND FEDERAL FORCES

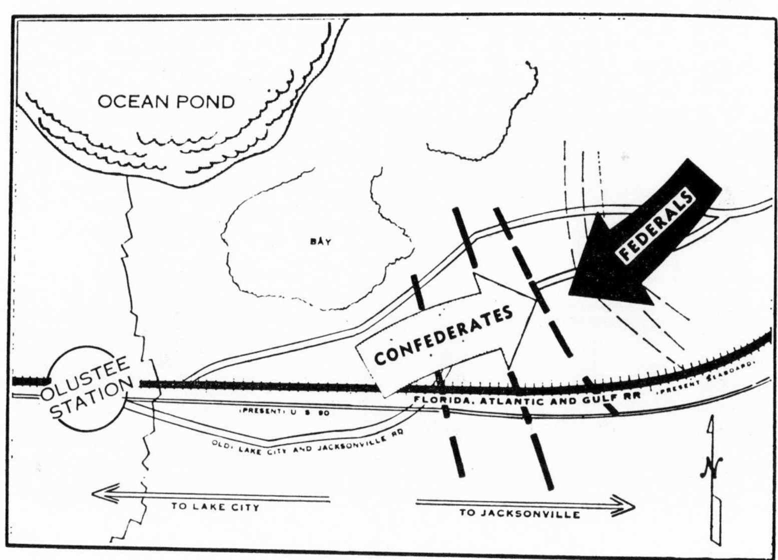

FROM *Dickison and His Men*

RECROSSING THE ST. JOHNS RIVER WITH PRISONERS, WAGONS, AND OTHER CAPTURED STORES

THE POST QUARTERMASTER'S HEADQUARTERS DURING THE FEDERAL OCCUPATION OF ST. AUGUSTINE IN 1864

THE NATIONAL ARCHIVES

II

FOR WHOM DO YOU CONSENT . . . ?

WHEN SECESSION APPEARED INEVITABLE, the Florida senators at Washington, David Levy Yulee and Stephen Russell Mallory, had started to prepare for the possibility of war. Realizing that the seizure of all United States forts within Florida and the raising of state troops would become an immediate necessity upon secession, the two senators gathered information that would aid Florida in accomplishing these two acts.

On December 21, 1860, Yulee wrote to Secretary of War John Buchanan Floyd, requesting the name and rank of all officers in the United States Army who had been appointed from Florida.[1]* This information was received and undoubtedly sent to the secession leaders in Florida, probably to Governor Perry. On January 2, 1861, Yulee and Mallory jointly requested that the war department inform them as to the strength of the garrisons at the various military posts in the state and the amount of arms and ammunition at the various forts and the arsenal. This information was denied to them on the grounds that it was not in the best interests of the service to make the information public.[2] Yulee, realizing the need for haste, wrote to the secession convention at Tallahassee that "the *immediately* important thing to be done is the occupation of the forts and arsenal in Florida. The naval station and fort at Pensacola are *first* in consequence." He felt that Georgia would cooperate by sending a force to Pensacola after the state seceded. He feared, however, that the federal government would soon reinforce the forts and cautioned that no time should be lost.[3]

The leaders of the convention had also considered the problem of the forts and decided not to delay their seizure. Taking advantage

*Notes to Chapter II begin on page 219.

of the adjournment of the convention over January 4, the day of fasting and prayer, the radical leaders held an informal and confidential meeting at which they authorized the governor to seize Fort Marion at St. Augustine and the arsenal near Chattahoochee.[4]

Acting upon their authority, Governor Perry on January 5 ordered a Colonel Dunn to raise a company of picked men and seize the arsenal and its supplies. He was cautioned to act with secrecy and discretion *but was given* authority to call out the entire Seventh Regiment of Florida Militia if it was needed. Similar orders were issued concerning the seizure of Fort Marion.

On the morning of January 6, four days before the formal secession of the state, the Quincy Guards seized the arsenal near Chattahoochee. Ordnance Sergeant Powell, in command, notified the federal authorities that he had surrendered the arsenal because his forces were too weak to defend it. He attempted to save honor by first refusing to surrender the keys to the magazine and the armory, but after communication with Governor Perry, Colonel Dunn insisted that the keys also be surrendered.[5] "If I had had a force equal or even one-half the strength of yours," Powell is reported to have said to Dunn, "I'll be damned if you would have entered that gate. You see I have but three men."[6]

Across the state at St. Augustine a company of 125 state artillerymen marched resolutely on Fort Marion in the early daylight hours of January 7. When asked by what authority they were acting, an aide-de-camp of the governor showed Perry's letter of instructions to seize the fort, directing him to use force if necessary. No force was needed as the entire garrison of the fort, consisting of one lonely sergeant, well advanced in years, decided "upon reflection . . . that the only alternative . . . was to deliver up the keys, under protest, and demand a receipt for the property."[7]

The seizure of these two relatively unimportant garrisons boosted the morale of the Tallahassee convention but the rest of the South was not impressed. The *Charleston Mercury* spoke for many Southerners when it published an open word "to our friends in Florida." "There are two powerful strongholds . . . in Florida—Pensacola and Key West." These should be seized and held, the paper asserted, because there were probably "no fortresses along our Southern Coast more important than those of Florida."[8]

The importance of these facts had also been foreseen by Federal officers. As early as November 10, 1860, Captain Montgomery C.

Meigs, of the United States Engineers at Tortugas, was calling for reinforcements to be moved into the forts at Key West, Tortugas, and Pensacola. Unless this was done immediately, he feared that "a few ardent, desperate men," seeing those great fortifications unoccupied by troops, "may emulate the fame of Ethan Allen" by seizing some of the fortifications.[9]

On December 11, 1860, Captain John M. Brannan, commanding at Key West Barracks, informed the war department that there was every indication that Florida would secede from the Union. He had reliable information, he continued, that as soon as the state seceded an attempt would be made to seize Fort Taylor.

> I therefore request instructions what I am to do—endeavor at all hazards to prevent Fort Taylor being taken or allow the State authorities to have possession. . . . These instructions are absolutely necessary now as it may be too late after the State secedes.

Before an answer was received, the secession crisis arrived. When word of the seizure of the arsenal and Fort Marion reached Key West, Captain Edward B. Hunt, the commander at Fort Taylor, called upon Captain Brannan for aid in defending the fort. Brannan, not waiting for orders from Washington, responded to this appeal by moving his entire command into Fort Taylor. He informed the war department that he had four months' provisions and would defend the fort "to the last moment against any force attempting to capture it." He added, however, that his command was small, and, without reinforcements and naval cooperation in defending the harbor, he could not withstand a siege by a well-organized army.

The Buchanan administration, realizing the importance of the forts at Key West and Tortugas to United States commercial interests and as a base of operations in the event of war, had determined to hold them in case Florida seceded from the Union. On January 4, 1861, the war department dispatched orders to Brannan to move his command into the fort and defend it. These orders had not arrived when the captain determined upon a policy of resistance if attacked, but they served as official sanction for his action.[10]

On January 10, the day that the Florida convention passed the Ordinance of Secession, Major Lewis Arnold, in command of a force of sixty-two enlisted men and four officers, was sent by the war department to reinforce Fort Jefferson on Tortugas. This force arrived on January 18 and immediately began cooperating with Captain Brannan at Fort Taylor. By January 23, naval vessels were escorting supply ships between Tortugas and Key West and the construction of defensive positions was proceeding at a rapid pace. The general situation improved so rapidly that by February 6 Brannan informed the war department that "it is very doubtful now if any attempt will be made on this fort." The captain was correct. The forts at Key West and Tortugas were never attacked.

The situation on Pensacola Bay was to be more involved. There were five Federal installations on the bay, only two of which were occupied with more than a caretaker garrison. Fort Pickens, the largest of the forts, was located on Santa Rosa Island and was unoccupied. Fort McRee, on the bay, was also unoccupied except for a sergeant and his wife. Fort Barrancas was unoccupied, but Lieutenant Adam J. Slemmer was stationed with a company of forty-six artillerymen at Barrancas Barracks. The Pensacola Naval Yard at Warrington was an active installation.

Early in January of 1861 rumors began to circulate around Pensacola that citizens of Florida and Alabama intended to seize the fortifications in the area. Realizing the seriousness of the situation after he received word that the fort at Mobile and the arsenal at Chattahoochee had been seized, Lieutenant Slemmer on January 8 requested orders from the war department at Washington. In the meantime, in an effort to clarify the situation locally, he had opened conferences with Commodore James Armstrong of the naval yard. The commander, in the absence of orders from Washington, decided it was inexpedient to cooperate with Slemmer in any joint defense of the bay.[11]

There was much confusion as to the policy to be followed at the naval yard. Commodore Armstrong, an officer of great distinction, had been in the service for fifty years. His age made him temporizing and cautious. The executive officer, Commander Ebenezer Farrand, was from New Jersey but his southern wife was an ardent Secessionist. The remainder of the officers were Southerners. The ships at the yards all had southern commanders but many of their junior officers were strong Unionists. "Nothing was talked about," said one of the junior officers, "except this infernal secession of the states."[12]

During the period of confusion among the Union officers at Pensacola, Governor Perry appealed to the governors of Alabama and

Mississippi for aid. Consequently, troops from those states assembled in West Florida, or reported to Mobile so that they would be available at Pensacola when needed.[13]

Lieutenant Slemmer, realizing that he could expect little assistance from the naval yard, prepared to defend himself. He removed the powder and other munitions of war from the exposed areas of Fort Barrancas and began to fortify the more dependable parts of the fort. On January 8 he placed a sergeant's guard in the fort to defend it against intruders. Undoubtedly he had received information from Pensacola which caused this action, because that very night a body of men approached the fort with the intention of seizing it. When the corporal of the guard sounded the alarm, however, the assailants retreated into the night without firing a shot.[14]

The morning mail of January 9 brought orders from Washington. These orders, enclosed in a "pink envelop and addressed in a woman's hand,"[15] directed Lieutenant Slemmer to take any measures necessary to prevent the seizure of the fort at Pensacola. He was to consult with Commodore Armstrong and the two were to cooperate in the defense of public property. An immediate conference was held, and Slemmer and Armstrong decided that the military force available could not hope to defend more than one of the forts. They decided that the defense should be made at Fort Pickens because it completely commanded the harbor and the other Federal installations on the bay. Furthermore, in case of necessity it could be more easily reinforced or evacuated.

The move to Fort Pickens was not a harmonious one. The U.S.S. *Wyandotte* began transporting Lieutenant Slemmer and his command across the bay to Santa Rosa Island on the morning of January 10 at about the same hour the convention at Tallahassee began its final debate on the Ordinance of Secession. The move had no more than begun before sharp differences arose over the use of the vessels at the naval yard and removal of Federal supplies. Lieutenant Slemmer desired two vessels to anchor under the protection of Fort Pickens so that he would be assured of support, but Commodore Armstrong refused his request except as a temporary measure. The commodore also refused to assume the responsibility for providing the fort with supplies of food or munitions.[16]

The crisis completely stunned Armstrong. He made no preparations for an active defense of the naval yard and refused to allow the destruction of any munitions of war. The antagonism between the pro-southern and pro-northern officers in his command grew more bitter. Accusations were hurled back and forth and once reached the degree of actual violence.

Lieutenant Henry Erben, a pro-northern junior officer of the U.S.S. *Supply*, decided to destroy the munitions at Fort McRee without authority. With a boat's crew he rowed up the bay to the fort and demanded the keys to the magazine. The sergeant in charge of the fort was away in town and his wife, a rabid Secessionist, refused to surrender the keys. Lieutenant Erben and the boat crew broke down the doors to the fort and "destroyed several thousand pounds of powder" by throwing it into the sea. Meanwhile, the sergeant's wife had sent for assistance from the settlements near the fort. A group of men was hastily organized and began pursuit of the fleeing Lieutenant Erben. Unable to catch the lieutenant, the men fired several shots which did no damage. Their shots (which fell harmlessly into Pensacola Bay) were the first shots of the Civil War fired in Florida.

Returning to the naval yard, Lieutenant Erben went to Commodore Armstrong and requested permission to destroy everything in the naval magazine and ordnance department. The commodore refused on the ground that his orders called upon him to protect the public property. "I did all I could to get his permission," Erben stated, "but failed."

> He went to the parlor door, called his orderly, and sent him for Commander Farrand; then I knew it was all up. There was some violent talk after Farrand came; he asked the Commodore to put me under arrest, and send me back to the ship, that I was crazy. . . . The Commodore refused to do this; then Farrand rose, seized his chair, threw it at my head, and left the room. I remained with the old Commodore a while; his face was buried in a handkerchief and he was crying like a child.[17]

Preparations meanwhile were being made in Pensacola for the occupation of the Federal property, by force if necessary. Major William Chase, a retired army officer living in Pensacola, was appointed by Governor Perry as commander of all the Florida troops in the area. Since the entire bay area was within the boundaries of Florida, Chase also assumed command of the militia from other states as they arrived. The first out-of-state militia to arrive in Pensacola were 225 men from the Second Alabama Volunteers who arrived on the night of January 11. These were but the vanguard of hundreds of troops that began to converge on the area from Louisiana, Mississippi, Alabama, and Georgia—as well as, of course, Florida.[18] Demands for action by the troops immediately began to grow throughout the South. Senator Stephen R. Mallory, later Confederate Secretary of the Navy, telegraphed Major Chase from Washington that "All here look to you for Pickens and McRee."[19] Governor Joseph Emerson Brown of Georgia was growing impatient with the inactivity of the Florida forces but was assured by Governor Perry on January 12 that Florida realized the forts must be taken and that he had tried to seize them "by Strataquee [sic] but failed" and that the only course now open to the state "is for the troops of a Southern Confederacy to be used."[20] Governor Albert Burton Moore of Alabama was also becoming impatient. Writing to Colonel Tennent Lomax, the commander of Alabama troops at Pensacola, he said:

> The possession of all the fortifications . . . of Pensacola is of the last importance of the safety of the seceding states on the Gulf of Mexico. No other place on the Gulf is safe while Federal troops hold possession of the commanding fortifications at Pensacola.[21]

Moore ordered Colonel Lomax to push for immediate seizure of the fortifications.

Word was received in the naval yard on January 11 that troops from Alabama and Florida were preparing to march out from Pensacola to seize the yard. The junior officers of the ships and the marine detachment wanted to defend it. Commodore Armstrong, however, decided to make a show of force and hoped it would prevent an attack upon the yard. Extra sentinels, armed with loaded muskets, were placed along the wall and a howitzer or two were positioned near the gate. The assault did not materialize, and at dusk Commander Farrand ordered the extra sentinels removed and the cannon returned to the regular position.

The next morning, January 12, nothing was done to meet the force that "every man, woman, and child knew . . . was coming, and for what purpose." A detachment of about five hundred Alabama and Florida troops, accompanied by many citizens of Pensacola "who had come along to see the fun," arrived at the gates of the naval yard just before noon, after having first seized the naval magazine.[22]

Hearing that the force was at the gates demanding surrender,

Commodore Armstrong destroyed the naval signal books and prepared to meet with the commissioners, Captain Victor M. Randolph, late of the United States Navy, and one Campbell, a Pensacola lawyer, who were conducted to the commodore's office by Commander Farrand. Arriving at the office, Captain Randolph, a service friend of the commodore, renewed acquaintances and then stated, "We are commissioners appointed by Florida to demand the surrender of their Navy yard." The commodore replied that it was a very unexpected thing to be attacked by his own countrymen and that he could offer no resistance as his force was so small. He demanded, however, that honorable terms of surrender must be given. The commissioners then sent for Colonel Lomax, commander of the Alabama troops. Lomax, upon arrival, read his instructions to seize the naval yard under the authority of the government of Florida. The commodore later testified that as Lomax read his instructions he was as "embarrassed as I was . . . [and] I concluded that he felt for my position for which I felt very grateful to him." The commodore, seeing resistance was futile, immediately surrendered the yard. "To my great surprise," Armstrong said later,

> the first lieutenant of the yard, who was sitting back of me, . . . spoke out in a very audible voice: 'Commodore, shall I haul down the flag?' I looked at the man astonished; it appeared to arouse me from a dream. I bowed, and turned my head away.[23]

The details of the surrender having been worked out, orders were given to William Conway, an old seaman from Camden, Maine, to haul down the flag. Conway refused to execute the order, and Lieutenant Frank B. Renshaw of Pennsylvania, whose wife was an ardent Secessionist, stepped forward and hauled down the flag.[24]

The vast majority of the employees of the naval base—Commodore Armstrong estimated nineteen out of every twenty—remained at their jobs in the service of Florida. These workers were organized into a company and furnished with arms by Major Chase, the commander of the Florida troops. Military officers drilled them one hour each day and they were incorporated into the regular defense forces of the area.[25]

Word that the naval yard was besieged reached Lieutenant Slemmer at Fort Pickens. He immediately requested Commodore Armstrong to release the marine detachment at the yard to his command before formal surrender occurred. With the Florida and Alabama troops on the move, the lieutenant wanted all the men he could get to reinforce his small detachment of soldiers and sailors which had taken refuge in the fort. He received no answer, however, and the garrison at Fort Pickens stood hopelessly by and watched the lowering of the flag at the naval yard. The eighty-one officers and men in the fort were now all that stood between Florida forces and their complete domination of Pensacola Bay. Fort Pickens must be taken, the Florida leaders realized, because without it the best natural harbor on the Gulf of Mexico would be useless to the South.

The defenders of Fort Pickens did not have long to wait. That evening just after retreat, four gentlemen from the mainland "presented themselves at the gate of the fort and demanded admittance as citizens of Florida and Alabama." The guard refused to admit them and sent for Lieutenant Slemmer. Upon his arrival at the gate, Slemmer was informed by Captain Randolph, the spokesman for the commissioners, that they had "been sent to demand a peaceable surrender of their fort by the governors of Florida and Alabama." Slemmer refused to surrender the fort unless ordered to do so by the President of the United States or the General-in-Chief of the Army. With the situation at an impasse, the commissioners withdrew.[26]

Preparations for the ensuing struggle were hastened on both sides of the bay. The garrison at the fort hastily constructed defensive works and manned the guns day and night. The Florida forces on the mainland continued to drill and practice assault tactics. The naval yard employees were assigned the task of building scaling ladders to be used on the walls at Fort Pickens, and gun carriages that could be maneuvered on the sands of Santa Rosa Island were rapidly constructed. Reconnoitering expeditions landed on the island to determine the progress of work at the fort. One of these expeditions, sent out by Major Chase on the night of January 13, exchanged shots with the guards at the fort but no one was killed or wounded.[27]

In an effort to avoid bloodshed, Major Chase, on January 15, conferred with Lieutenant Slemmer at Fort Pickens. Chase had crossed over to the fort under a flag of truce, accompanied by Commander Farrand, who had served as Commodore Armstrong's executive officer at the naval yard, and was now a member of Chase's staff. During the conference, Chase asked Slemmer to surrender the fort and read him a written statement which said that the governor of Florida desired the fort to be taken and that it should be done peacefully if possible. The fort would be held by the state subject to any agreement that might be entered into between Florida and the United States government in Washington. Chase promised the lieutenant that the officers and men in the fort could keep all personal property and that they would be paroled on their oath and taken to Barrancas Barracks where they could remain unmolested until final disposition of the fort was worked out. The major also stated:

> I would not counsel you to do aught that was dishonorable; on the contrary, to do that which will secure for you the commendation of all Christian gentlemen; and if you refuse and hold out, for whom do you consent that blood shall flow—the blood of brethren? Certainly not for the deadly enemies to the assaulters, for they are not such, but brethren of the same race.

Lieutenant Slemmer, after promising to deliver an answer to the major on the following day, conferred with the commanding officer of the U.S.S. *Wyandotte*. When it was ascertained that the vessel could remove his troops from the island if they were in danger of being overwhelmed, Slemmer decided to refuse the major's request. He informed Chase that he was not going to surrender and that if any blood was shed, Chase would be responsible for it as he would be the aggressor.[28]

Major Chase immediately notified Governor Perry and United States Senators Yulee and Mallory of Slemmer's refusal to surrender and asked for instructions. The situation was acute. If he were ordered to fire on Pickens, the war might begin at once; if he did not fire on the fort and it was reinforced, Pensacola Bay might well be lost to the South. This problem was faced squarely by the Southerners. A delegation of southern senators, Stephen A. Mallory of Florida, Benjamin Fitzpatrick of Alabama, and John Slidell of Louisiana, conferred with President Buchanan and his Secretary of the Navy, Isaac Toucey. At this meeting, the President and the Secretary assured the Southerners that there was no need to attack either Fort Pickens or Fort Sumter in Charleston, South Carolina, where a like situation had developed. An attack on these forts, they argued, would play into the hands of the Republicans who desired hostilities to commence before the inauguration of Lincoln. It was agreed by both sides that there was no need for shedding blood. To prove his good faith, Secretary Toucey sent a special messenger, one Captain

Barron of Virginia, to Fort Pickens with orders for Lieutenant Slemmer to allow no Federal vessels to land at Pensacola.

The South accepted the agreement and a delegation of southern senators telegraphed Major Chase on January 18 as follows: "Yours received. We think no assault should be made. The possession of the fort is not worth one drop of blood to us. Measures pending unite us in this opinion. Bloodshed may be fatal to our cause."

In an effort to be certain that there was no bloodshed at Pensacola, Mallory and Yulee appealed directly to Governor Perry to see that Chase made no attack. "First get the Southern Government in operation," they urged. They added that "the same advice had been given as to Charleston and will no doubt be adopted there."[29]

Governor Perry and Major Chase followed the senators' advice. No attack was made, but preparations for an assault continued unabated. Troops continued to arrive at Pensacola and enter into intensive training for action that many feared would never come. A period of watchful waiting had begun.

While the opposing forces at Pensacola waited, Florida moved rapidly to prepare itself for war. The militia system had been ineffectual because of the sparse population and lack of communication and transportation.[30] As the sectional controversy grew during the late 1850's, Governor Perry called annually for a strengthening of the militia system. He was unable to secure an adequate revision of the returns at all.[31] Floridians had not yet caught the martial spirit, but 1860 there was such a lack of interest that seven counties made no returns at all.[31] Floridians had not yet caught the martial spirit, but this lack of interest was dispelled as the sectional crisis approached. Following the nomination of Abraham Lincoln by the Republican party, vigilance committees and squads of "Minute Men" were organized throughout the state. Upon Lincoln's election, many of these offered their services to the governor.[32] By January 1, 1861, Florida citizens had become convinced that a military organization within the state was needed and gave their support as the governor, the legislature, and the convention made efforts to bring order out of the chaotic condition of the state militia.

On February 4 Governor Perry appealed to the General Assembly for legislation to stabilize and to give direction to the raising of troops. He emphasized the fact that the governor and the legislature had the duty to protect the newly proclaimed sovereignty of the state, and that the recent refusal to surrender the Key West fort and Fort

Pickens would likely put this sovereignty to the test of actual combat. In his opinion, legislation was needed which would provide for calling troops into the service of the state in "such a number . . . as may be equal to our defense, when assisted as we shall be by our sister states." He also desired special appropriations for the pay and maintenance of troops, for the purchase of munitions, and for other expenses incidental to the defense of the state. Florida should take this action immediately, he felt, because the Montgomery convention would most certainly form a provisional government which would need troops and money. "The quota of Florida will not be large," he concluded, "but we should proceed to organize the force which we are likely to be called upon to furnish."[33]

The General Assembly responded by passing a series of acts which exempted the horses, arms, and accouterments owned by any member of a company of cavalry or mounted men from levy, sale, or taxation.[34] Governor Perry made provision for the defense of the ports of Apalachicola, St. Marks, Cedar Key, Egmont Keys, St. Augustine, Fernandina, and other seacoast locations until the duty of protecting the ports of Florida could be assumed by the Confederate States of America.[35] These two acts—one by the General Assembly and one by the convention—were to cause much confusion. The first actually led to the formation of many more companies of mounted men than were needed and presented a problem which was not solved until March, 1862, when the state troops were disbanded. The second caused the legislature and military leaders to prepare for a short period of defense. Hence, adequate defenses were not planned, and when the Confederacy failed to emphasize the defense of Florida, the state was left exposed to the enemy.[36]

The legislature did adequately revise the militia system. On February 14, a law was enacted which created Florida's Civil War Militia. The adjutant general was to prepare and distribute blank lists of enrollment to every captain and lieutenant then holding a commission from the state. These blanks were to be distributed by these officers throughout their militia area. When a blank was signed the individual designated that he was liable for six months' service in the forces of the state and would report promptly upon receiving orders. The responsibility for securing signatures to the lists was left to individual citizens; however, they were not to allow any male under fifteen years of age or "persons manifestly unable to do military duty" to sign. The adjutant general was to take the completed lists and divide the men into companies, regiments, and brigades according to geographic location. No company was to have less than sixty-four, nor more than one hundred men.

Each company was to elect, on April 1, a captain and two lieutenants. Each regiment, on the same date, was to elect a colonel, a lieutenant colonel, and a major. The entire militia was to be commanded by a brigadier general appointed by the governor with the advice of the senate. Any citizen of the state or any United States Army officer who had resigned his commission was eligible for election to any of the command positions.

The act also provided for the appointment of surgeons, chaplains, and other noncombatant elements of a military establishment. The office of adjutant general was created and located in Tallahassee; the adjutant general was to be appointed by the governor with the advice of the senate.

The governor was authorized to raise at once two regiments of infantry and one of cavalry. Elaborate rules were formulated for the administration of the state's army, which during the first year of the war remained a separate organization from the Confederate Army.[37]

The formal organization of the Confederate Army began on March 1, 1861. On that date, Secretary of War Leroy P. Walker informed the governor that under a congressional act of February 28, 1861, the President of the Confederate States was authorized to receive volunteers for twelve months and to assume control of all military operations between the Confederate States and any "foreign power." On March 6, the Confederate States Army was created by an act of Congress. The President was authorized to employ the militia, military, and naval forces of the Confederate States of America, and to accept as national troops a maximum of 100,000 twelve-month volunteers. The volunteers were to furnish their own clothing, and, if mounted men, their own horses and equipment. The volunteers were to be armed by their states, or by the Confederate government. When called into actual service of the Confederacy, they were to be refunded the cost of their clothing and equipment.[38]

The first requisition for troops was addressed to the governors by the Confederate War Department on March 9, 1861. It called for a total of 11,700 troops, 5,000 of which were to be sent to Pensacola. Georgia, Louisiana, and Alabama were asked to furnish 1,000 soldiers each for duty at Pensacola, Mississippi, 1,500, and Florida, 500. "If you can supply this requisition immediately without publication of your order, it would be better to do so," stated Secretary Walker, "as it is advisable . . . to keep our movements concealed from the Government of the United States."[39]

By the middle of March, the mobilization of Florida troops, both state militia and Confederate, was well under way. Wild enthusiasm prevailed throughout the state. Men rushed to the military units being formed in their locality. Doctor Edward Bradford, a planter, not only volunteered himself but dismissed every white man in his employ so that he might volunteer.[40] The Governor Guards, a militia company at Tallahassee, changed its name to the Howell Guards in honor of Mrs. Jefferson Davis.[41] Patriotism for the new government ran high as planter, farmer, artisan, and worker rushed to be among the first to sign the rolls of new companies. Newspapers were filled with notices by prominent men that they were forming companies for state or Confederate service. The press aided in recruiting by publishing patriotic editorials, appeals for enlistments, and slogans to foster the martial spirit.[42]

These newly formed companies began to assemble at Tallahassee, Apalachicola, Quincy, Marianna, Monticello, Pensacola, Chattahoochee, Fernandina, Jacksonville, and other designated localities.[43] Often they were ordered to camp with very little notice. A Palatka correspondent of the *St. Augustine Examiner* wrote on March 9 that the town was quite "stirred up just now in consequence of orders from Governor Perry to our Guards to report themselves to Fernandina at once. They are to leave on Thursday. This is moving on short notice." In spite of all the hurry and confusion, regiments soon began to take shape and move off to war. The first regiment organized was known as the First Florida Infantry and was composed entirely of West Florida volunteers. The troops entered their camp of instruction at Chattahoochee and on April 5 were mustered into Confederate service for twelve months. Upon completion of its organization, the regiment left for Pensacola where it arrived on April 12.[44]

On April 8, before the First Regiment reached Pensacola, the Confederate government made a new call for volunteers. The requisition to Florida this time was for fifteen hundred men. On April 16 two thousand more troops were called for,[45] and a requisition for the Confederate Reserve Corps was sent out on June 30. Florida was asked for one thousand men. The reserves were to be called to camps of instruction under the control of the Confederate war department and could be mustered into service at the President's discretion.[46]

During 1861, the Confederate War Department levied Florida for five thousand troops. These troops were grouped into four infantry regiments, one cavalry regiment, nine unattached companies of infantry, four of artillery, and three of cavalry.[47] Most of the unattached companies were in the state militia, which numbered only 762 troops by January, 1862.[48] The militia steadily decreased in numbers, the governor stated, "owing chiefly to the desire to enter the Confederate service for short periods and certain pay," and because of the popularity of the cavalry. "Almost every man who has a pony," the governor stated, "wishes to mount him at the expense of the Confederate Government."[49]

The outfitting of troops entering the state militia and the Confederate Army presented Florida with a grave problem. Arms, ammunition, accouterments, tents, and even clothing were purchased from any locality in the South that would sell them. Most of the supplies, however, came from such cities as Charleston, New Orleans, Mobile, and Columbus, Georgia.[50] The purchase of arms in an inflated market soon exhausted the $100,000 appropriation of the legislature without securing sufficient weapons for the troops.[51] The situation became so desperate by early summer of 1861 that Governor Perry sent James Banks as a personal representative to confer with Governor John Willis Ellis of North Carolina in an effort to secure arms from that state. Governor Ellis felt that public sentiment would not allow him to send military supplies out of North Carolina to equip other troops. He suggested, however, that the Florida troops be sent to Virginia by a route which would cause them to pass through Raleigh. The sight of unarmed soldiers on their way to battle, he felt, would so touch the public sentiment that he could equip them with bayonets and muskets. No military assistance was secured in this manner, however, because the government at Richmond refused to accept the unarmed Florida troops into Confederate service.[52]

As the summer of 1861 progressed, the acquisition of weapons became more and more difficult. Companies of half-armed troops were combined so that a fully armed unit could be formed.[53] Other companies remained in camps of instruction until rifles could be procured.[54] The inactivity because of the lack of ammunition and supplies naturally gave rise to many complaints against army life. Lieutenant Gann, commander of a company of cavalry which had neither arms nor horses, ordered his men into line one evening following a day of complaining by his troop. "So you wish to mount," he shouted. All his troops responded with a lusty "yes." "All right," responded the lieutenant, "if one half of you will mount the other half, I'll soon see how many of you are capable of making cavaliers." The men, seeing the joke, mounted and the lieutenant drew his sword and led a lusty cavalry charge. "This," stated the Tallahassee *Florida Sentinel,* "has now become the favorite camp sport."[55]

Many of the arms secured for the Florida troops after midsummer of 1861 were parts of cargoes brought into one of the state's numerous bays or river mouths by blockade runners. A profitable business awaited any vessel that could safely reach the Florida coast with arms, ammunition, or supplies purchased in nearby Cuba or in the Bahama Islands. Blockade-running reached such a proportion that when the steamer *Salvor,* owned by James McKay of Tampa, ran aground and was captured in October, 1861, her cargo consisted of 21,000 stands of rifles, 100 boxes of revolvers, 6 rifled cannon, and large quantities of ammunition.[56]

The problem of arming the troops was never completely solved by the state. As late as May, 1862, the commanding general of the military department of East Florida, Brigadier General Joseph Finegan, issued a special address to the people of Florida appealing to them to give up enough of their private weapons to equip one or two of the Florida regiments then in camps of instruction. The general appealed for any type of arm but preferred "shot guns, double and single barreled, rifles, and muskets."[57] Enough of these were secured by purchase, by gift, and from the Confederate government to outfit the Florida troops leaving for the battlefields. These troops received all available arms, however, and no reserve stock of weapons was provided by the state. In September, 1863, the state quartermaster general reported that he had only nineteen usable rifles and only twenty-five percussion pistols in the quartermaster warehouse.[58]

In addition to the arms problem, the state had to solve the problem of clothing for the troops. Prior to the establishment of the Confederate Quartermaster Department, volunteers were required to furnish their own clothing. Most of the first volunteers were able to purchase resplendent uniforms, but soon many could not clothe themselves. Soldiers' aid societies were formed and before the end of 1861 many counties, towns, villages, and families were contributing directly to support soldiers in the field. At first, this aid reflected the romantic concept of war. Company colors were presented by young ladies amid the cheering of friends and relatives. Embroidered flags and banners for the newly formed companies and regiments were purchased and presented by political and business leaders.[59] Grim realities soon stripped the war of its tinsel glory, however, and the assistance became more practical.

The first organized effort to aid the soldiers was at Pensacola. By May, 1861, the Pensacola Committee of Relief was purchasing such necessary items as cartridge boxes, knapsacks, canteens, and lint.[60] This committee was composed of the leading citizens of Escambia County and was supported by volunteer contributions.

Other towns and villages organized to purchase supplies. The citizens of Alachua County in a mass meeting at the courthouse on July 1, 1861, decided to assess each county taxpayer 30 per cent of his state taxes. This money was to be paid in cash and administered by a Central Committee for the purchase of clothing and supplies for troops from the county. The Central Committee appointed one person to collect the money. The committee was also empowered to make additional assessments if the need arose. Those in service were exempt from the tax. The plan was to be enforced by publishing the names of all persons on the tax roll with a statement explaining whether or not he had paid his assessment.[61]

Unfortunately, this first attempt at county-wide taxation ended with bad feelings between the companies, the committee, and many of the townspeople. The Alachua troops at first cheerfully accepted the offer of assistance from the Central Committee and said, "We are all very much in need of clothing, shoes and hats."[62] These items were ordered by the committee and the troops informed of the purchase. Before all the supplies were delivered, however, the committee learned that the troops had been paid and that in addition to his full pay each man had received a $21 allowance for a uniform.

The committee wrote to Company H, commanded by Captain B. W. Powell, a company which had received no aid from the committee, stating that it was presumed that the needs of the company could now be filled without aid from the committee. This infuriated Company H as it had been bragging to other companies about how well Alachua County was caring for its troops. Captain Powell declared that the company had been insulted, and rejected all further aid from the Alachua Central Committee. "No other county in the state," he concluded, "would have felt justified on such grounds in refusing aid and comfort to the volunteers in the field."[63]

The Alachua company which had received aid felt that it too had been insulted. Its commander, Captain Thomas J. Meyers, wrote the committee, "If the gentlemen who furnished our company with tents and other articles will inform me of the amount expended, I will refund it, with interest, as they being a part of your committee must have treated us well unintentionally."[64]

Another major cause of the dissension between the soldiers and the Central Committee was the fact that pressure was applied to those citizens who did not pay their assessment. The soldiers were very vehement in their denunciation of the plan to publish the names of those taxpayers who had and who had not paid their assessment. Captain Thomas J. Meyers' company published a notice in the *Gainesville Cotton States* explaining that the company opposed the taxation of the poor for the benefit of Alachua soldiers.[65]

This conflict between the soldiers and the Central Committee was unfortunate because it destroyed the only effort in Florida to aid soldiers in the field by direct taxation. It prompted many Alachua taxpayers to delay or to refuse payment. Gainesville taxpayers were assessed $826.73 and paid only $345.77.[66] George Washington Means, committee agent at Micanopy, reported that most of the taxpayers in his precinct would pay, but many of them decided to pay later in the year or to pay by personal note.[67] The only precinct to meet its total assessment was Waldo. The Alachua Central Committee was disbanded during the last week in September, 1861. During the three months of its existence the committee collected and disbursed $1,802.25. This money was used to provide Alachua troops who would accept aid with tents, and clothing.[68]

Pride and misunderstanding had destroyed the one means of a fair and systematic method of aiding the troops in the field. The committee felt that the families and friends of the soldiers had written them "wicked and mischievous" reports of the action of the committee in an effort to avoid taxation.[69] The soldiers believed these reports and, feeling that they had been insulted, refused further assistance. Throughout the remainder of the war, the soldiers were aided, but not from a central fund supported by taxation: Ladies Aid Societies now became the principal source of assistance to the troops.

After June 30, 1861, the question of recruitment, mobilization, and regimental organization became matters of concern to Confederate officials. No more requisitions for troops were sent directly to the governor of Florida. The state was divided into military districts commanded by Confederate officers. The dual military system was eliminated when a special session of the Convention of the People of Florida met in January, 1862, and despite strong protests from Governor Milton abolished the state militia. The Confederate Conscription Act of April 16, 1862, ended all question as to the control of Florida men entering military service. Only the future would demonstrate the effectiveness of Confederate forces within the state.

III

FORT PICKENS

AT THE BEGINNING of the secession crisis, President James Buchanan determined that no act of his should increase the excitement in either the North or the South. If the political conflict was to end in civil war, it was his purpose not to commence it, or to furnish an excuse for it by an act of the federal government.

The President held the conviction that no state had the constitutional right to secede from the Union. But if a state should secede, President Buchanan felt that he had no right, under the Constitution, to coerce the state by making aggressive war upon it. Congress, he believed, was the only tribunal possessing the power to meet the existing emergency. "To them," he stated, "belongs the power to declare war, or to authorize the employment of military forces . . . and they alone possess the power to remove grievances which might lead to war, and to secure peace and unity in this distracted country. On them, and on them alone, rests the responsibility."

The President, however, just as firmly believed that it was his constitutional duty, as chief executive officer under the Constitution, to continue to collect the public revenues and to protect the public property, "so far as this might be practicable under existing laws," in the seceded states.[1*]

To headstrong men, both North and South, the position of the President was ridiculous. Buchanan was not a headstrong man, however. He was an adept lawyer following the course which he believed was correct both constitutionally and politically. His greatest desire was to avert bloodshed and he sought consistently any means to prevent a clash of arms. "If the seceding States abstain," he stated, "from any and all acts calculated to produce a collision of arms,

*Notes to Chapter III begin on page 221.

then the danger so much to be deprecated will no longer exist." His policy, he continued, was and would be "defense and not aggression."[2]

The President was no fool. He realized that a serious breach existed between North and South. "I still hope the storm may blow over, but there are no indications of it at present," he wrote George M. Wharton in December, 1860. "On the contrary," he added, "the spirit [of secession] is rapidly extending to states which were quiet a few weeks ago."[3] Time did not change his opinion. In January, 1861, he urged Congress to act upon the crisis and warned that "The fact cannot be disguised that we are in the midst of a great revolution."[4]

Buchanan's theories of government faced the acid test at Charleston Harbor and Pensacola Bay. To surrender Fort Sumter to South Carolina and Fort Pickens to Florida would be a submission to the demands of the Secessionists, and for Buchanan a breach of faith with his constitutional duties. To reinforce the forts would initiate the armed conflict which he bitterly opposed. Faced with this dilemma, Buchanan vacillated and compromised in an effort to postpone any precipitate action which would mean war. "Time," he stated, "is a great conservative power."[5]

The senators from Florida withdrew from Congress on January 21, 1861.[6] Mallory left two days later for his home at Pensacola.[7] Governor Perry had appointed him Judge of the Court of Admiralty for the Southern District of Florida.[8] Yulee remained at his home in Washington a few days longer.[9] Prior to their withdrawal from Congress, both Mallory and Yulee had become convinced, as had other southern leaders who had attended the conference with President Buchanan and Secretary Toucey, that no blood would be shed at Pensacola. The immediate problem, they believed, was to establish the Confederacy. Then the question of the forts could be met.[10]

Consistent with his policy of nonaggression and his determination to protect the public property, Buchanan decided to reinforce Fort Pickens, looking upon it as an "errand of mercy and relief."[11] The reinforcing troops, one company of artillery commanded by Captain Israel Vogdes, were not to attempt any reoccupation or recapture of Federal property and were to confine themselves strictly to defensive action.

On January 28, Yulee, who was still in Washington, telegraphed the news of the President's decision to reinforce Fort Pickens to the leaders at Pensacola. This news greatly disturbed ex-Senator Mallory. He immediately telegraphed John Slidell, R. M. T. Hunter, and Governor William Bigler, who were still in Washington, that news of the proposed reinforcement had reached Pensacola. He urged that they see the President and impress upon him that no attack upon Fort Pickens would be made as long as it was not reinforced. Any attempt to strengthen it, however, would be taken as a hostile act. "Impress this upon the President," he stated, "and urge that the inevitable consequence of reinforcement . . . is instant war."

This message from Mallory was a direct challenge to the President and his "errand of mercy and relief." The decision for war or peace now rested with Buchanan. Had he been headstrong, the war would have started at Pensacola Bay. He was not headstrong and he did not desire bloodshed during his administration; therefore, he retreated from his position. On January 29, he directed Joseph Holt, Secretary of War, and Isaac Toucey, Secretary of the Navy, to issue jointly the following order to the Union commanders at Pensacola:

> Upon receiving satisfactory assurances from Mr. Mallory and Colonel Chase that Fort Pickens will not be attacked, you are instructed not to land the company on board the Brooklyn unless said fort shall be attacked or preparations shall be made for its attack. The provisions necessary for the supply of the fort you will land. The Brooklyn and other vessels of war . . . will remain . . . and be prepared at a moment's warning to land the company at Fort Pickens, and you and they will instantly repel an attack on the fort.

This was the beginning of an official armistice on Pensacola Bay—an armistice known as the Fort Pickens Truce.

The *Brooklyn* arrived at Pensacola on February 6. Captain Israel Vogdes, commander of the troops aboard the vessel, went ashore at Fort Pickens and assumed command of the station. He inspected the fort and found that it was at the mercy of the Florida and Alabama troops. Only fifty-four cannon were in position and fifty-seven embrasures had no guns at all. Most of the embrasures were protected only by wooden shutters. There was no ammunition for many of the guns. The defenders of the fort, outnumbered twenty to one, were exhausted, as one-half of the garrison stood watch every other night. The thirty ordinary seamen at the fort had become insubordinate and could not be depended upon in the event of an attack. "In fact," Captain Vogdes declared, "had it been the intention of the government to place the fort in the state to render its defense impossible, it could not have been done more efficiently than it has been done."[12]

By February 6 there were approximately one thousand troops from Mississippi, Alabama, and Florida encamped along Pensacola Bay. They were busily engaged in erecting batteries, making sandbags, and performing other duties common to preparation for either defensive or offensive warfare.[13] On March 7 Brigadier General Braxton Bragg of the Provisional Army, Confederate States of America, was placed in command of all troops in the Pensacola area.[14] General Bragg was a West Pointer. He had served with distinction in the Mexican War and then retired from the army to become a planter and businessman in Louisiana. "I know every inch of Pickens," he said to William Howard Russell, a London *Times* correspondent, "for I happened to be stationed there as soon as I left West Point."[15]

A change of policy as well as a change of administration took place with the inauguration of President Abraham Lincoln, March 4, 1861. As rapidly as possible the new administration took up the various civil, military, and political subjects demanding attention. Among the matters of immediate interest were those which related to the few military posts in the South that were retained by the United States government.

General Winfield S. Scott of Mexican War fame, as Commanding General of the United States Army, approved the Fort Pickens truce. Upon the inauguration of Lincoln and the subsequent change in attitude concerning the South, however, the general began to demand that his small garrisons at Pickens and Sumter be reinforced.[16] In accordance with Scott's desire and with the knowledge of President Lincoln, Secretary of the Navy Gideon Welles ordered Commander T. A. M. Craven, commander of the U.S.S. *Crusader,* to carry special orders to Captain Vogdes aboard the *Brooklyn* at Pensacola.[17] These orders, dated March 12, instructed Captain Vogdes to land his company and strengthen Fort Pickens "at the first favorable moment."[18]

Because of delay in sailing and inclement weather on the voyage, the *Crusader* did not reach Pensacola until April 1. Upon receipt of his orders, Captain Vogdes immediately contacted Captain Henry A. Adams, senior naval officer, and requested boats for landing his men. Captain Adams refused. He did not consider himself under the orders of General Scott but rather bound by the orders of ex-Secretary Toucey to prevent any disturbance of the status quo on Pensacola Bay. The captain stated his position in a special dispatch to Secretary of the Navy Gideon Welles and requested new orders if his position was contrary to new policies of the navy department.

Secretary Welles received Adams' dispatch on April 6, and at once carried it to the President. The information that Adams refused to land reinforcements without further orders proved to be extremely embarrassing, because the administration had been engaged for some days in fitting out an expedition to relieve Fort Sumter. A major part of the strategy had been to strengthen Fort Pickens first. It was felt that Pickens was the more vulnerable of the forts and could be easily seized by the Confederates if they became aware of the President's plan. The President and the Secretary decided that the movement to build up Sumter could not be delayed as the expedition was scheduled to sail that day. The only hope of saving Pickens, they agreed, was to dispatch a special messenger overland to Pensacola.[19]

Lieutenant John L. Worden, U.S.N., left Washington late that afternoon with orders for Captain Adams to assist in reinforcing Fort Pickens. Hurrying with all possible speed he arrived in Pensacola on April 11. After an interview with General Bragg in which he assured the general that his mission consisted merely of delivering a verbal communication to Captain Adams, Lieutenant Worden was granted a pass to visit the naval fleet.[20] He was put on board the *Sabine* on April 12, where he communicated his orders to Adams. That night the squadron's boats, under the command of Lieutenant Albert N. Smith, successfully landed Captain Vogdes' artillery company, consisting of 86 men and a detachment of 115 marines.[21] The Fort Pickens truce was broken. The successful reinforcement of the fort was of immense importance because it saved the most important fort on the Gulf of Mexico for the United States government. The bombardment of Fort Sumter by Confederate forces commenced on the morning of April 12. War was now an actuality.

Both the United States and the Confederate States governments had anticipated an end to the truce at Pensacola. The expediency and necessity of providing additional troops and supplies for Fort Pickens once it was reinforced by Captain Vogdes had been foreseen by the Lincoln administration. On April 1 General Scott appointed Colonel Harvey Brown as commander of an expedition to strengthen the fort still further.[22] Colonel Brown and his expedition reached Pensacola on April 17 and immediately assumed command of all Union military forces on Santa Rosa Island.[23] Reinforcements continued to arrive, and by the end of June Colonel Brown commanded a total of 2,088 officers and men on the island.[24]

The Confederate troops ordered to Pensacola by the war department in its troop requisition of March 9 began to arrive during the first days of April. Alabama had been the first state to send troops into Florida. Then followed militia from Mississippi, Louisiana, and Georgia, in the order named. "It is a matter of impossibility for me to keep you advised of the arrival of troops," General Bragg wrote Secretary Walker on April 14. "They come under such various orders, and fail so often to report at all, that they are [here] for days sometimes before I hear of them."[25]

One newspaper correspondent commented:

The influx of troops into Pensacola the past week is unprecedented and astonishing. Although they remain only long enough to take a boat for the Navy Yard, they afford all patriotic citizens an opportunity for inspection by parading once or twice around the public square. Mississippi pours in her companies almost daily, Georgians from Augusta, Atlanta, and Columbus, Zouaves from New Orleans, with females habited *A la Fille du regiment* at their head.[26]

"The boys," said Ellen Call Long, "think it great fun, and regard the trip [to Pensacola] as an excursion."[27]

By the end of May the Army of Pensacola was over five thousand strong.[28] The task of shaping these militia into a trained and well-disciplined army was attacked with vigor by the Confederate officers, many of whom had seen service in the Mexican War or in European wars.[29] Sessions on tactics and army regulations were held daily and all troops received instruction in the use of arms. When not receiving instruction, the troops busily engaged themselves preparing gun emplacements and defensive positions.[30] "We have been rolling cannon balls to the cannon all day," one Confederate private wrote. "We pile them near the cannon, ready for instant use. Others are cutting wood for the Hot Shot furnace. We hope this means that action is not far off."

Action did not come, but preparations continued. During the summer of 1861, all combustible material, including doors, windows, and weather stripping, was torn out of the forts and removed from the premises. Troops slept fully clothed with rifles at hand. Wood was cut, supplies distributed, cisterns built, batteries erected, and other preparations made for the expected battle. The inactivity and newness of the troops in the Confederate Army of Pensacola led to a lessening of the individual soldier's zeal for military discipline. Many slept while on guard duty. At first the officers tried to humiliate the offenders by sentencing them to a fort dungeon for eight days on a diet of bread and water. After release from the dungeon the offender wore a ball and chain for another thirty days or rode a wooden horse for a specified time before his fellow soldiers. Later the death sentence was used against such offenders.[31]

Liquor was consumed in some quantity and frequent disorders resulted. The problem became so serious that General Bragg outlawed the introduction of liquor into an area reaching five miles beyond the camps of his army.[32] This did not solve the problem as many citizens of Pensacola continued to earn their livelihood by selling whiskey to the troops. The situation was accentuated on December 2, when two drunken soldiers entered the home of an aged widow in Pensacola and destroyed all her furniture. The next day Bragg threatened to place Pensacola off limits for his troops because over one-half of the court-martial cases in his army arose out of drunkenness. More serious than that, he added, was the fact that his army had "lost more valuable lives at the hands of the Whiskey Sellers than by the ball of the enemy."[33]

There was little diversion for the soldier of either side at Pensacola. At first there was much indiscriminate firing of rifles by the Confederates. When accosted, the offender claimed to be "practicing for the Damn-Yankees," and doing nothing more than he had done at home when he had fired his rifle when he pleased.[34] In October, Bragg forbade indiscriminate target practice and allowed only the advance guards to carry loaded rifles.[35] The chief diversion for the Union forces on Santa Rosa Island was swimming. Occasionally the tide and current would force a swimmer to the mainland, usually in the vicinity of Fort McRee. Upon capture, the swimmer was considered an ordinary prisoner of war.[36]

Another diversion was sending propaganda messages to the opposing force. Confederate troops built a small vessel with three sails on which were inscribed the names of Beauregard, Davis, and Johnson. Into this vessel they put the latest newspapers containing speeches of Clement Laird Vallandingham, the Ohio Secessionist, accounts of the Battle of Manassas, and speeches of Jefferson Davis. When the wind and tide were right to take the vessel to Fort Pickens it was set adrift. Union soldiers read the dispatches "as attentively as a college student applies himself the night before his examinations," and replied by floating northern newspapers, attached to planks or other timbers, to the Confederates. A simpler system was soon developed by the Confederate troops. A few men would row a boat into the bay and throw a dog overboard. The dog would swim to Santa Rosa Island as it was the nearest land. Tied around the dog's neck was a sealed bottle containing the insulting message or news dispatch the Confederates wanted to deliver.[37]

The strength of Confederate fortifications at Pensacola was exaggerated in the southern press. Actually the Confederates constructed only thirteen batteries against Fort Pickens. These contained approximately eight cannon and described an arc of 135 degrees for about three miles around Pickens. The average distance from the fortifications to Fort Pickens was one and one-third miles. There was a chronic ammunition shortage, and much of that on hand was of inferior quality. "Altogether," stated an English newspaper correspondent who visited both Confederate and Federal garrisons, "I was quite satisfied that General Bragg was perfectly correct in refusing to open fire on Fort Pickens and on the fleet, which certainly ought to have wrecked his work about his ears . . . on the whole, I should prefer to be inside than outside Pickens in case of bombardment."[38]

Spring passed and summer came. Action started in earnest in other places but still no shots were fired at Pensacola. Sickness increased in both camps. Scurvy broke out in such severity at Fort Pickens that medical officers recommended the removal of an entire company from Santa Rosa Island.[39] The Confederates, who were not issued vegetables but who could purchase them from farmers, escaped scurvy but suffered severely from other diseases such as malaria and diarrhea.[40] As the summer progressed, the problem of fresh food increased for both commanders. After May 14, 1861, Pensacola Bay was almost desolate of vessels because of the blockade and counterblockade.[41] Provisions were shipped by boat from the North to Pickens and hauled in by wagon and train for the Confederates. Salt meat and crackers became the troops' main diet.[42]

The monotony of the limited diet and hot weather was broken early in May, 1861, when General Bragg, realizing that he could not expect naval superiority in any struggle at Pensacola, set out to block the principal passages from the gulf into the bay. On the night of May 4, the Confederates sank four old vessels in the channel between Fort Pickens and Fort Barrancas. "It was expected certainly that we would be fired into when that was done," said one of the participants. "Lights were thrown up on Fort Pickens so that there is no doubt that all was known to those in the fort," he added, "but not a gun was fired."[43]

Near the naval yard was anchored the huge "million dollar dry dock" which had been acquired by the Secessionists upon the surrender of the yard. At first it was thought that the dry dock would be of great value to the Confederate cause, but it soon became apparent that Confederate vessels could not enter the bay for repairs and the dock could not be taken elsewhere. Not only was it useless but it was blocking the channel near the naval yard and was also being used as a blind for schooners at Fort Pickens.[44] As a result, General Bragg decided to use it to block the principal channel between Fort Pickens and Fort McRee.[45] Colonel Harvey Brown, commanding at Pickens, saw what was contemplated and on the night of September 2 sent out a boat with twelve carefully selected regulars under Lieutenant Alexander Shipley to destroy the dry dock. They met no resistance, boarded the dry dock, placed live shells and combustibles on its floor, applied the torch, and retired without loss. The dock caught fire and was destroyed. Not a shot was fired.[46] This was soon followed by a bolder stroke.

At two o'clock on the morning of September 14 a launch and three cutters, from the Federal warship *Colorado,* succeeded in reaching the armed Confederate vessel *Juda,* moored at the docks under the guns of the naval yard batteries. Lieutenant John H. Russell of the *Colorado* commanded the expedition of one hundred men. Approaching the *Juda* with muffled oars, two of the boats attacked her while the others attacked the naval yard battery as a diversion. The plan was well executed and most of the attacking party was aboard the *Juda* before they were discovered. In the savage hand-to-hand combat which resulted, they drove the Confederates from the vessel. While the surprised sentries at the naval yard were sounding the alarm, Union seamen set fire to the ship and hastily withdrew under the cover of darkness. They left behind three of their number dead and eight wounded. This was the first bloodshed of the war in Florida.

Colonel Harvey Brown, at Fort Pickens, realizing that there would be retaliation for the two raids of Confederate property, prepared for and expected a bombardment of Pickens.[47] But General Bragg had a more drastic reprisal planned. On October 8, preparations were completed for a night attack upon the Federal encampment on Santa Rosa Island. The detachments destined for this work assembled at the naval yard and were transported by water to Pensacola on the steamer *Time*. While proceeding up the bay, Brigadier General Richard H. Anderson, commander of the expedition, issued final orders for the division of the assault troops into three battalions. The first battalion, 350 strong, commanded by Colonel James R. Chalmers, was composed of detachments from the Ninth and Tenth Mississippi Infantry and First Alabama Infantry; the second battalion, 400 strong, commanded by Colonel J. Patton Anderson, was composed of detachments of the Seventh Alabama Infantry, First Florida Infantry, and two independent companies of Louisiana Infantry; the third battalion, 260 strong, commanded by Colonel John K. Jackson, was composed of detachments from the Fifth Georgia Infantry and an independent battalion of Georgia infantry. In addition, an independent company of fifty-three men was taken to spike guns, destroy ordnance, and set fire to the enemy camp.

At Pensacola these troops were transferred to waiting barges and flatboats and towed across the bay to a point on Santa Rosa Island some four miles from Fort Pickens by the small steamers, the *Ewing* and the *Neaffie*. They disembarked rapidly in good order and formed on the beach at a little after two o'clock on the morning of October 9.[48]

Between the Confederates and Fort Pickens lay the camp of the Sixth New York Volunteer Infantry. Billy Wilson's Zouaves, as the Sixth New York was commonly called, had arrived on Santa Rosa Island on June 24.[49] Unaccustomed to the sun and the brightness of the sand, Wilson and his officers ordered that the sand at the camp be covered with pine branches. Also, company streets were covered with arbors of branches. These branches dried under the hot summer sun and made the camp a veritable kindling pile.[50]

The master strategy of the Confederates was to advance in three columns: the First Battalion along the north beach; the Second Battalion along the south beach or the gulf side; the Third Battalion to advance at the rear of the other two to be used as reserves; and the Special Company to follow in the rear and destroy the camp and ordnance supplies. Enemy pickets were to be captured, if possible, before they could spread an alarm. It was hoped that before the enemy was warned, the attackers could be in a position between Wilson's camp and the fort.

The advance was arduous. The Confederates encountered numerous sand dunes and thickets which exhausted the men and which would have made a silent advance difficult had it not been for the sound of the surf.[51] After marching some three miles, they came suddenly upon an outpost of the camp. The Federal pickets fired ineffectually and were soon shot down. With the element of surprise gone, General Anderson ordered a direct assault upon the Zouave camp.

The first volleys served to alarm the camp. Colonel Wilson dispatched a messenger to the fort for aid, then set about organizing resistance. The camp was attacked from both flanks and the front. The Confederates entered the camp on the first rush and applied the torch to the tents, storehouses, and sheds. The flames from these, plus the dried branches, soon covered the entire camp. The sight of an undetermined number of attackers appearing and disappearing amid the flames and smoke of their camp proved too much for the Sixth New York. It broke and ran for the protection of the batteries at the rear of Fort Pickens.[52]

Colonel Wilson later defended his men, saying, "My men did well. They have smelt gunpowder, now they are all right." One Confederate assailant was not as charitable in his account of Wilson's action. He reported that:

> The gallant Colonel took to his heels with nothing but a brief skirted nether garment to cover his nakedness, and the race between him and his valiant braves presented a struggle for precedence more closely contested than any ever witnessed on the race course. Bulls' Run was nothing in comparison to it.[53]

Following the seizure of the Federal camp, the Confederates were reorganized with a view to proceeding against the batteries at the rear of the fort. The assault was not renewed, however, as daylight was fast approaching and any chances of surprising the batteries had vanished. Anderson, therefore, ordered his troops back to their boats. About halfway between Wilson's camp and the point of disembarkation, a sharp skirmish occurred between the withdrawing

Confederates and two companies of United States regulars that had been sent out from Fort Pickens. The regulars were driven off and the withdrawing troops boarded their barges without further incident. After some delay, caused by the fouling of the propeller of the *Neaffie,* the expedition recrossed the bay to Pensacola,[54] narrowly escaping before United States naval vessels arrived.[55]

The first offensive action by a Confederate force in Florida was a limited success. It had not destroyed or captured Fort Pickens but it had completely destroyed the camp and almost all of the equipment of the Sixth New York Volunteers. The destruction of property in the conflagration was very great. Large stores of provisions, supplies of clothing, camp and garrison equipage, arms, and ammunition were completely demolished.[56] In addition, the expedition had killed fourteen and wounded twenty-nine, and captured twenty of the enemy, among them Major Israel Vogdes. This had been accomplished at a loss of eighteen killed, thirty-nine wounded, and thirty taken prisoner.[57] In all probability the attack would have been more successful if General Anderson had not tried to maneuver a group of raw recruits divided three ways during a night action. The complicated attack caused confusion in Confederate ranks and reorganization lost the attackers much valuable time.

The attack on Santa Rosa Island brought a realization of the horrors of war to Florida communities. Captain Richard H. Bradford was killed while leading his troops during the attack, and Private William Roth was killed during the engagement with the United States regulars. Both men were from the same neighborhood in Leon County. Captain Bradford's body was returned home by special train for burial. The captain, being the first casualty from the area, lay in state at various towns along the route. A large number of prominent citizens, including John Milton, attended the funeral. "When the services at the grave were over," Mrs. Eppes wrote, "a military company came forward and fired three times across his grave, it was horrible. . . . War is even worse than I thought."[58]

Colonel Brown considered the assault upon Santa Rosa Island "an insult so gross to the flag of my country . . . [that] I designed immediately to take appropriate notice of it." At once he began preparations to bombard Confederate positions on the mainland. Conferences were held with Flag Officer William McKean of the United States Navy, and a coordinated bombardment by both Fort Pickens and the vessels under McKean was planned.

The Confederate positions, arranged in an arc along the mainland shore of Pensacola Bay, consisted of two forts, McRee and Barrancas, and fourteen batteries. The combined armament of forts and batteries was only fifty effective pieces of light artillery and twenty-five ten-inch Columbiads. The Federal position on Santa Rosa Island was stronger. The armament of Fort Pickens consisted of seven separate batteries mounting thirty-five heavy guns, twelve of them eight- or ten-inch Columbiads. In addition, there were five batteries—Cammeron, Lincoln, Totten, Scott, and "Spanish Fort"—mounting twenty-two pieces, including four ten-inch Columbiads, two forty-two pounders, eight ten-inch seacoast mortars, one twelve-inch mortar, and one thirteen-inch mortar.

The guns of Fort Pickens and its outlying batteries, assisted by those of the U.S.S. *Niagara* and the U.S.S. *Richmond,* opened fire at ten o'clock on the morning of November 22. The Confederate batteries returned the fire and an artillery duel developed which lasted until darkness. The main Federal attack was against Fort McRee. The ships, the heaviest batteries, and a large portion of the guns of Fort Pickens devoted their entire time to shelling the fort. Before nightfall, McRee was silenced. Half its armament was disabled and its magazines were laid bare to the Federal shells constantly exploding near them. Recurring fires within the fort added to the discomfort of the garrison. As a result, it was proposed that the fort be abandoned and blown up. General Bragg refused, however, because of the effect such an act would have on the morale of his troops as well as of the enemy troops. Repairs were made throughout the night, and by dawn the fort was prepared for the resumption of the onslaught. Losses on both sides had been insignificant during the first day. The Federals had suffered only one killed and six wounded. Confederate losses were one killed, twenty-one wounded, and six smothered to death in a magazine cave-in.

The conflict was renewed at ten o'clock the next morning. Heavy firing continued until dark. A few random shots were fired throughout the night until four o'clock in the morning. Firing on the second day was slower and more deliberate. At three o'clock in the afternoon, the villages of Warrington and Woolsey went up in flames from the hot shots of the Federal batteries and the blaze soon spread to the naval yard. Two churches and a number of private dwellings were destroyed in the village but prudent action by the garrison saved all but one important building at the naval yard.

The action did not resume on the twenty-fourth. Over five thousand cannon shots had been fired during the duel of the forts but only eight lives had been lost. "It was grand and sublime," stated General Bragg. "The houses in Pensacola, 10 miles off, trembled from the effect," he added, "and immense quantities of dead fish floated to the surface in the bay and lagoon, stunned by the concussion. The bombardment, though inconclusive, together with the unsuccessful Confederate attack on Santa Rosa Island, demonstrated that with the forces at hand neither side could take a decisive action.

Only once more did an artillery duel occur between the two forces. On the afternoon of January 1, 1862, a small vessel at the naval yard was fired upon by Fort Pickens. The Confederates answered, and a general bombardment occurred which lasted approximately four hours. The Confederates suffered no casualties but lost a storehouse of supplies. The Federals suffered only two minor casualties and little damage.[59] This ended the duel of the forts. Action elsewhere, even in Florida, now engaged the attention of the opposing forces.

IV

RAID AND BLOCKADE

PREPARATIONS FOR WAR were pushed throughout Florida during 1861. Troops were raised, organized, and sent to Virginia, Tennessee, and Kentucky. Others were placed in strategic positions to repel an expected enemy attack upon the state's exposed coastline. There was nothing approaching a fortification from Pensacola around the coast to St. Augustine except the works at Key West and Tortugas, and they were in possession of the enemy. The attempt to strengthen the state's defenses was hampered by the lack of arms, ammunition, men and competent leadership.

Brigadier General John B. Grayson, assigned as commander of the Department of Middle and East Florida on August 21, 1861,[1]* reached the state on September 4. He went immediately to Fernandina, considered the most likely place for an enemy attack in his district, and found the situation so confused that he wrote Secretary Walker:

> The whole population of Florida may well unite with me, as they do, in deploring the condition of the State. . . . As sure as the sun rises, unless cannon powder, etc., be sent to Florida in the next thirty days, she will fall into the hands of the North. Nothing human can prevent it. There are not 4,000 pounds of powder at every post combined. The batteries are incorrectly put up and not finished. The enemy can land where they please. Guns and chassis are lying on the beach. . . . There is not an officer to put up the guns or an officer to superintend their instruction when put up. . . . I trust . . . that you will . . . have the ordnance stores and various officers sent at once.[2]

*Notes to Chapter IV begin on page 223.

The arms, ammunition, supplies, and officers were not sent. Governor John Milton, only recently inaugurated, became exasperated and telegraphed Secretary of War Judah P. Benjamin, who had replaced Walker, "Florida wants arms, she has never received a musket from the Confederate States."[3] Still no arms or ammunition were sent. The governor next turned to President Jefferson Davis: "We need troops and munitions of war, and officers of military education, ability and experience." He warned that Florida citizens "have almost despaired of protection from the Confederate Government—[and] will lose confidence in it."[4] Aid did not come, however, and preparations for the defense of the state continued to lag.

The situation on the west coast of Florida was almost as deplorable. Apalachicola, the entry port for the rich cotton region of West Florida, Southeast Alabama, and Southwest Georgia, was almost undefended. A battery of six outmoded cannon at St. Vincent's Island twelve miles from town comprised the principal defense. The land approaches to the town were unprotected except for local militia companies. The East Pass, a principal sea approach, was totally unguarded. "Insecurity and apprehension are the predominant feelings now," wrote a delegation of citizens seeking better defenses for the town.[5] These citizens rightfully felt apprehensive. Only eight companies of troops were stationed on the entire Gulf coast below Pensacola. Three of these were on St. Vincent's Island, two near St. Marks, one at Tampa and two at Cedar Keys.[6]

The situation in East Florida was no better. Fernandina, where General Grayson expected an attack, remained without adequate defenses. By the end of February, 1862, a total of only thirty-two guns had been mounted in Fort Clinch and on all of Amelia Island. Most of these were outmoded and mounted incorrectly.[7] Jacksonville, dominating the St. Johns River route into the interior of East Florida, was dependent upon militia for its protection. In an effort to bolster these defenses, most of the cannon were removed from Fort Marion at St. Augustine. Four were sent to Fernandina, four to a battery at St. Johns Bluff on the river below Jacksonville, and others elsewhere in the Confederacy until Fort Marion was left with only five cannon mounted in the water battery to defend the city.[8] With virtually no cannon available, the artillerymen stationed at Fort Marion were removed and the duty of defending St. Augustine was given to the St. Augustine Blues and the Jefferson Beauregards, two companies of the Third Florida Infantry.[9]

Adequate defensive preparations within Florida were also deterred by a lack of Confederate military leadership. General Grayson was in the last stages of tuberculosis when he reported as commander in Florida. He was unable to render effective generalship, and his command degenerated into a center of petty cabals among the junior officers. "Dissipation and disorder prevails," Governor Milton informed Secretary of the Navy Mallory.[10] General Grayson's inadequacy became a state political issue. Those officers who were appointed before Governor Perry relinquished office supported the dying Grayson and defended his fitness for command. The friends and appointees of Governor Milton desired an active commander.[11] Grayson was relieved on October 10, 1861, eleven days before his death, and Brigadier General Edmund Kirby Smith was assigned to the Department of Middle and Eastern Florida. But General Smith never reached Florida. His orders were changed assigning him to the Army of the Potomac and Brigadier General James H. Trapier, a South Carolinian, was assigned to the Florida command.[12] Trapier, however, delayed his departure from Charleston and did not arrive for a month after his appointment.[13] Florida, therefore, did not secure a Confederate commander capable of performing his duties until November 21.[14]

Events outside the state ended any attempt by the Confederate government to fortify and hold coastal Florida. Early in 1862, battles in Kentucky and Tennessee seriously threatened the safety of the lower South. Fort Henry fell on February 6, and Fort Donelson capitulated on February 16. The Confederate government found itself faced with disaster. Unless General Ulysses S. Grant was stopped, the rich and productive regions of Mississippi and Alabama would soon be under his control. More troops were needed if the Confederate commander, Albert Sidney Johnston, was to save the West. Troops could not be sent from the Army of the Potomac because the Union commander, George B. McClellan, was openly preparing a spring offensive. The Confederate government turned to the lower South for the reinforcements needed by General Johnston. The withdrawal of men from Florida was but a small part of a general movement of Confederate troops to the North and West, but it was to have a tremendous effect upon the state.

Events moved rapidly. On February 15, 1862, the day before Fort Donelson fell, General Bragg called for an abandonment of Florida by the Confederacy. "On the Gulf coast," he advised Secretary Benjamin, "we should only hold New Orleans, Mobile, and Pensacola; all other points, the whole of Texas and Florida should be abandoned, and our means there made available for service elsewhere." On February 18, Secretary Benjamin informed General Bragg that "the heavy blow which has been inflicted on us by the recent operation in Kentucky and Tennessee renders necessary a change in our whole plan of campaign, as suggested in your dispatch." The war department had anticipated Bragg, however, and had made the decision prior to his dispatch. Bragg was ordered to proceed as promptly as possible to withdraw his troops from Pensacola and Mobile "and hasten to the defense of the Tennessee line." All cannon and munitions were to be removed and no force was to be left in the area.[15]

The actual withdrawal from Pensacola Bay was executed under the command of Brigadier General Samuel Jones, as Bragg had hastened to Tennessee.[16] General Jones assigned the removal of guns, ammunition, and supplies to the Twenty-seventh Mississippi Infantry commanded by Colonel Thomas M. Jones.[17] While the other troops were hastening to the battle front, Colonel Jones and his regiment systematically removed everything of value from the Confederate positions at Pensacola. By unremitting labor, all the heavy guns and nearly all the smaller guns were saved. The cannons were removed at night and wooden imitations placed in position by morning. All the powder and most of the large shot and shell were removed. The naval yard was successfully stripped of its machinery. The busy colonel and his regiment even saved such articles as rain gutters, lightning rods, window weights, bells, and all articles of copper, brass, lead, or iron. All commissary stores were saved.

The removal of supplies and equipment had been in progress for two months before the area was finally evacuated. On the afternoon of May 7, Brigadier General John H. Forney, commanding the Department of Alabama and West Florida, informed Colonel Jones that a number of Federal vessels were steaming along the Alabama coast. Pursuant to previous orders, the colonel was to evacuate Pensacola immediately and aid in the defense of Mobile if the Alabama port was attacked. Colonel Jones, deciding that an attack on Mobile was imminent, set about preparing for a general evacuation of the Pensacola Bay area. Three cavalry companies were brought from Montgomery to aid in the destruction of public property that could not be carried to safety.

On the evening of May 9, the Confederate troops marched quietly from their camps toward Oakfield. Sentinels were posted as usual on the beach but withdrew an hour after the troops had left. When the marching infantry was out of range of Federal guns on Santa Rosa Island, the cavalry took up previously assigned positions to begin the necessary destruction at a signal from the colonel, who stated:

> Precisely at 11:30 o'clock, when everything was perfectly quiet, both on the enemy's side and ours, the most painful duty it ever fell my lot to perform was accomplished, namely, the signalizing for the destruction of the beautiful place which I had labored so hard night and day for over two months to defend. . . . The two blue lights set off by Colonel Tattnall and myself . . . were promptly answered . . . and scarcely had the signals disappeared ere the public buildings, camp tents, and every other combustible thing from the navy-yard to Fort McRee were enveloped in a sheet of flames.[18]

The destruction of private property was scrupulously avoided; the only property destroyed in the city was that of unquestionable use to the enemy. Previous to the general evacuation, however, General Samuel Jones ordered the demolition of all saw mills, planing mills, sash factories, lumber, baled cotton, and boats of every description located on or near Pensacola Bay. In all, $764,500 worth of property was put to the torch under this order.[19]

The fires which consumed the last of the Confederate property also signaled the end of any challenge by the Confederacy of Federal control over Pensacola Bay. The next morning, a small detachment of Federal troops crossed the bay and demanded the surrender of Pensacola. The duly elected city officials had fled along with over 90 per cent of the population. The acting mayor, one Brosenham, assured the Federal troops that the remaining citizens were loyal and would remain orderly and quiet. On May 12, one thousand Federal troops under the command of Brigadier General Lewis G. Arnold crossed over from Santa Rosa and formally took possession of the city.[20] From then until the end of the war, Pensacola Bay was effectively under Federal control.

Pensacola itself, however, became a ghost town by March, 1863, when the exigencies of the military situation in the West forced a second evacuation of the city. The campaigns on the Mississippi caused Federal commanders to desire a concentration of their forces. "Evacuation Week," as it was called, occurred between March 17 and March 22. A census taken by the Federal troops upon withdrawal revealed that only ten men, thirty women, and thirty children remained.[21] Pensacola, the largest city of West Florida, became a city of deserted homes, "deprived not only of their furniture, but mostly of doors, and windows." The unused streets became filled with high weeds and bushes.[22] Neither army attempted to control the city, for it was no longer considered strategically important. Warfare in the Pensacola Bay area continued spasmodically but degenerated into bushwhacking or raids by troops of both sides with no firm control exercised by either the Federals or the Confederates.[23]

The Confederate military disasters in Kentucky and Tennessee also affected the defense of East Florida. General Robert Edward Lee, commander of the coastal defenses in South Carolina, Georgia, and Florida, immediately called for a restudy of those of eastern Florida. General Lee suggested that most defense establishments located on islands be evacuated because of the enemy's superior naval forces. Confederate strength, he felt, should be concentrated in the interior of the state and used to contest an enemy landing after it had taken place rather than to attempt keeping coastal defenses strong enough to repel the initial landing.[24]

These suggestions never went into effect. When the magnitude of the defeats in the West became known, the Confederate government determined to evacuate most of Florida. General Lee ordered Colonel William F. Dowd's Mississippi Infantry Regiment to proceed immediately from Fernandina to the Tennessee line. "The only troops to be retained in Florida," Lee informed General Trapier, Confederate commander in East Florida, "are such as may be necessary to defend [the] Apalachicola River, by which the enemy's gunboats may penetrate far into the state of Georgia."[25]

This order, if carried out, would leave Florida helpless before the enemy. Governor Milton protested it. His protest was not based upon the withdrawal of Confederate troops but rather upon the lack of any plan whereby Florida citizens could be armed to defend the state.[26] The order was modified and explained in more detail on March 13, 1862. Florida was not to be completely evacuated unless the defeats in the West continued. The number of troops in eastern Florida would be reduced, however, to a point where coastal defense would not be possible. The best Floridians could hope for would be a force adequate to safeguard the interior.[27] The Confederate government had decided on a calculated risk in Florida. It was willing to allow the enemy to occupy the coastal regions with the hope that no concentrated effort would be made to move inland. The validity of the risk received its first test even while the Confederate government was determining its policy.

Fernandina, the principal east coast port, was extremely attractive to the Federals. It was the eastern terminus of the Florida Railroad and an entry point for blockade runners; but above all, it contained a deep-water harbor which could be used by the United States Navy as a depot for vessels on blockade duty.[28] The town, on Amelia Island, was dependent upon steamship service with Charleston for most of its merchandise and much of its food.[29] Following United States naval operations during the first two weeks of November, 1861, which resulted in the seizure of Port Royal and other islands off the South Carolina and Georgia coasts, Fernandina became isolated from her chief source of supply to the north. This factor, plus the need for a naval base, strengthened the Federal government's determination to seize the town and Amelia Island.

The Federal expedition against Fernandina left Port Royal on February 28, 1862. The fleet comprised some twenty-six vessels, of which eighteen were gunboats or armed transports. On board were a battalion of marines commanded by Major John G. Reynolds, and an army brigade commanded by Brigadier General Horatio Wright. Flag Officer Samuel F. DuPont of the United States Navy was in command of the vessels and naval personnel.[30]

Four days prior to the sailing of the Federal squadron, General Trapier requested and received permission to evacuate both Amelia and Cumberland islands.[31] The evacuation had not been completed, however, when the Federal flotilla made its appearance on the morning of March 2 in Cumberland Sound which separates the two islands.[32] Flag Officer DuPont received news of the Confederate evacuation when an escaped slave rowed out to the Federal vessels to report that "the rebels were at that moment retreating from the islands." In an effort to halt the exodus, DuPont ordered the gunboats and steamers of light draft to proceed immediately to Fernandina. Navigation was so intricate, however, that only one gunboat, the *Ottawa,* was able to reach that portion of Cumberland Sound that separated the city from the mainland, and then not until three o'clock on the afternoon of March 3.

Meanwhile, the Confederate withdrawal from the city and the

island had been accelerated. Official word of the flotilla's destination had been received in Fernandina at eight o'clock on the evening of March 2. By noon the next day the garrison and most of the residents had fled the island for the interior of Florida. This rapid evacuation of troops, supplies, and civilians was accomplished by effective planning which used trains to shuttle persons and goods across Cumberland Sound to the mainland. The last train was leaving when the *Ottawa* steamed down Cumberland Sound. Seeing the train, the Federals opened fire, but the train was not damaged and escaped across the trestle to the mainland. The Federals were successful in capturing the *Darlington,* a small Confederate steamer attempting to escape with a cargo of women, children, and supplies. Fort Clinch, abandoned by the Confederates, was occupied by a detachment of sailors from the *Ottawa* that afternoon and Fernandina early the next morning by a detachment of sailors and marines from the gunboat flotilla.[33] The Confederate loss of equipment while leaving Amelia Island was not great considering the haste of the withdrawal: the entire loss consisted of twenty of the thirty-three artillery pieces on Cumberland and Amelia islands and a small quantity of commissary and quartermaster stores.[34] Civilian losses were greater because most of the evacuees were compelled to leave their household goods since the military did not have sufficient time to move private possessions. All civilians, however, who wished to leave the island were safely carried away. Most of the Negroes and the whites of northern birth remained to welcome the Federal troops.[35]

Fernandina, destined to remain under Federal control for the rest of the war, soon became a haven for escaped slaves from Georgia and Florida. Nearly every home in the city was occupied by Contrabands, as the runaway slaves were called. Fernandina "is now but a hive of Negroes," recorded one Federal officer. The few white natives of the town, mostly women, remained indoors and were rarely seen by the occupying troops. Throughout the war these women were able to keep in contact with the mainland by the use of an intricate system of signals. The Federals, at first apprehensive over spies, tried to stop this signaling from the island. However, they soon found out that the signals were primarily between wives and husbands or sweethearts and no arrests were made.[36]

As the war progressed, Fernandina became a rest center for Federal troops and a base for expeditions along the Florida east coast.

The duties of the Federal soldiers stationed on the island consisted primarily of drills and parades. Officers were joined by their wives, and the post developed a highly intricate social system based upon rank, and whether or not the husband was a regular or a volunteer. Feelings between the groups became so bitter that all volunteer forces were removed to St. Augustine in 1863.[37]

The Confederate forces fleeing Fernandina followed the railroad to Baldwin. At Baldwin, Colonel William Scott Dilworth divided his troops, sending the larger portion to the interior of the state to regroup and prepare to contest any invasion of the interior counties. The smaller portion was sent to Jacksonville for transportation up the St. Johns River to Enterprise to move any arms or ammunition in the area to the safety of the interior.[38]

The occupation of Fernandina encouraged the Federal commanders to continue operations against the east coast. Only three localities, Jacksonville, thirteen miles inland on the St. Johns River, St. Augustine, and New Smyrna, were of any importance. Of these Jacksonville and St. Augustine were the most significant. Jacksonville was the gateway to the interior of eastern Florida, while St. Augustine was a potential threat to the blockade as Fort Marion could provide a safe refuge for blockade runners. Other influencing factors were the desire to eliminate bases for possible operations against Federal shipping lanes to and from the Gulf of Mexico, and to pacify an aroused minority of the northern press which feared that England or Spain would attempt to regain Florida if the United States did not occupy it. Major General George B. McClellan had no such important motives, however, when he ordered Major General Thomas W. Sherman to occupy St. Augustine. The city, he wrote, "might as well be occupied by the way of an interlude, while awaiting the preparations for Charleston."[39]

On March 8, a Federal squadron of four gunboats, two armed launches, and a transport carrying the Fourth New Hampshire Infantry sailed from newly occupied Fernandina for Jacksonville and St. Augustine. The occupation of Jacksonville was to be temporary and was considered a reconnaissance in force. The ships arrived at the mouth of the St. Johns and crossed the bar on the afternoon of March 11. Since it was necessary to land a company of soldiers to protect the mouth of the river, the Federals decided not to proceed to Jacksonville until the following morning.[40]

Jacksonville was defenseless. No adequate preparations to defend the city had been made by the citizens or by the Confederate government. "Our city is cursed with a Mayor who will do nothing but oppose what others suggest," wrote a resident. Jacksonville, a seaport and resort area, also had a large percentage of northern-born residents in its population. Most of these remained after the war began, but many were not loyal to the Confederate cause. "At least one-half of the population of the city would tamely submit to Lincoln," complained a rabid Secessionist.[41]

News of the occupation of Fernandina and knowledge of the decision to abandon the river defenses reached Jacksonville almost simultaneously. Those who desired to leave the city were faced with the problem of how to get out and where to go. Drays were scarce and the few to be had were monopolized by the merchants who had valuable stores of goods to move.[42]

On Tuesday afternoon, March 11, news of the arrival of the gunboats at the mouth of the St. Johns reached Jacksonville. News was also received that a large number of Confederate troops was coming to burn the city to the ground. The troops arrived late in the afternoon and assured the population that only strategic places would be burned and that no harm would be done to dwelling houses.[43] This assurance caused a general relaxation of tension as the pro-Unionists had felt that the Southerners were sent to burn their property as punishment for their sentiments.[44]

The Confederates systematically burned eight steam sawmills near the city and over four million board feet of lumber stored near them. In Jacksonville, an iron foundry, the ironworking shop close by, and a gunboat under construction for the Confederate government were burned.[45] Groups of irregular troops began to arrive in the city around midnight. These irregulars, composed chiefly of refugees from Fernandina and men who had fled Jacksonville at an earlier date, came solely to intimidate the Union sympathizers. They began indiscriminately burning private homes, chiefly those of Unionists. Three Unionists were killed: one Remington, a commission merchant, was shot dead in the street, and the other two were killed while attempting to escape in small boats. The Judson House, the largest hotel, was set on fire, shooting was widespread, and panic seized the city. The Confederate officers disclaimed all responsibility for the shootings or the fire. The inhabitants piled their household furniture into the streets as no one knew whose home would be burned. Unionists fled across the river and found safety in hiding until picked up by the Federal troops. Large groups of frightened women and children stood in the open all night. The city was saved from complete destruction by a heavy rain that fell shortly after midnight and extinguished the fires.[46]

The next morning, March 12, as the Federal gunboats were proceeding up the river toward the town, rumors spread that the irregulars were returning to burn the property of all who attempted to remain in Jacksonville. A desperate rush to leave the city resulted. Men offered $10 for a dray, and all available light boats were seized to go either up or across the river—depending upon the affiliation of the individual. The gunboats arrived at noon and all escape by the river or by railroad was cut off.

As the Federal vessels moved slowly up the river and took positions before the town, a few men rushed to the wharf and waved their hats in greeting. Some females—"I could not tell whether they were white or black," wrote one observer, "but they certainly were not of the first circles"—waved their handkerchiefs. The same observer remarked that the owners of those waving hats and fluttering handkerchiefs were known and that if the Federals ever left Jacksonville, those owners, "if they value their lives, will leave when the Federals do." A deputation from Jacksonville headed by one Burritt, "a Northern man," boarded the flagship of the flotilla and surrendered the town.[47]

When the Federal troops landed from the gunboats and occupied Jacksonville, a new phase of the war was begun. The troops were not aware of the fact and neither were their commanders, but as soon as they were ashore they became involved in domestic politics in Florida. The Union sympathizers at Jacksonville were mostly merchants, lumbermen, and real estate operators who remained in the town to protect their investments. They wanted the Federal forces to remain permanently and sought to influence the military commanders to abandon their intention of shortly evacuating the area. These "Union men" cooperated with the occupying troops and suggested that Union sentiment in the area was so strong that if given an opportunity, the people would immediately return to the Union. To evacuate Jacksonville, they contended, would be a grave mistake, since the city was the center of this loyalty to the Union. Instead, the argument continued, the occupation should be made permanent and a civil government loyal to the United States established.[48]

A meeting of the loyal citizens of the "United States of America" was held on March 20. This meeting, attended by "about seventy loyal men," condemned the right of secession, asserted that the secession of Florida was illegal and that Florida was still a state within the United States, petitioned the Federal government to maintain sufficient forces at Jacksonville to protect their "persons and property," and called for an immediate "convention" of "all the loyal citizens" of Florida for the purpose of organizing a state government loyal to the United States. These efforts by the Jacksonville Unionists were temporarily successful. The occupying force was not immediately withdrawn; in fact, it was strengthened to a total of sixteen companies of infantry.[49]

Confederate forces, after leaving Jacksonville, retired to Baldwin, twenty miles west of the city. Here, at the junction of the Florida Railroad and the Florida, Atlantic, Gulf Central Railroad, Colonel W. S. Dilworth began preparations to resist an invasion of the interior. When the invasion did not occur, Dilworth determined upon a series of raids against enemy pickets and foraging parties. On March 25 they attacked the Federal pickets in West La Villa, a suburb of Jacksonville. Four pickets were killed and three captured with the loss of but one Confederate. The raids continued and the Confederate force grew until Dilworth had 2,700 men in and around Baldwin.

These raids on the outposts and information that the already large Confederate force was to be reinforced by two Georgia infantry regiments caused the Federal garrison at Jacksonville to request immediate reinforcements. They were refused and Jacksonville was ordered evacuated "in view of the . . . already too extended line of operations of our forces in this district." Arrangements were to be made for the safety of "loyal citizens" before withdrawal and notices were posted that any retaliation against noncombatants by the Confederates would be punished.

The Federal garrison evacuated Jacksonville on April 9. Prior to this action, three conferences were held between Colonel William Davis of the Confederate Army and General Horatio G. Wright, Federal commander at Jacksonville, concerning the safety of citizens. The two officers agreed that irregular bands of Florida refugees might return to the city and exact a heavy vengeance upon the residents who had refused to flee before the Federal occupation. As a result, regular Confederate troops moved into the city on the night of April 8 after the Federal garrison had retired to their transports anchored in the river. An unofficial truce was observed. The next morning as the Federal flotilla prepared to sail down the river, Colonel Davis and a company of Confederate infantry were already at work on the docks a few yards from the vessels.[50]

The Confederates never regularly occupied Jacksonville again. Small detachments would enter the town for intelligence purposes but would soon withdraw. The Federals were to return occasionally, however, for the control of the St. Johns River was advantageous to their plans for East Florida. Also, the seed of the political reorganization and reorientation of Florida had been well planted in the minds of United States officials—a seed which was to grow and develop until 1864 and the Battle of Olustee.

It will be remembered that part of the Federal naval squadron which set out from Fernandina on March 8 was ordered to St. Augustine. Federal gunboats arrived off the city on March 11. The city was defenseless because all Confederate troops and five hundred citizens had left the previous night. Early in the afternoon, Commander C. R. P. Rodgers and one Dennis, of the coastal survey, unaccompanied by troops, entered the harbor in a small boat. Mayor Bravo ran up a white flag from Fort Marion and met the commander at the wharf. Bravo then conducted Rodgers and Dennis to the city hall where the city council was in session. St. Augustine was promptly surrendered and remained in possession of the United States throughout the war.[51]

The people of St. Augustine seemed less perturbed about Federal occupation than those at Fernandina or Jacksonville. Only about one-fifth of the two thousand inhabitants left the city. Rodgers visited the local clergymen and assured them Federal forces wished to occupy the city in a peaceable and friendly manner. "I believe that there are many citizens who are earnestly attached to the Union," wrote Rodgers from St. Augustine, "and a large number who care very little about the matter." Nearly all the men, he felt, acquiesced in the occupation and would cooperate with the Federal troops.[52]

The only bellicose spirits left in St. Augustine were the women. "There is much violent and pestilent feeling among the women," Rodgers reported. "They seem to mistake treason for courage, and have a theatrical desire to figure as heroines," the commander concluded. Rodgers found that the flagpole had been cut down before he arrived so that the flag of the United States could not be hoisted.

The men said that the women did it, and one woman, a widow, admitted that they had not only cut down the staff but had chopped it into small pieces as mementoes of the Confederacy. "The men had behaved like cowards," she informed the commander to his face, "but there were stout hearts in other bosoms (striking her own)."[53] Nor did these patriotic women have any respect for the city officials who surrendered the town without resistance. Mayor Bravo and his council were referred to as "low ignorant Minorcans puffed up by their elevation to office."[54]

St. Augustine became a Union rest camp. Little attempt was made to enlarge the Federal-controlled territory around the city. The principal danger came from raids on work details by Captain John Jackson Dickison, a locally renowned leader of light cavalry. Toward the end of the war, St. Augustine was the base for Federal raids into interior Florida but no major operation had its origin in the Ancient City.

This series of reverses to the Confederate cause in Florida had an immediate reaction upon the people. A public meeting at Gainesville discussed the "present and pressing dangers" to the state. The meeting decided that James Bailey and Edward Haile should go to Richmond immediately "to impress in the strongest language upon the government of the Confederate States the great importance of keeping in East Florida an army as a nucleus around which the citizens might rally."[55] A similar meeting was proposed at Tallahassee. In obvious reference to the hasty evacuation of Fernandina, the call for the meeting urged the residents of Tallahassee to defend their city rather than to run off "like so many stampeded mules."[56]

Floridians generally fled the coastal areas for the interior. Nearly all the people living near the St. Johns River fled, with their slaves, when the Federals gained control of the river. Their homes were left unprotected and often filled with furniture because of the hasty flight. The commanders of the Federal gunboats cruising the river between Jacksonville and Enterprise, a distance of 150 miles, took good advantage of these abandoned homes. Landing parties removed the valuables before the homes were burned or shelled. Many Federal officers slept, ate, and drank in comfort, because of a voyage up the St. Johns. Much of the destruction was completely senseless, such as the many orange groves which were cut down.[57] Some of the refugees from the St. Johns region began to fear that the Confederate government would completely abandon Florida. In search of security of person and household property, they fled to Virginia in order to be in an area which they felt confident would be defended.[58]

The plight of these refugees is adequately stated by a recorder of the events of the time. Said she:

> The experience of those who had remained within the Yankee lines disposed all to run away; but the experience of "refugees," as they filled every town and hamlet, was equally severe. War was so new that no one knew what to expect. The imminent danger of the present, and the doubtful security of the future, made confusion confounded in the hurrying to and fro.[59]

The state press set about awakening the people to the stern realities of the defeats which the Confederacy was suffering. The true military situation was given and the overwhelming advantages which the North possessed were pointed out. The hopes of an easy victory over "Yankeedom" were effectively dispelled when one editor wrote in a front page column: "It is time that the evanescent chivalry in the South which has boasted that we could whip the Yankees ten to one had subsided, and that we take a common sense view of our position. . . . The enemy has the greatest array of artillery in the history of the world and an army that is twice as large as that of the Confederacy." These facts, he concluded, "mean that if the Confederacy is to win, every man, every woman, and child must do his utmost at all times."[60]

The influx of exasperated refugees into interior Florida and the campaign by the press to educate Floridians concerning the real danger to the Confederacy caused a growth of resentment against Brigadier General James H. Trapier, Confederate commander in East Florida. "General Trapier has met with the condemnation of every man, woman, and child in Florida," reported the *Savannah News* of March 14, 1862. The general, during inspection trips about the state, was jeered all along his route. Once a woman entered his railroad car and placing a basket at his feet announced loudly that it contained a new uniform for him. Upon opening the basket, the general found a complete change of women's clothing—hoop and all.[61] The feeling against Trapier was so intense and bitter that he was relieved of his command on April 8, and replaced by Brigadier General Joseph Finegan.[62]

The Confederate government became convinced that its calculated risk in not defending Florida coastal areas was the correct defense. Fernandina, Jacksonville, and St. Augustine had been occupied by the Federal troops and no invasion of the interior had followed. Therefore, on April 19, General Finegan, the new commander of Middle and Eastern Florida, was officially notified that Florida coasts were not to be defended as it appeared that the enemy would make no effort to occupy the state in force. Finegan was ordered to defend the Apalachicola and St. Johns rivers and to keep sufficient forces to protect any supplies which might enter the state after running the blockade. Except for the forces needed for these purposes he was to release all troops under his command for use in other parts of the Confederacy.[63] General Finegan, upon receipt of these orders, reported that he probably could defend the Apalachicola, but that the Federal gunboats were in firm control of the St. Johns as far upstream as Palatka.[64]

In accordance with orders, troops were rapidly moved from Florida to other parts of the Confederacy. Finegan had assumed command over 6,368 men. Of these, approximately 4,000 had adequate arms and equipment.[65] By the end of September, 4,000 had been ordered from the state and General Finegan was confronted with the problem of defending Florida with an army of 2,368 men.[66] The number of troops in the state remained stable throughout the rest of the year and during 1863.[67]

As the Confederate forces in Florida were reduced and withdrawn into the interior, the Federal government adopted a strategy of raiding coastal localities. These raids, usually carried out by sailors from the blockading vessels, could be executed with little loss to the raiding party. Throughout 1862 such raids caused extensive damage, and from April, 1862, until February, 1864, they constituted the principal hostile action by United States forces inside Florida.

The first raid in force by Federal naval vessels was against Cedar Key. The town, located on one of a series of islands on the Gulf Coast, was a terminus of the Florida Railroad and a center for blockade running. On January 16, 1862, a landing party from the blockading vessel *Hatteras* entered the town and destroyed the railroad depot, railroad wharf, seven freight cars, telegraph office, a turpentine warehouse, four schooners, three sloops, a ferry barge, and the abandoned Confederate defenses. "We were extremely successful, with the expenditure of very little powder and no one killed," reported Commander George Emmons of the United States

Navy.[68] No resistance was offered by the small Confederate garrison. One officer and twenty-two men had been detailed to protect Cedar Key. When the attack appeared imminent, however, the residents petitioned the Confederate lieutenant to offer no resistance as it would be futile and only bring revenge upon civilians.[69]

The lieutenant and fourteen of his men attempted to escape on a flatboat propelled by poles. The water was too deep for their poles to touch bottom, and the current swept them into the hands of the enemy. Four of them had measles, however, and since the physician of the *Hatteras* would not allow them on board, they were released. The Federal sailors and the Confederate prisoners who had had contact with them were quarantined for fear of a measles epidemic breaking out aboard ship.[70]

Apalachicola was defended early in the war almost entirely by state troops. After the state convention of January, 1862, ordered the disbanding of all state troops, by March 10 the city was left almost defenseless. Hence, most of the population fled to Ricco's Bluff on the Apalachicola River some ninety miles inland. The Union blockaders began to move inshore and prepared to seize the town. On the night of April 2, a small detachment of sailors and marines from the blockading vessel *Sagamore* entered Apalachicola, and early the next morning raised the Stars and Stripes amid ceremonies proclaiming the city officially surrendered to the forces of the United States. The only residents remaining were slaves and a few of the poorer whites—mostly women and children. Federal Commander Henry S. Stellwagen lectured them on the evils of secession and warned that any display of sympathy for the Confederacy would be suppressed. The commander granted them permission to fish in Apalachicola Bay, provided they did not use their vessels or their catches of fish to aid the Confederacy.[71]

The Union forces withdrew following the ceremony and never occupied Apalachicola permanently. Nor did Confederate forces reoccupy the town, and it became an area controlled by neither side. As late as June, 1864, General Pierre G. T. Beauregard, commander of the military department, and General Samuel Jones and General J. Patton Anderson, commanders in Florida, considered Apalachicola as enemy territory even though there were no Federal forces stationed there. Governor John Milton, however, considered this position absurd and continued to exercise civil authority over the town.[72]

The only raid costly to Federal forces during 1862 occurred at New Smyrna on March 22. A quantity of arms had been brought through the blockade into Mosquito Inlet. The Federals received news of this fact and dispatched a gunboat to capture the blockade runner and its cargo. The Confederate defenders of the cargo, having just evacuated St. Augustine without a fight, were eager for a battle. Upon learning of the Federal expedition, they prepared an ambush and succeeded in killing forty-two of the fifty-two Union men who came ashore.[73] Revenge was taken against New Smyrna by the United States Navy on July 26, 1862, when four vessels entered the inlet and fired over five hundred shells into the little settlement. A landing party then burned those houses which had escaped the shelling. The residents fled to the underbrush around the town and suffered no casualties.[74]

The heavy losses during the first raid did not deter Federal raiding parties. A small detachment from the *Kingfisher* landed near St. Marks on June 15, 1862, and burned several houses and the lighthouse.[75] Tampa was shelled by the Federal gunboats *Sagamore* and *Ethan Allen* on June 30 and July 1 after refusing an ultimatum to surrender. Very little damage was done to the city or the defending Confederate battery. The Confederates returned fire but were unable to damage the gunboats because their artillery was not powerful enough to reach them.[76] The Federal navy returned to Tampa Bay on October 16, and shelled Tampa while a landing party burned a vessel anchored six miles above the town in the Hillsborough River. As the raiding party was wading to the boats sent for them, a Confederate cavalry unit arrived and charged into the shallow water, attacking with sabers while the sailors defended themselves with pistols. Three Federals were killed, twelve wounded, and three taken prisoners. The Confederates lost six killed and seven prisoners.[77]

In accordance with Confederate strategy to retain control of the Apalachicola and St. Johns river basins, General Finegan prepared to block the St. Johns to Federal gunboats. During the summer of 1862, the Confederates erected batteries at Yellow Bluff and St. Johns Bluff below Jacksonville, which were successful in keeping the Federals from coming up the river. In an effort to reduce these batteries, a Federal force of 1,573 men left Hilton Head, South Carolina, on September 30 to cooperate with the gunboats in destroying the batteries and reopening the St. Johns to Federal vessels. The transports arrived at the river's mouth on October 1, and were joined by a flotilla of six gunboats. The expedition immediately began to move against the Confederate gun emplacements.[78]

The Confederate battery at St. Johns Bluff was the more formidable of the two emplacements. Containing six eight-inch guns and two four-inch guns, its capture was considered the key to the success of the raid on the river. The troops at the battery, commanded by Colonel Charles F. Hopkins, numbered approximately five hundred men. When the combined land and water expedition moved against him, he decided to abandon the position and withdrew his troops from the area. Removal of the guns and ammunition was impossible so they were ordered destroyed. This order was not executed, however, because the powder trail meant to blow up the magazine failed to burn evenly and the fire died out before reaching its destination. The Union landing party, therefore, captured all the guns and their ammunition.[79] The battery at Yellow Bluff was evacuated prior to the arrival of the Union gunboats. With the fall of the battery at St. Johns Bluff, Confederate control of the river once again was lost.

The Union gunboats proceeded up the river and Jacksonville was again occupied on October 5. For four days Union scouting parties were sent out from the city, and a few minor skirmishes occurred. Since the principal object of the expedition was to secure control of the river, there was little interest in holding the town. As a result, the Federal forces left Jacksonville on October 9, and returned to Hilton Head. The gunboats retained control of the river, however, and could reoccupy Jacksonville at their pleasure.[80]

The following spring, on March 10, Jacksonville was occupied for a third time by Federal troops. They came to collect Negro recruits, to plunder, and to satisfy the growing demand "by the Florida men" that Jacksonville and the St. Johns area be occupied so that a state government loyal to the United States could be established. "It was urged that it was worthwhile in the effort to hold Florida," stated Colonel Thomas Wentworth Higginson, commander of the expedition, "and perhaps bring it back into the Union." "My chief aim," he added, "was to get the men into action." The invading military consisted of two regiments of Negro troops called the South Carolina Volunteers. Two weeks later this force was reinforced by the Eighth Maine and the Sixth Connecticut regiments of white troops.

This expedition to Jacksonville marked the first use by the enemy of Negro troops in Florida. The "Florida men," Higginson reported, leaked the news of the proposed expedition to correspondents of the northern press. Immediately, the minor expedition was depicted as a "great liberating host of five thousand Negroes."[81] The Negro regiments were not looked upon as "liberators" in Florida, however. General Finegan issued a proclamation to the people of the state informing them of the presence of Negro troops in Jacksonville and calling upon all Floridians to organize into military companies for the defense of their homes.[82] Floridians did not become unduly alarmed over the use of the colored troops. One editor advised columnists and all those demanding that the Negroes be driven from the state that the military would be pleased to have them do their fighting in services of the Confederacy rather than in the parlors of young ladies.[83]

Federal troops raided and plundered the country adjacent to Jacksonville. Sharp skirmishes were fought at several points with Confederate cavalry, and several artillery duels occurred between the Federal garrison and a mobile Confederate battery.[84] The increase of Confederate troops in the vicinity of Jacksonville, and the shortage of plunder and Negro recruits made the occupation less attractive. As Union sentiment was practically nonexistent outside of the Union lines and deserters' camps, the Federal troops prepared to abandon Jacksonville for the third time.

The evacuation began on March 29. As part of the troops were moving to their vessels, flames suddenly burst up from several points in the town, and immediately the hoodlums among the Union soldiers began sacking private dwellings, stores, and churches. Doctor Alfred Walton, a Unionist who had practiced medicine in Jacksonville before the war and returned as a physician with the occupying forces, recorded in his diary:

Saturday, March 28, 1863 . . . at 9:00 A.M. some of the boys set fire to the Catholic Church, and it (together with the parsonage, all furnished) was destroyed. Two other houses were also burned.

Sunday, March 29, 1863 . . . Before we were ready to embark the boys began to set fire to the city, and soon we had to hurry up for the smoke was getting rather uncomfortable. . . . [I] ran into St. Johns Church and groping through the smoke and fire I took from the altar a large gift bound prayer book. . . . Further down on Market street I entered a burning building . . . and took . . . a manuscript map of . . . Jacksonville. Farther down I saw some negro soldiers setting fire, and from their songs and shouting they appeared to be having a good time.[85]

The town would have been almost destroyed by the fire had not General Finegan rushed all his available troops into the city to fight the flames. Almost six city blocks were ravaged.[86]

The passing of the ships bearing the departing military out of the St. Johns River marked an end to major raids in Florida during 1863. Jacksonville was to have quiet as Federal forces were not to return for almost a year. The raids against coastal areas had not seriously crippled Florida as a contributor to the Confederate war effort. They had not brought about serious loss of life, and with the exception of Jacksonville, the St. Johns basin, and New Smyrna, personal property losses had not been great. Floridians did not feel secure, however, with the specter of invasion of the interior ever present. Would it come and from what direction? Only the future held the answer.

V

A DERANGED STATE OF AFFAIRS

SECESSION DID NOT PRODUCE any major change in the form of state governments in the South. Transition from the Federal Union to the new Confederate Union was accomplished simply, directly, without much change in constitutions, and with little experimentation. The conduct of a major war, however, even under favorable conditions of internal stability often results in confusion in government. In the individual southern states, the urgency of the war situation demanded assumption of governmental functions which were new to them. The states found themselves suddenly confronted with functions of defense, control of the manufacture and transportation of essential goods, aid to indigent families, and the financing of these and related war measures. Under such extraordinary circumstances, it is not surprising that the stability of the state governments underwent severe trial. Florida experienced these stresses and demoralizing influences to a lesser degree than some of her sister states in the Confederacy, but she too had adjustments to make.

The secession convention and the state legislature, by ordinance and statute, provided for some of the exigencies of the moment. New financial and industrial institutions were incorporated, or given the authority to increase capitalization. Some of these newly-provided-for institutions would be needed in event of war, while others demonstrated a feeling of confidence in Florida's future stability.[1]* Funds were appropriated for the fiscal year,[2] and temporary arrangements made to meet the expense incurred during the meeting of the convention.[3] Banks were required to pay all liabilities in specie,[4] and a regular method of bank examination was adopted. Regulations concerning commercial fishermen were adopted and

*Notes to Chapter V begin on page 225.

provision made for harbor improvements.[5] Arrangements were made for state representation in the Confederate Provisional Congress.[6] Money was issued by the state,[7] and many other measures which logically followed the secession of Florida were enacted. Although passed in the face of impending war, none of this legislation was designed as war legislation. The General Assembly of Florida made the transition from the Federal Union to the Confederacy with no display of fanaticism.

But war brought many problems to the state. Thousands of her citizens marched away to join the Confederate armies; the cordon of the Federal blockade tightened; the food supply diminished perceptibly; financial confusion spread and security steadily fell in value; private business interests tried, by fair means or foul, to adjust themselves to wartime conditions; Confederate armies fought a losing battle to uphold the Confederate government. Faced by such problems, the state legislature briefly demonstrated competence, then became more and more inept and enacted restrictive and arbitrary laws.

The courts proved ineffective almost from the beginning. Cases pending in the federal courts were transferred to a system of state circuit courts established by the legislature in February, 1861.[8] These new courts were almost paralyzed by the suspension of action concerning debts. All process at law for debts was arrested until the first Monday of 1862.[9] All process at law was also forbidden to any citizen of the United States of America until that government recognized the independence of the Confederate States.[10] Active warfare brought such disorganization that the courts voluntarily suspended much of their business. The holding of court became uncertain; the judge of the Western Circuit temporarily suspended court because it was impossible to secure a petit jury.[11]

In December, 1862, the legislature passed an act allowing certain county courts either to omit sessions entirely or to hold them at more convenient places, provided that in each case due notice was given.[12] Another act authorized the trial of individuals in counties other than those where crimes were committed if regular court procedure was interrupted by the enemy.[13] State law compelled circuit judges to hold court at regular sessions or at a time and place which had been duly advertised. As Federal raids became more numerous and Federal occupations within the state became firmly established, judges were often unable to comply with the law. The legislature refused to repeal the statute but passed a "Resolution of Relief" to the effect that the errant judge had "good and sufficient" reason for noncompliance with the law. Hence no punitive action was taken.[14]

Only probate courts continued to function with any regularity in the areas exposed to the enemy and in the isolated southwestern area of the state. Liaison was so poor between the southwest and Tallahassee that when the solicitor for the Southern Circuit entered the army in 1861 it did not become known to state officials until April, 1864, when he applied for his salary.[15] The circuit courts in central Florida remained more stable and the Suwannee Circuit held regular sessions in Gainesville. This court caused a great deal of annoyance to Confederate military authorities in cases involving impressment of goods and supplies. The most important conflict over impressment adjudicated in the Suwannee Circuit arose from seizure of property belonging to the Florida Railroad.[16]

Criminal justice fared badly during the war. Most localities had no local law enforcement agency and depended upon the sheriff for protection of person and property. The sheriffs were handicapped by state law, however, for they could have no deputy of conscript age.[17] Consequently, localities large enough to have a municipal government depended upon the mayor to enforce town laws.[18] The counties with large slave populations turned to the county patrol as an agency of protection against violence. The legislature in December, 1863, increased the age group of those subject to patrol duty to embrace all males between sixteen and sixty years of age. This was not as effective in combating crime as had been hoped, and by June, 1864, one editor was decrying the fact that "stealing and all kinds of villainy, is the order of the day, and it seems more difficult to detect the rogues now than in time of peace."[19] Another editor lamented that "there was a time when a man might go to sleep and leave his house open with impunity . . . but we fear that time has passed away."[20]

Enforcement of all law on the local level became more difficult as the war progressed. Complete collapse of the local governmental agencies did not occur, however, except in the fringe counties in eastern Florida and in the isolated southern section of the state. This collapse was the result of the dislocation of persons, the activity of the enemy, and the growing number of desertions from the army. St. Johns County, in East Florida, had no county officials performing their duties after the summer of 1864;[21] and Volusia and Duval counties suffered from the desertion of officials to the enemy.[22]

The collapse of local government greatly affected state income because taxes could not be collected.[23] As early as December, 1862, the state gave up efforts to collect taxes in the counties "that are now abandoned, held, possessed, or controlled by the enemy."[24] Floridians abused the provisions of this act by claiming immunity from taxation if any Federal troops entered their county. The tax assessor of Clay County, seeking to clarify the legislation as it concerned his county, wrote to Walter Gwynn, the state comptroller:

> Mr. Comptroler, Dir Sir the yankeys has bin thru my countey twice and has landid at green cove springs as mutch as three times dus this clean tha Countey From paying taxis ples let me no.[25]

The Comptroller refused to comply with the request and informed the assessor that taxes would be collected from the time of the withdrawal of Federal troops.[26]

As local government collapsed in the fringe areas, it became impossible to comply with tax laws. The state greatly complicated matters by refusing to assume the risk of allowing tax revenue to be sent to Tallahassee by mail. Collectors were notified that for all revenue sent by mail they would be held liable by the state.[27] This dilemma did not worry the collector of Nassau County. Upon receipt of the notification, he informed the comptroller that he had $895 on hand. Refusing to mail the money because of the liability and refusing to take it to Tallahassee "because of farming operations," he plainly told the comptroller that if the money ever got to Tallahassee someone would have to come and get it.[28]

By the middle of 1864, popular opposition forced most tax assessors and tax collectors in the fringe areas to suspend operations. "My services are in demand as a soldier [in the newly created militia]," one assessor informed the comptroller, "as my fellow citizens think it of more importance to defend the county than to assess taxes."[29] The problem faced by these officials is aptly stated in this report from Manatee County:

> It is out of the question for the Tax Collector of this county to come up to the letter of the law the men are all Soldiers either for or against us and it is a difficult matter to see the owners of the property to get his tax and if I was to offer property for sale I would

not get a bid and besides the Yankees and Torries are strolling around trying to capture all sivel officers send me the Books [tax books] and I will do my best . . . the revanue will be smawl as nearly all the property has bin removed to outher counties or captured.[30]

Realizing the futility of attempting to enforce the letter of the law, state officials early in January, 1865, adopted a plan of assessment allowing the property owner to assess his own property, under oath, and the state accepted the tax payment without question.[31] This was a frantic effort to salvage a small portion of the income lost by the collapse of local government. Based upon the optimism that the plan was workable, tax books were sent to twenty-five of Florida's counties less than a month before the end of the war.[32] The end being apparent, however, and demoralization on the home front growing daily, the state received less than $5,000 in depreciated currency under the novel policy.[33]

Amid the chaos that wartime conditions produced in all branches of government, it was the governor upon whom the responsibility of running the government ultimately rested. It was natural, too, that the influence of the executive was greatly increased during the war. Successful prosecution of a war is largely a matter of effective administration, for myriad problems require immediate settlement. Laborious resolution of issues by deliberation in a popular legislative assembly must give way, through broad legislative delegations of discretionary power, to a combination of administrative planning and execution. When a country is united and confident of its persisting democratic institutions, this transition is easily effected; but when the situation is aggravated by the internal dissension of civil war, it is difficult to make such an adjustment. It is not surprising, therefore, that the powers and the prerogatives of the governor of Florida became an immediate issue.

Existing political arrangements were not calculated to help the state adjust. Governor John Milton was elected in October, 1860; but he did not take office until October 1861. Between Milton's election and his assumption of office the state seceded from the Union, entered the Confederacy, and became engulfed in a full-scale war.

The mood of the greater part of the population changed during this interval from one of anxious waiting to an inflamed belligerency. Governor Perry, a native of South Carolina who served as governor from 1857 to 1861, assumed a very radical position. His message to the legislature in November, 1860, was full of strongly worded exhortations against the North, ending with an appeal for a secession convention. "For myself, in full view of the responsibility of my position," he stated, "I do most decidedly declare that in my opinion the only hope the Southern States have for *domestic peace and safety,* or future respectability and prosperity, is dependent upon action now; and that the proper action is—Secession."[34] When the convention met early in January, 1861, he was not only in complete sympathy with successful radical demands for immediate secession but aided in creating an atmosphere favorable to the radicals throughout the state by sending troops to take over the Federal arsenal at Chattahoochee,[35] Fort Marion at St. Augustine,[36] and the Pensacola Naval Yard.[37]

Governor Perry was a realist. Upon the secession of Florida from the United States, he warned that military preparations were necessary. "Is it not our duty," he asked, "to prepare to sustain, by arms, what we have determined upon in our councils?"[38]

Under Perry's guidance the General Assembly passed the legislation necessary for raising troops, purchasing munitions of war, and other expenses incidental to the defense of the state. Perry was not a good administrator during a period of crisis, however. Army commissions were issued with great rapidity and with little thought of creating a balanced defense force.[39] Personal friendship often proved more important as a prerequisite for acquiring a commission than military competency.[40] Troops were ordered into service more rapidly than they could be equipped; and instead of combining the armed companies into completely armed regiments, Perry allowed most regiments to remain only partially armed.[41] Much unnecessary expense was incurred in procuring weapons for the state troops,[42] and the expense of civil government was increased to a point where the state was in severe economic crisis before the end of the summer of 1861.[43]

By way of contrast, Governor-elect John Milton was a mild conservative. Born in Jefferson County, Georgia, April 20, 1807,[44] he was graduated from the University of Georgia, after which he read law and was admitted to the Georgia bar. He first entered Georgia politics in 1833 as candidate for Congress and an advocate of nullification. He was defeated and soon moved to Mobile, Alabama, where he became a successful attorney and an officer in the Alabama militia. When the Seminole War began in 1836 he left his law practice to command a company of Alabama militia in Florida. At the conclusion of hostilities, Milton moved to New Orleans where he maintained a law office on Canal Street until 1845, when he moved to his newly acquired plantation, Sylvania, in Jackson County, Florida. Jackson County, with Marianna as its county seat, was in the heart of the cotton region of the western part of the state. Here be became a wealthy planter and increased his land and slave holdings. By 1859, he owned a total of 7,326 acres of land, and, by 1861, 52 slaves.

Milton entered Florida politics in 1850 as a candidate for the lower house of the General Assembly. He was successful and made an outstanding record as a legislator during that crisis year in national politics. Many violent speeches were made in the Florida legislature during the course of the debates over the nation's problems, but John Milton did not make them or author them. Instead he used his energies in diligent work on such important committees as militia, Indian affairs, judiciary, and schools and colleges. Milton did not offer for re-election but had become known throughout the state as a conscientious person whose political philosophy contained both liberality and idealism.

The year 1860 with its ominous issues was an appropriate one for Milton to re-enter the political arena. He served as chairman of the Florida delegation to the Democratic convention at Charleston and worked zealously to keep the party united. When this unity proved impossible, he joined his more radical colleagues in denouncing the northern Democrats and in calling for a repudiation of the theory of Squatter Sovereignty. Milton, now looked upon as a radical by many Floridians, became the Democratic gubernatorial candidate after a bitter convention struggle in which the predominantly conservative areas of West Florida supported him. The so-called South Carolina Ring, led by Governor Perry, had opposed Milton. The Democrats won the state elections in a closely contested campaign, and John Milton became governor-elect of Florida as the state was entering the secession crisis.[45]

During the long interval between his election and his inauguration, Governor Milton, whose military experience made him aware of the gravity of war, spent much time inspecting the state defenses. He did not like what he saw. On October 2, 1861, five days before he was inaugurated, Milton wrote confidentially to Mallory, "The fact is, our State is in a most deplorable condition." "In the present deranged state of affairs," he continued, "I shall be inaugurated and enter upon the duties of governor on next Monday with a heavy heart and a fearful apprehension."[46]

Upon assuming office, Milton became very dissatisfied with the administration of the state military organization. He found the direction of military affairs in the hands of the radical followers of Perry, who, Milton felt, lacked the capacity for military organization and leadership. This was especially disagreeable to Milton as he was personally opposed to Perry and his followers. "Governor Perry," he wrote to President Jefferson Davis, "is, I reckon, as you would have perceived, a man of strong prejudices, without very extraordinary intellectual abilities."[47] Milton at once implored the Confederate government to review "the illegal appointments of Governor Perry," and used the power and influence of the state executive office to curb the more odious appointees.[48]

The defense of the Apalachicola River basin was a prime factor in Milton's plans for the state defense. This basin formed the center of communications not only from the Gulf to East and West Florida, but also from Florida to Alabama and Georgia. Milton had given the defense of the basin much thought prior to his inauguration and was completely dissatisfied with the arrangements made by Governor Perry. As a result, he immediately protested the actions of the ex-governor and the dying Confederate commander in Florida, Brigadier General John B. Grayson. Grayson had appointed Colonel Edward Hopkins, a friend of Perry, commander of the defenses in the Apalachicola region. Milton protested this action to the war department and attacked Hopkins' ability as a military leader. [49]

The war department did not take immediate action to relieve Colonel Hopkins from the Apalachicola command; therefore, Milton took action as Governor of Florida. Declaring that "the public good requires a change, *prompt and decided,*" he relieved Hopkins of the responsibility of defending all areas around Apalachicola except St. Vincents Island. Colonel Richard F. Floyd, of the state troops, became the commander of all mainland defenses of the city. Floyd was to conduct only "official" intercourse with Hopkins and was not to "permit him [Hopkins] in any manner, however slight, to interfere with your command."[50]

Milton began immediate agitation for the removal of Confederate troops from St. Vincents Island as a method of removing Colonel Hopkins from the area. The war department cooperated and the Island was evacuated.[51] Hopkins was transferred to Fernandina by the war department after the governor threatened to arrest him for delay in the evacuation.[52]

The transfer of Colonel Hopkins to Fernandina was not a complete victory for the governor. A struggle had already developed between the Perry appointees at Fernandina and Milton. The controversy centered upon the legality of an artillery battalion created by Perry. The former governor had organized five companies, intended to be a part of the Fifth Regiment of Florida Volunteers, into an artillery battalion and appointed a very close friend, D. P. Holland, as its commander. Milton said that this action was illegal under any circumstance, and he urged the Confederate government to send the companies into a camp of instruction or retire them.[53]

The commanding officer at Fernandina, William Scott Dilworth, a friend of Perry, struck back at Milton by defending the legality of the artillery battalion. "I trust," he wrote to Judah P. Benjamin, "the officious meddling of scared politicians, who have never raised voice or hand for our independence, will receive that merited rebuff from headquarters it deserves for meddling with the acts of better men."[54] The Secretary of War, however, refused to accept the artillery battalion into Confederate service because investigation showed "that this battalion possesses but a single battery . . . barely sufficient for a single company."[55]

Colonel Dilworth did not cease his efforts in behalf of Holland. Upon the death of General Grayson and the subsequent delay in the appointment and arrival of a successor, Dilworth, as senior officer, became acting Confederate commander in Florida. When this occurred, Milton, as commander of state troops, ordered Holland's battalion to disband immediately. This order was ignored and Dilworth mustered the battalion into Confederate service as light infantry attached to the Fourth Division of Florida Volunteers.[56] The governor challenged this action and appealed directly to President Jefferson Davis. Calling the election for commanders of the Fourth Regiment illegal, Milton wrote:

> The time of the election was only known a day or two before it occurred, and was intended to secure the command to D. P. Holland, who happened to be a pet of Governor Perry, and whose character was so odious that he was beaten by Hopkins [Colonel

Edward Hopkins whom Milton had removed from command at Apalachicola]—the only man . . . in the State that if the election had been properly advertised, Hopkins could have defeated.[57]

The Confederate government intervened in the dispute by disallowing the action of Dilworth and ordering General James Trapier to Florida as Confederate commander.[58] Holland's battalion was not received into Confederate service, and he lost his position as second in command of the Fourth Regiment. He later entered the Confederate service as an adjutant of the Seventh Florida Infantry with the rank of first lieutenant.[59] Milton had won a clear victory over the radical Florida Democrats in military service. It was to be a costly victory, however, for it united the radical forces against him.

Financial troubles, of course, added to the trying problems of military organization. The actions of the Convention of the People of Florida and the General Assembly contradicted one another on the methods by which money was to be raised.[60] Confusion also existed concerning what would be legal tender for the purchase of public land.[61] The radical Democrats, who had seen their friends ousted from leading military and political positions and replaced with moderate Democrats or ex-Whigs, determined to use the growing financial crisis against the governor.[62] The convention was the one body that could correct these contradictions and aid in alleviating the financial crisis. It was also the only body that could limit the power of the state executive and thus re-establish radical leadership. So the radicals campaigned to reassemble the convention.[63]

The secession conventions of the various southern states operated, implicitly if not always directly, under the sovereignty theory formulated by John C. Calhoun. This theory was based on the idea that sovereignty was illimitable, indivisible, and inalienable. Although sovereignty was an attribute of the whole people of the state, it was exercised through a convention especially chosen as a device by which the people could act in a sovereign capacity. The convention itself thus became in fact the sovereign people, exercising unlimited powers. Calhoun held that this rigid doctrine was necessary to sustain the right to secede and his arguments were largely seized by southern radicals.[64]

The Florida convention, bolstered by the Calhoun doctrine, first met on January 3, 1861, as previously described. Before it adjourned in April (after having recessed from March 1 until April

18), it had passed the secession ordinance, approved a revised state constitution, accepted the Confederate constitution, and passed a number of ordinances necessary for the operation of the state government. In adjourning, the convention not only left the way open for a future meeting, but also insured against any other "sovereign" convention being called during the remainder of the year. Its adjournment resolution stated: *"Resolved,* that this Convention now adjourn sine die, unless convened by the President on or before the 25th of December next. Adopted April 27, 1861."[65]

Nothing further was heard from the convention until its president, John C. McGehee, visited Tallahassee on December 10, 1861. While he was there, many conferences were held and McGehee decided to act because of "circumstances of difficulty and embarrassment in the affairs of . . . [the] Commonwealth, which could not be relieved by any other than *the sovereign power of the state."* Accordingly he issued a call on December 13, 1861, for the convention to reassemble on Tuesday, January 14, 1862, at Tallahassee.

This call and the subsequent actions of the convention raised serious questions as to the legitimacy of the session. In the first place, there was a question as to whether, in scheduling a meeting of the convention for a date later than that established by its own adjournment resolution, the convention was not acting illegally. And secondly, the more important question of the powers of the convention was reopened.

McGehee, as convention president, lightly dismissed the matter of the late date of the meeting with a semantic argument. He construed the word "convene" in the adjournment resolution to mean "call" or "convoke"; by issuing the call prior to December 25, 1861, even though the meeting date was later, there was no violation of the adjournment resolution.[66] Governor Milton disagreed with this logic and requested the attorney general, John B. Gailbraith, "to take steps for the purpose of testing the validity of . . . the Convention." The attorney general refused to challenge the convention's legality, however, as he desired to remain aloof from the struggle between the radical Democrats and the governor.[67] The larger question of the power of the convention was not throughly debated until its actions were complete.

Following the call for the convention, the radicals increased the force of their attack upon Milton. Personal correspondence and the newspapers of the state were filled with demands that the governor's power be limited. "Home affairs are in a very bad way," wrote one of the radicals:

Milton it [is] admitted by all will Bankrupt the state if his hands are not tied. The Convention is called again to meet on the 10 of January . . . it is assembled for the purpose of Either deposing his Excellency or limiting his power. . . . He is as fickle as the wind and surrounded by counsellors who know more about the management of harems than States. . . . The whole State is corrupt and if the war does not soon close we will all go to the devil.[68]

The press, led by the *Florida Sentinel,* had actively argued the case for calling another convention session. Milton was accused of violating "the plainest ordinances of the Convention" and rushing the state into economic disaster by his refusal to disband the state troops. On the opening day of the convention the *Sentinel* defended its legality and suggested that it investigate the administration of Governor Milton. The governor's aides were attacked as being grossly ignorant of "our type of government," and the editor suggested that Florida imitate South Carolina in the creation of an executive council for "the public would rest more confidence in . . . such a council."

As the convention began its deliberations the *Sentinel* intensified its attacks upon the governor. Milton was called "a master of humbug" whose "diploma is brass." His "chief competency," continued the editor, "is the practice of . . . conceit . . . and [a] vulgar leer that makes him disgusting." The governor was characterized as suffering from such a corrupted conceit that it caused him to believe "himself so immaculate as not to be impugned and his dictum so authoratarian as not to be disputed." The editor conceded that he should be charitable and agree that Milton was a good man, but could not decide what was good about him. "Florida," concluded the editorial, "is now Thy paradise lost and never to be regained, by Milton."[69] The only newspaper which unqualifiedly defended the governor was his home county paper, the *Marianna Patriot.*[70]

The convention, with very little debate, corrected the conflict between its action in 1861 and the General Assembly concerning the raising of money. The confusion over legal tender for the sale of public lands was also easily corrected.[71] These issues having been settled, the radical Democrats began their attacks upon Milton.

The governor, during the General Assembly session of 1861,

had called for a law which would prevent any citizen of Florida from monopolizing goods or services for the purpose of speculation. This antimonopoly law had been a capstone of his legislative program for the session and was passed by the General Assembly. The Convention repealed this act[72] despite warnings from Milton that such action would immediately open the "floodgates . . . of villainy."[73]

The radicals, attempting to embarrass both the governor and General Trapier, began an investigation into the reasons for Trapier's decision to establish his headquarters at Tallahassee rather than at Fernandina.[74] Milton assumed all responsibility for the location of the headquarters and reminded the convention that Tallahassee was not only the seat of the state civil government, and therefore the logical location for the military headquarters, but was also centrally located for the defense of both coasts.[75] With this indisputable logic, the moderates in the convention were able to defeat narrowly a resolution of censure against Trapier.[76]

Meanwhile, a committee was investigating the financial condition of the state government. The committee's report contained a sharp criticism of the governor. "Your Committee," the report read, "cannot omit to note the fact $21,000 of the funds of the State were in the hands of the Governor . . . and no information given thereof."[77] Milton was unable to answer publicly this open attack upon his honesty because the state treasury was empty except for $21,000, and he considered it necessary to keep this fact secret. He requested a committee of "discreet men" from the convention, explained the situation to them in confidence, and requested continued secrecy as the money was needed to pay the state troops rather than to meet civil expenses. This was done, and although the *Florida Sentinel* questioned the governor's honesty,[78] Milton did not openly defend himself until the troops were paid.[79]

The capstone of the radical attack upon the power of the governor was the creation of an executive council. The parallels between the action of the South Carolina convention and the Florida convention are too striking to be ignored. The Florida radicals had looked to South Carolina for leadership during the secession crisis and it was natural that they would imitate that state when they sought to curb the governor's power.

The South Carolina executive council was composed of the governor, the lieutenant governor, and three other members selected by the convention. The council was vested with almost unlimited war powers. In fact, it went far beyond a cabinet system and was in actuality a council of safety of which the governor was merely another member. The appointed members were influential political figures who rapidly seized the initiative from the elected officials. The convention had previously abolished nearly all state cabinet posts; these appointed members of the council, being paid a full annual salary, became extremely active and were able to create and assume the leadership of departments in the state administration.[80]

In contrast with the South Carolina council, the Florida executive council was never important in the functions of the executive branch of the state government. It was created in 1862 by Ordinance Fifty-two of the convention, entitled "An ordinance for strengthening the Executive Department during the exigencies of the present war." The council was composed of four members elected by the convention. Although the text of the ordinance did not include the governor in its membership, the implication was plain that he was to act for all purposes as a council member. The ordinance made it clear, however, that the council was to share fully in "the discharge of the duties imposed and in the exercise of the power conferred" upon the governor.[81] In other words, the convention had decided that extraordinary powers had of necessity to be vested in an administrative authority of the state, that the governor was not to be the sole unchecked depository of these powers, and that an instrumentality of the convention's own creation should be set up which would, in effect, act as a thorough check on the governor by sharing directly in the exercise of these powers. The convention created in legal form a plural executive, and conferred upon it some of the governor's traditional powers and many additional war powers as well.

The powers of the Florida council were identical with those which the South Carolina convention had granted to its council. The governor and council of Florida, acting together, had the power to declare martial law, to arrest and detain all disloyal and disaffected persons, and to order the disposition or appropriation of private property for public uses subject to the owner's right of just compensation. In addition, the council and the governor could make and cause to be executed all orders, regulations, and amendments for bringing into public service the whole or any part of the population. They could maintain the police; make, secure, and employ arms and munitions of war; constitute agencies and appoint the agents necessary to carry out their powers; and draw money from the treasury on warrants from the comptroller for effecting these measures. The council was given the power of appointment over military officers which had previously been in the hands of the governor, as well as certain other appointive powers. The council was also allowed to fill vacancies in its own membership, although Ordinance Fifty-eight amended this provision by providing that the president of the convention could fill the vacancy if caused by death or failure of one of the members to accept the position.[82] The governor was authorized to consult the council in the discharge of all other duties and powers of his office, and if the need arose he could require the council's advice in writing.

The first meeting of this new executive body was to be held, upon the call of the governor, within twenty days of the adjournment of the called session of the convention. If the governor did not issue the call, the council was to assemble on February 28, 1862, and thereafter set its own times of meeting. The governor and any two of the council were to constitute a quorum, and a majority vote of all those present was sufficient for action. Council members were required to take the same oath of office as the governor and were subject to the same disabilities as the governor for malpractice in office. Their pay was equivalent to that of members of the legislature.

Some checks were established against the council's use of arbitrary power. A full record of its proceedings was to be presented to the legislature on the opening day of its session, and were subject to legislative review, even to the extent of revision or repeal of the council's actions.

The executive council members were elected individually by the convention: James A. Wiggins of Marion County won on the first ballot; Mariano D. Papy of Leon was the second member selected, polling a clear majority on the eighth ballot; W. D. Barnes of Jackson won on the tenth ballot; and Smith Simkins of Jefferson won on the eleventh.[83] Among these men only Mariano D. Papy remains a lasting name in Florida political history, having served as attorney general of the state from 1853 to 1860. He was also one of the five commissioners sent to Washington after the surrender of the Confederacy to inquire as to the status of Florida in relation to the Union. Later he participated in framing the Black Code of 1865.[84]

Having enacted these ordinances designed to curb the power of the governor and having struck the governor's plan for state defense a death blow by abolishing the state militia,[85] the convention was ready to adjourn. Although it never met again, it was not prepared to surrender its sovereign status by adjourning sine die. The ordinance creating the council also empowered the president of the convention to reconvene the body if petitioned to do so by any thirty-five of its members. A special committee of five members was created to insure the call in the event of the death, resignation, or disqualification of the president. Thus protected, the convention adjourned at 12:15 A.M. on January 28, having been in session for fourteen days.[86]

Reaction to the new ordinances varied with the attitude of the individual toward Governor Milton. The *Florida Sentinel* of January 28, 1862, hailed the action of the convention and declared that the governor had not been honest in his statements to the convention. The establishment of the executive council and the abolition of the state militia was cheered by the *Sentinel* as an effective means of insuring honesty and frugality in the state government. The *Marianna Patriot* as usual strongly defended Milton and called upon him to become "the defender of the finances and credit of the state" by causing each member of the "unnecessary Convention to pay his own expenses."[87]

The governor, himself, was unalterably opposed to the actions of the convention for he considered the called session an illegal body. Upon its adjournment, Milton immediately requested John Gailbraith, attorney general of Florida, "to take steps for the purpose of testing the validity of the proceedings of the Convention . . . with the view of declaring the entire proceedings of that body null and void." The attorney general refused and informed the governor that he considered the called session a legal continuance of the original convention.[88] Milton, therefore, took no legal action.

But he did not relent in his personal attack upon the legality of the convention. When Papy, Wiggins, and Simkins presented themselves to him on February 28, in accordance with the directives of the ordinance establishing the council, he registered his opposition in cogent terms. His arguments against the convention's legitimacy were grounded in the idea that it was created for the limited purposes of deciding the expediency of secession and the time of secession, if that action was decided upon. At no time, the governor contended, did the people of Florida grant legislative, judicial, or executive authority to the convention. All its authority, Milton stated, was delegated for the specific purpose of secession and for making such amendments to the state constitution as might be necessary to a "free, sovereign, and independent state." The convention had no right, therefore, to create an executive council and "invest it with supreme power over the liberty, lives, and property of the citizens."

The Florida executive council, then, began its life under strained relations, never achieving the prominence of its counterpart in South Carolina. The council met five times: February 28, April 3, April 11, April 26, and May 1, 1862. These sessions lasted from two to three days but were not well attended. Papy and Simkins were more conscientious in attending than Wiggins and Barnes, Papy being present on all five occasions, Simkins on four, Wiggins on two, and Barnes on only one.[89]

By far the greater part of the council's activities were devoted to the approval of resolutions designed to allow the governor to prosecute the war effort more vigorously. A comparison of the council's resolutions with the governor's attitudes on the war and his subsequent requests to the legislature gives strong indications that the council was largely engaged in ratifying decisions which Milton had arrived at independently. With only two exceptions, the council acted unanimously on all matters.[90]

Not many of the council's decisions can be construed as broad policy decisions. Approval of appointments and delegation of authority to the governor in various problems of war administration occur most often in the record. The council granted the governor permission to order the seizure of private arms and to employ the coast guard as part of the state defense until it could be turned over to the Confederacy. The governor was also authorized to take up and use elsewhere specific railroad and telegraph installations which otherwise might fall to Union troops, to declare martial law, and to halt any vessels engaging in blockade-running which did not have his special permission.

Larger and more controversial issues than these also came before the council. The convention's action disbanding the state militia effective March 10, 1862, was most unfortunate. Apalachicola, defended entirely by Florida militia, was expecting an attack at any hour. Its capture would give the Federal blockading squadron an excellent port and at the same time close the mouth of the very important Apalachicola River. Confederate troops were unavailable because most units were being shifted from the deep South to protect the northern borders of the Confederacy. Florida would be defenseless if the governor complied with the convention's action and abolished the militia.

In an attempt to forestall a complete collapse of defenses, the executive council ordered the state troops at Apalachicola to remain on duty until they were relieved by troops of the Confederacy,[91] and also passed a short-lived resolution reorganizing the militia for the entire state. Under the new plan, all nonexempt able-bodied males between the ages of sixteen and sixty were subject to military duty.[92] These men were to be enrolled in the militia company nearest their residence. Each company was to consist of not less than seventy-eight nor more than one hundred men, who would drill at least once a week. Men between eighteen and fifty were subject to active service in the Confederacy, and the various companies were to furnish an equal share of the men required for such service. The older and younger men were to remain organized for home defense when those subject to Confederate duty had been called.[93]

Objections were quickly raised to this plan. The *Florida Sentinel,* previously so eager to give full credence to the extravagant claims of power made on behalf of the convention, now raised the strongest objections to the council's action. Actually the *Sentinel* was beginning a gradual change from its previous outspoken opposition to the governor to a moderate support of Milton. "Where," asked the *Sentinel,* "does the Executive Council get its authority to reorganize the militia? Where does it [get] the power to legislate at all?"[94] And a little later the paper asserted that the council's claim to authority by virtue of the convention ordinance was not valid because, granting that the convention had legislative powers, it had no authority to delegate those legislative powers to any other body. The *Sentinel* made it clear also that it was ashamed of the council for including its own members in the list of those exempt from compulsory military service.

The council heeded the arguments of the opponents of the militia and repealed the reorganization resolution on April 26, 1862.[95] News of the Confederate Conscription Act of April 16 had reached Florida and made the action of the council more acceptable to those desiring a strong militia.

During its lifetime, the council passed a total of about thirty resolutions or ratifications of gubernatorial orders. When it adjourned its fifth session Thursday, May 1, the council scheduled a meeting for the first Monday in July, unless the governor should call a session sooner. On May 15, Milton received a message from Papy, directed to him and the council, in which Papy tendered his resignation without stating the grounds for his action. None of the council attended the meeting called for the first Monday in July, and neither the council nor the governor called a subsequent one. In fact, Milton reported to the legislature in November that he had not seen a member of the council since the adjournment of May 1.[96]

The legislature, realizing that the council was ineffective, and in fact already dead, heeded the governor's arguments and made the demise of the council legal. On December 4, both the House and the Senate repealed Ordinance Fifty-two of the convention and Florida's experiment with a plural executive was at an end.[97]

The experiment had never been a success. The council had incurred the antipathy of many of its earlier supporters by refusing to ride roughshod over Governor Milton. Many were alienated when the council ordered the reorganization of the militia and otherwise assumed legislative functions. The governor weakened the council by refusing to recognize its legality, and thereby declined to be dominated by its actions. Once the highly emotional state of the population in the early days of secession and war had passed away and a cooler appraisal of events was possible, it became obvious that Milton was a competent administrator and that his planning and execution of the affairs of state were adequate, especially in the light of the adverse conditions under which he worked. The *Florida Sentinel* seemed to express the desires of the state in the fall of 1862 when it declared that the coming legislative session should be very cautious how it dealt with governmental institutions and should not "embarrass the state with experimental projects." "At the present," the *Sentinel* concluded, "we must be content to keep pace with the revolution—we cannot be ahead of it."[98] Later the *Sentinel* referred to the governor's message to the legislature as an "able and patriotic paper," and called upon that body to support the governor and his program.[99] Milton had won his fight with the radicals and against the plural executive because public opinion came to support his position. In short, Floridians wanted a return to traditional methods of government.

The rise in public support for the governor also meant that the General Assembly would be more cooperative. This cooperation was hastened by a technicality. A regular election for all county officers, registrar of public lands, a solicitor for the western judicial circuit, and for the two-year-term senators was scheduled for Monday, October 6, 1862.[100] Prior to the election, Governor Milton requested a formal opinion from the attorney general as to the effect the new constitution drawn up by the convention of January 3, 1861, would have on the state senatorial elections held prior to secession. Gailbraith ruled that the new constitution had revised the election code and that all state senators must stand for re-election in 1862—even those who had been elected to four-year terms in 1860.[101] Thus the entire Florida Senate was forced to stand for election.

The voting took place in a calm atmosphere and without undue excitement. There was no great pressure on the voters, and, in general, very little campaigning. "The question was," reported the *Sentinel,* "not what a man has been, but what he is now? . . . We never witnessed an election at which the voters appeared so profoundly impressed with the importance of the occasion."[102]

The results clearly demonstrated the change to a more moderate stand. In Jackson County, a West Florida hotbed of radicalism in 1861, the original Secessionists were defeated and men of moderate views elected to county office and to the General Assembly.[103]

The radicals, however, were not to take defeat at the polls easily. When the Senate convened on November 17, 1862, an immediate contest of seats arose from four senatorial districts. The contest in each instance involved a challenge by a senator who had been elected for a four-year term in 1860 and had been defeated in 1862.[104] The ensuing investigation by a Senate-appointed select committee developed into a question of the validity of the opinion of the attorney general which had forced the defeated senators to stand for election. The select committee upheld the attorney general and decided against the defeated candidates.[105] Thus men elected in the quiet atmosphere of 1862 replaced many of the radicals who had been elected in the emotional era of October, 1860.

Governor John Milton now dominated the political structure of Florida. The radicals had been met and defeated in all areas of state government. Their defeat did not mean their extinction, but they were never to challenge seriously the governor's authority or leadership throughout the remainder of the war.

VI

FLORIDA'S WARTIME FINANCES

PROBABLY NO QUESTION was more vexing to the Confederacy or to its individual states than the problem of finance. Florida was no exception.

Florida had had a sad experience with banks during her territorial days, and as a result it was not until 1853 that a general banking law was passed.[1]* Two years later, the first chapter under the act was issued to the Bank of the State of Florida at Tallahassee. The capital was to be $500,000 in shares of $100 each. By 1859, the capital paid in amounted to $130,000.[2] Only two other institutions were chartered before Florida left the Union. These were the Bank of Fernandina and the Bank of St. Johns at Jacksonville. The aggregate paid in capital stock of the three was $350,000.[3] Florida also had thirteen private banks by June, 1861, but since the state had very limited control over these institutions, little is known about their capital stock or their financial condition.

Besides the notes of these state banks, another kind of currency common in Florida at the outbreak of the war was "railroad money," commonly spoken of as change bills. These change bills were of varying denominations, but as a rule never exceeded $3. They were not legal tender, but were paid out by the railroads to any person who would take them in payment for services rendered, and in return were acceptable by the railroad for all payments to it.[4]

In addition to the lack of ready capital, Florida was handicapped financially by the fact that the counties were negligent in the assessment of taxes and slow in their collections. Hence the receipts at the Treasury hardly balanced expenditures, and it was impossible to build a reserve fund with which to meet any future emergency that might arise.[5] This situation was graphically demonstrated in

*Notes to Chapter VI to begin on page 228.

1856 when there was an Indian uprising and the state found itself unable to pay its volunteers. It was necessary to vote a $500,000 bond issue for the sole purpose of paying off state debts. The bonds did not sell in the open market, however, and Governor Perry was compelled to negotiate a loan in April, 1859, through the agency of John W. Parsons, from banks in Savannah and Charleston. The total amount of the loan was $241,300, payable in twelve months, and from this the state realized $222,015. Security from the state was provided when the legislature authorized a total of $346,000 of the 1856 bonds to be hypothecated for the purpose of retiring this debt when it matured in April of 1861.[6] Thus it can be seen that when Florida withdrew from the Union in 1861, she faced a grave financial situation naturally much aggravated by war.

One of the primary tasks of the General Assembly and the convention, therefore, was to make provision for the quick raising of money to support the government. The treasurer was authorized to make temporary arrangements with state banks, or any person or corporation, to obtain sufficient funds to meet the expenses of that session of the General Assembly. For security, the treasurer was authorized to grant whatever he deemed proper, provided his action did not entail more than 8 per cent interest.[7]

The need for expanded capital manifested itself in the chartering of several new financial institutions. The Planters and Merchants Bank of Pensacola, with capital up to $1,000,000, the Bank of Commerce at Fernandina, capital up to $500,000, the Bank of Tallahassee at Tallahassee, capital up to $500,000, the Western Bank of Florida at Apalachicola, capital up to $300,000, and the German Savings and Building Association at Jacksonville, with capital up to $50,000, were chartered in rapid succession.[8]

New commercial legislation was also consistent with the desire to build domestic capital. All trade, except traffic in whiskey and ammunition, with the Indians of Florida was now legalized and encouraged.[9] At the same time, it became unlawful for any person other than a citizen of Florida to establish a fishery or take fish out of Florida waters. The tax assessors and tax collectors of each county were made fish commissioners for their respective counties and had the duty of issuing licenses to commercial fishermen. The fee for these licenses was set at $500 per boat, and the revenue received was to be used within the county for harbor improvements.[10]

The mere passage of an act chartering a bank does not create banking capital or state revenue. Hence, Florida followed the easiest and most direct course open to her: the rapid expansion of state credit.

State public lands were to be used as a basis for the expansion of credit. These lands had been increased by 7,653,953 acres when at secession the state assumed control of all the land formerly belonging to the United States. By Ordinance Forty-nine of the convention of 1861 valuation of this land ranged from 10 cents per acre to $1.00 per acre, the total evaluation being $4,603,162.99.[11]

Two forms of security issued by the government in expanding credit were treasury notes and 8 per cent twenty-year bonds. On February 14, 1861, the legislature authorized the governor to expand credit to a maximum of $1,000,000. This was to be done by the issue of $500,000 in bonds as described,[12] and $500,000 in treasury notes.[13]

The bonds could not be sold at less than par and did not meet a ready sale. The treasury notes were to be issued in denominations of ones, twos, threes, fours, fives, tens, twenties, fifties, and hundreds. These notes were to be receivable by the state in payment of all dues and demands, including public lands. They could also be used by the treasurer to pay demands on the state provided the holder of a warrant was not compelled to receive them, and provided that they were accepted at par value by the person holding the warrant.

In an effort to stimulate circulation of the notes at par, the legislature provided that no person or private corporation, except railroads, could issue any note of less than $5 in denomination after January 1, 1862. It also provided that any bank which refused to receive state treasury notes at par would have its minimum note denomination raised to $20 and forfeit its right to transact business within the boundaries of Florida.[14]

The same session of the General Assembly made it unlawful for a citizen of any nonslaveholding state forming a portion of the United States to institute or maintain a suit, including litigation for the collection of debts, in any Florida court until its independence or that of the Southern Confederacy was fully recognized by the United States government. Enemy aliens were likewise forbidden to prosecute to judgment any case involving a debt which was to come due on or after May 21, 1861.[15]

The General Assembly was not the only organ of government

which was interesting itself in the state's finances. The convention, which assembled for the second time on February 26, 1861, to recognize the Provisional Confederate Government, was also concerned. This fact led to great confusion because the convention and legislature often passed conflicting ordinances and legislation.

The General Assembly had directed that the issue of treasury notes be acceptable for all debts to the state. The convention, on the contrary, instructed the registrar of public lands to receive only gold and silver coin in payment for the purchase of public lands. The convention also repealed the act of the General Assembly authorizing a loan of $500,000 upon state bonds, but left in force the act authorizing the issue of treasury notes to the extent of $500,000 and its ordinances calling for the governor to borrow $500,000 upon the state's 8 per cent coupon bonds. But Governor Milton found that the bonds would not sell, and the only source of state income left was treasury notes.

The situation was so critical that even though the convention had adjourned sine die after its third meeting in April, 1861 (unless called on or before Christmas day of 1861), the president called it together for a fourth time on January 14, 1862. At this session, the convention reviewed the financial situation and remedied the conflicts between its program and that of the General Assembly. Had the convention then adjourned, the General Assembly would have been the sole governmental agency legislating on matters of domestic economy and finance. The convention did not adjourn, however, until it reviewed the legislation passed by the General Assembly in November and December, 1861.[16]

The legislature in 1861 had attempted, among other things, to combat monopolies and the rising tide of speculation, and to make supplies for the armed forces more easily obtainable. With this in view, it forbade the export from Florida of any beef cattle, dried or pickled beef, hogs, pork or bacon, corn or corn meal, salt or provisions of any kind, except for the use of the state of Florida or of the Confederate States. The maximum profit from the sale of provisions was set at 33 per cent, and the governor was granted power to seize "any provisions for the use of the public service," provided just compensation was granted to the owners.[17] The purchase of provisions by private individuals or corporations with the object of producing a scarcity in the market was declared illegal under the threat of $1,000 fine and imprisonment not exceeding one year.[18]

The convention again confused the situation when it repealed the act which controlled exports, fixed prices, and provided for the seizure of supplies by the state. This action was deplored by Governor Milton, but he found consolation in the knowledge that the convention had adjourned sine die and that no more ordinances would be issued to contradict him or the legislature.[19]

Financial planning in Florida can best be considered by examining the manner in which certain basic financial and economic problems were met. It must be remembered that Confederate government policies affected Florida to a large degree.

The solvency of banks in Florida, as in the Confederacy, presented a primary problem. The few prewar banks and the newly chartered banks, if they were to serve the state, had to be geared to the wartime economy. A great hindrance to this adjustment were Sections 6 and 11 of the General Banking Law adopted in 1853. Section 6 provided that if a bank or corporation failed to redeem its notes upon demand in lawful money of the United States, the comptroller, after sixty days' notice, could pay the person making the demand out of the trust fund that the bank or corporation had posted with the comptroller's office. Section 11 provided that if the comptroller was forced to make the payment for the bank or corporation, he was empowered to sell the stock of the bank or corporation at public auction.[20] The legislature in 1861 suspended the operation of these two sections until twelve months after the cessation of hostilities.[21]

Danger of immediate invasion along the state's lengthy and undefended coastline caused unrest in Florida banking circles. To allay the bankers' fears, and to make certain that the funds of their banks did not fall into the hands of the "public enemy," the legislature authorized any bank to transfer its assets and place of business "when the safety of such assets may be in danger."[22]

The banks' major difficulty was the question of specie payment. All banks chartered by the state were compelled by law to be specie banks. After the election of President Lincoln, however, and especially after South Carolina had taken the lead in seceding from the Union, southern banks began suspending specie payment.

The Virginia banks, first to act, suspended specie payment on November 20 and 21, 1860. North Carolina banks followed on November 24, and Georgia banks on November 30.[23]

As suspension of specie payment spread throughout the South, a Joint Select Committee on the Judiciary was appointed by the General Assembly to investigate the desirability of suspension by Florida banks. This committee communicated with the three institutions chartered by the state and used its findings as the basis for its report.

The committee found that the banks were in sound financial condition but divided on the question of suspension of specie payment. The Bank of Fernandina did not desire legislation authorizing suspension, and since it had ample coin to meet its liabilities, probably would not suspend specie if authorized to do so. The state bank of Florida at Tallahassee desired suspension legislation, but its president doubted that the board of directors would allow the bank to take advantage of any such act. The Bank of St. Johns at Jacksonville did not communicate with the committee, but it was public knowledge that it had suspended specie payment with no apparent ill effects either to its stock or to its notes. This fact caused the committee to make an unfavorable report upon the proposed legislation, reasoning that this evidence was "conclusive proof that it is better to compel the banks to trust the generosity of the public, than the public to trust the generosity of a bank legally authorized to repudiate its obligations."[24]

The failure to suspend specie payment by legislation in 1861 gave rise to the question of the validity of notes which were circulating in Florida from banks in states where suspension had been legalized. This matter became so critical that the General Assembly was forced to pass legislation defining the conditions on which a bank note could be considered a solvent bank bill. It was declared that any bills of banks in the states of Georgia, South Carolina, North Carolina, Alabama, and Virginia that were received on deposit by their neighboring banks should be considered as solvent bank bills and receivable for all obligations to the state of Florida.[25]

The Joint Select Committee on the Judiciary saw danger in this situation. It feared that a serious situation would develop within the state banking system if currency from states which had suspended specie payment continued to be received in Florida upon the same terms as the specie-paying currency of the state.[26] Individual banks also saw this danger and suspended specie payment without waiting for authorization from the General Assembly. This authorization was forthcoming, however, at the next session of the legislature.

On December 14, 1861, suspension was legalized until twelve months after the cessation of hostilities. The purpose of this legislation was to "relieve the community" and to provide an "adequate and reliable currency for commercial intercourse." To guard against excessive issues of notes, all banks which suspended specie payment were required to present quarterly reports to the governor. And if it was discovered that banks were making unlawful issues, the attorney general was empowered to take action in the circuit court of the district in which the bank was located.[27]

The state's banks were in a sound financial condition at the close of 1861. Their circulation had fallen to $116,252 but their specie had risen to $55,071. The loans had risen from $350,000 in January, 1860, to $424,262. The deposits had declined from $120,000 to $108,606.[28] The decline in circulation was no doubt due to the increased number of Confederate and state treasury notes. These notes had increased so rapidly that they actually forced bank notes out of circulation by the end of 1862, and checks were drawn only in treasury notes.[29]

These treasury notes presented the paramount problem in finance to both the Confederacy and the states as they were their principal means of expanding credit. Here both governments were to enter a morass and, because of the lack of proper policies, flounder on deeper into the mire until they were finally engulfed in confusion and disaster.

The first Confederate notes were issued in March, 1861. These bore interest and were modest in amount—only $1,000,000 and in denominations of not less than $50. These notes, in fact, were more like bonds, as they required endorsement each time they were passed. But after the First Battle of Manassas in July, 1861, when the war assumed serious proportions, the Confederacy began its downward road to financial ruin through an inflated currency. In August, 1861, it issued $100,000,000 in notes in denominations of $5 and above, and at the same time provided for $100,000,000 in 8 per cent bonds. The following year millions of notes under $5 were issued and in 1863 a law was passed allowing the treasurer to issue $50,000,000 monthly. But also in 1863 a law was passed which attempted to stabilize the circulation of treasury notes at $175,000,000. This attempt at reduction of the currency failed, and the amount of currency outstanding in the spring of 1864 was approximately $973,000,000.[30] The fact that these Confederate notes circulated in the states simultaneously with state notes served to add to the confusion.

By an act of February 14, 1861, the Florida General Assembly authorized the governor to issue $500,000 in treasury notes. By mid-January, 1862, the conflict between the convention and legislature had ended; thus the notes issued were to be legal tender for all purposes within the state, and the citizens were encouraged to convert them into 8 per cent coupon bonds.[31]

This problem of currency was soon to prove as baffling to the government of Florida as it was to the Confederacy. To declare nonchalantly that notes be issued and to print them proved easy as long as the paper lasted, but to induce the people to accept them at face value was impossible.

The legislature tried unsuccessfully to uphold the value of its notes by law. Notes of solvent banks which received treasury notes at par would be received for taxes, and all state taxation on such banks would be suspended. Those banks which refused to receive the treasury notes at par were forbidden to issue any note smaller than $20.[32]

Throughout 1861 the currency problem in Florida was not critical. The bank note circulation seemed a deterrent to the wild issue of treasury notes for several months. In fact, by November 26, 1861, only $75,000.00 in treasury notes had been engraved, and of this amount only $25,680.00 had been signed by the governor. Of the amount signed, $11,654.55 had been spent for military purposes and $13,838.45 had gone for payment of civil claims. It is significant, however, that of all the treasury notes engraved, none was for a denomination larger than $3.00.[33]

The large issue of low-denomination notes was ample evidence of the drastic need for small bills. This need was further emphasized in December, 1861, when the legislature amended the Treasury Note Act of February 14, 1861, so that persons other than employees or servants of a corporation could circulate "change bills" which had been issued by railroad companies.[34] The legislature also empowered the city of Pensacola to issue $25,000 in small bills. These "shin plasters," as they were popularly termed, were to circulate as currency and had the faith and resources of the city pledged for their redemption.[35]

No such moderation with the printing press was to be displayed during the rest of the war. One of the deterrents to the issue of large amounts of notes in 1861 was a matter of physical limitation—the governor did not have time to sign them. This was remedied as the legislature authorized the governor to appoint five "suitable persons" to the task of signing the authorized treasury notes,[36] providing for a more rapid issue. The first of these was forthcoming in December, 1861, when the governor was authorized to have an additional issue of $500,000 printed for the purpose of meeting the Confederate war tax. These notes were to range in denomination from $5 to $100 and thus did not relieve the shortage of change bills in the state.[37] This shortage remained serious throughout 1862; so serious, in fact, that when Union troops captured Jacksonville in the spring of 1862 they discovered that funds necessary to continue work on a Confederate gunboat could only be raised by issuing promissory notes, valued at 25 and 50 cents. These notes circulated as currency in the area and were known as "gunboat money."[38]

The need for more revenue could not be questioned, and the necessity was so pressing that a further issue of $300,000 of treasury notes was authorized. The state now proceeded to take charge of the business of supplying change and ordered $50,000 of the above sum to be issued in fractional parts of a dollar. Of the rest, $30,000 was to be in 1's, 2's, 3's, 5's, and 10's each, $25,000 each in 20's and 50's, and $50,000 in 100's. Thereafter it was unlawful for any person or corporation, unless expressly authorized by law, to issue or put in circulation change bills of $1 or less under penalty of a fine not exceeding $5,000. After ninety days no others were to be paid out or circulated under a penalty of not more than $1,000.[39] In an address to the legislature, the governor said that it was early discovered that too many large bills had been issued, and that there was a great demand for small bills and fractional currency. He had had small bills engraved, in lieu of the $50,000 of 100's, and suggested that they be paid out only in exchange for 20's or bills of larger denominations.[40] The legislature assented to the change of denomination but not to the suggested contraction of the currency.[41] Instead, an additional issue of $300,000 was authorized for the relief of soldiers.[42]

By the end of the fiscal year of 1863, a total of $1,535,550 of treasury notes had been issued. Of these, $13,622.00 had been destroyed, $48,439.55 had been redeemed, and $382,979.41 was still on hand. This meant that a total of $1,090,509.04 of the state's treasury notes were in circulation. During the fiscal year of 1864, $351,090.15 of new bills were issued,[43] making a total issue of $1,886,640.15 up to December 5, 1864. Of this amount,

$88,824.15 had been redeemed by land sales and destroyed, and there was $311,214.72 still on hand. Thus a total of $1,486,601.28 of state treasury notes was in circulation on December 5, 1864.[44]

During the last days of the war, the legislature became desperate and reckless. In January, 1865, it authorized an issue of $40,000 of 50's, $120,000 of 100's, and $190,000 of 500's, and in April, $363,500 of 50's. This last issue was recorded as having gone to the governor for signature, but it is unlikely that much of it was put into circulation.[45] The size of the denominations of these last issues is of primary importance as an index to the depreciation that struck the state's notes in the closing months of the conflict. The total value of all treasury notes issued during the war came to $2,236,640.35. Of this total, $379,370.36 had been redeemed. Thus at the end of the war, Florida had a total of $1,857,269.99 of state treasury notes in circulation.[46]

The appearance of Confederate notes as a circulating medium had tested the financial loyalty of Florida. Since the state notes were secured by public land, they were worth more than the Confederate notes and it was soon observed that people were paying their taxes and other dues in Confederate currency. This served to undermine the state notes by depriving the state of an opportunity to receive its own notes as payment of dues, and therefore made any large scale redemption of the state notes impossible.

Governor Milton, as a Confederate nationalist, deplored this situation. He blamed the entire depreciation of Confederate notes on blockade running and unnecessary expenses of the Confederate government. Blockade running caused depreciation, he stated, because cotton which had been bought with Confederate notes passed through the blockade and sold at a higher price in specie. The specie thus received was invested in merchandise and brought into the Confederacy and sold at exorbitant prices—payable in notes or cotton. This contention was proved by the fact, he continued, that calicoes which cost from 10 cents to 30 cents per yard in specie were sold for from $4 to $8 per yard, and rum which cost 15 cents to 20 cents per gallon in specie was sold at from $40 to $80 per gallon in Confederate treasury notes.

In order to reduce unnecessary expenses, Governor Milton declared that the number of government employees should be decreased and the combat strength of the army increased. He felt that the "uniform has ceased to be the honorable badge of position in military service, because its admirers cannot distinguish the gallant officer, who has fought bravely in many battles, from the peaceful citizen who has measured thousands of bushels of corn and potatoes, or conducted a thousand cars upon a railroad."[47]

The General Assembly did not seek explanations of the causes of the depreciation. It forthwith branded discrimination against Confederate notes as "unpatriotic" and "traitorous," and provided by law that any person guilty of such discrimination should no longer be exempt from military service.[48] No speech of the governor nor any law of the legislature, however, could keep Confederate treasury notes circulating at par. The state had attempted to aid the central government, but since it could not compel acceptance of its own notes at face value, no wonder it failed with Confederate notes.

The principal bonds issued during the Civil War by Florida were the $500,000 of 8 per cent coupons provided by the convention. These bonds did not meet a ready market, and the state used them to pay such creditors as were willing to receive them, or deposited them with the Confederate government as security for an advance in funds.[49]

Bonds were also issued by the state in December, 1862, in order to repay the money which had been withdrawn from the school fund and the seminary fund in December, 1860, for the purchase of arms. These bonds were to draw 8 per cent interest but could be redeemed before the date of maturity if the state so desired.[50]

The state's bonded indebtedness in 1863 was as follows: bonds of 1861, deposited in Richmond, $297,500; bonds of 1856, $206,000; bonds of 1861, issued for Indian war claims, $4,125; bonds issued to school fund, $99,500; and bonds issued to the seminary fund, $60,992. Thus the state had a total bonded indebtedness of $668,117 as of October 31, 1863.[51] This amount was reduced to $462,117 in December, 1863, as a resolution of the legislature ordered the destruction of the $206,000 of 1856 bonds.[52]

During the four war years Florida's expenses increased enormously. The 1860 budget had been less than $150,000. The yearly budgets during the war averaged more than $500,000. This revenue was expended principally for: (1) provisions for state troops; (2) the payment of Florida's quota to the Confederate direct tax of 1861; (3) supplies for soldiers' families and indigent persons within the state; and (4) the maintenance of hospitals for Florida troops at home and abroad.[53]

To meet this increased expense the state government did not increase its tax rate. The property tax rate, 1/6 of 1 per cent, remained unchanged during the war and actually yielded less than it had in 1860. Florida made an attempt to shift the burden of paying for the war to the future. Many believed that Florida's fertile soil and good climate, together with the fact that the western states would "for many years be exposed to the depredations of Indians, Mexicans, and abolitionists," would stimulate immigration into the state. Thus in a few years taxes to pay off the debts would be "light and would be cheerfully paid."[54]

In a mood of optimism, the General Assembly suspended the collection of taxes for the year 1860-1861 until the next year,[55] and the time for tax returns was changed from January 1 to May 1 of each year.[56] Special consideration was given to any person who had been mustered into the Confederate Army as a private for three years or for the duration; he was exempt from paying any poll or capitation tax. Furthermore, his property up to $1,000 valuation was exempt from taxation, if he so desired.[57]

The periodic invasion of both Florida coasts increased the strain upon the tax structure for it meant actual occupation of certain counties and dislocation of the economy and population in others.[58] Tax assessors and collectors also became very slow in making their assessments and in reporting their tax returns to the comptroller. By December, 1862, fourteen counties had failed to report and of these, two had not reported since 1859 and one not since 1858.[59] Consequently, in 1863 the state required tax collectors and assessors to forward to the comptroller a complete book of the property in each county and its assessment on or before July 1 of each year. Failure to do this meant the forfeit of all commissions for that year and also a fine of $100. An additional fine of $100 was provided for each month that the report book was overdue.[60]

By 1864 Governor Milton had become greatly disturbed about the state tax structure. The tax yield amounted to only approximately one-fifth of government expenditures. Although in sympathy with the expansion of state credit by the issue of treasury notes, Milton felt that this credit had reached a critical point and should not be extended. He, therefore, urged the General Assembly to double the tax rates. This action, he felt, would increase the value of the depreciated treasury notes, and also reduce the state debt and the subsequent need for future heavy taxation. This advice was not heeded; Florida continued to have the lowest tax rate of any Confederate state during the entire war.[61]

Florida did not fare as well under the taxation of the Confederate government. This taxation rested fundamentally upon three statutes: namely, the War Tax of August 19, 1861, the Impressment Act of March 26, 1863, and the General Tax Act of April 24, 1863.

The War Tax was 1/2 of 1 per cent tax on all real and personal property in the Confederacy. This was shifted from the individuals to the state in Florida, and, as we have seen, was paid by an issue of state treasury notes to an amount not to exceed $500,000.

The Impressment Act was the legal recognition of what had been occurring out of military necessity since 1861. This practice was so odious even to the most loyal Confederates that Congress passed legislation regulating the procedure by which articles were to be impressed.[62] Hence Confederate agents were authorized to impress food products and other articles useful to the military. The person from whom the article was seized received compensation at a rate fixed by boards created by the President and the state governors.[63]

The third Confederate General Tax Act authorized a yearly levy of 8 per cent on the value of all naval stores and agricultural products produced within the country. It also provided for large license fees on various occupations, an income tax, a sales tax, and last, but not least, a tax in kind of one-tenth of all agricultural products.[64]

Confederate taxation and impressment of goods brought hardships, but many Floridians were suffering untold privations before the act was passed. One factor causing general distress, in addition to the disruption of an agricultural economy by war and blockade, was the dislocation of population caused by refugees from the coastal areas. Another factor was that able-bodied men by the thousands had marched off to war leaving the women and children to provide for themselves. It is not surprising, therefore, that a grave problem within Florida during the war was the care of indigent families. A program for their relief was begun early with funds raised by three methods: an increase in local taxation, state appropriation, and an issue of treasury notes.

In December, 1861, the county commissioners of each county were given authority to levy annually a separate and distinct tax, not exceeding 50 per cent of the state tax, on all the property subject to taxation within their respective counties. The funds from this tax were to be reserved for the relief and support of indigent families of the soldiers within their respective counties.[65] The following year the county commissioners were authorized to levy an additional local tax of not more than 100 per cent of the state tax. These funds were to be used to purchase clothing or supplies for the men of their respective counties who had joined the Confederate service.[66]

This system of local support proved inadequate. Consequently, a Joint Select Committee of the General Assembly was appointed to consider the entire problem of aid to soldiers' families. This committee found that from $500,000 of the war tax note issue only $233,000 had been needed to pay the tax. This left $267,000 from that issue which had not been placed in circulation, and $159,625 of this was on deposit in the several banks of the state. In addition, there was on deposit in banks a total of $275,000 from the issue of February 14, 1861. The committee requested that these notes be issued to furnish funds for the relief of needy families. The committee realized that these funds would be insufficient, but this amount added to money raised by local taxation would be adequate. The legislature on December 6, 1862, authorized the governor to issue the notes which had not been issued under the acts of 1861. Of this sum, $200,000 was set aside for the needy.

The justices of the peace were required to make lists of persons eligible to receive aid and forward the lists to the comptroller. The entire aid program was to be under the direction of the governor, but actual distribution carried out by the individual county commissioners. The money was to be used for clothing, provisions, cards, spinning wheels, and other necessary family provisions.[67]

The relief program also included a provision for the education of all orphan children of Florida soldiers killed in service. The several boards of county commissioners were required to send the children to the most accessible school. If none was available, they were to establish a school and find teachers for it. The funds for this program were to come from a special tax of 1/3 of 1/6 of 1 per cent on all property taxed by the state.[68] Since this act was not passed until December, 1864, it is highly unlikely that any schools were founded under its provisions.

The Florida aid program was indeed a large enterprise. The state sent between 14,000 and 15,000 men into the Confederate service. During 1862 and 1863, 3,431 families including 11,744 individuals received $186,638.94 in aid from the state. During 1863 and 1864, 3,633 families including 13,248 individuals received

$291,443.40 in aid.[69] In other words, the state government was contributing to the support of approximately one noncombatant for every soldier it had placed in the field.

The cost of supporting the war effort and providing for the non-combatants at home was enormous. As has been seen, the principal method of financing the war had been the issuance of state treasury notes. Of the total amount issued, $1,857,269.99 of these notes were still in circulation and unredeemed.[70] Nor had the $500,000 worth of 8 per cent coupon state bonds, authorized by the convention of January, 1862, been sold during the war. The total bonded indebtedness of the state at the close of the war was $370,617.00.[71] Thus it can be seen that the war cost Florida $2,227,886.99 in governmental debt besides the incalculable costs to individuals through the loss of savings, destruction and depreciation of property.

Florida's economic problems were not essentially different from those of the other southern states during the war. All had rural societies based upon the concept of a staple-crop agriculture. All were victims of the same economic weakness of such a system. All suffered, to a greater or lesser extent, from dislocation of population and destruction of goods by the enemy. All lacked the necessary capital to survive the blockade. When one surveys these factors, it is not surprising that financial chaos followed secession and the subsequent war.

VII

A TISSUE OF ABSURDITIES

ON OCTOBER 7, 1861, John Milton, not without realization of the seriousness of the problems before him, was inaugurated Governor of Florida. His sentiments were expressed in a letter to Stephen R. Mallory, Confederate Secretary of the Navy and a personal friend, when he said:

In the present deranged state of affairs, I shall be inaugurated and enter upon the duties of Governor on next Monday with a heavy heart and a fearful apprehension of my inability to perform the duties of the office creditably and very usefully; but to the best of my judgment I will encounter surrounding difficulties.[1*]

Milton had good reason to be despondent. His predecessor, Madison Starke Perry, had all but destroyed the state militia by allowing its members to volunteer for Confederate service as individuals or in small units with no thought of a systematic approach to the problem. Milton also found Perry's friends directing the remnants of the military organization. Both factors were severe blows to Milton; he was the champion of a strong militia, and also was personally opposed to Governor Perry and his followers. Thus, the new governor found himself in a position of opposing Confederate policy concerning the acceptance of militia volunteers, and of opposing the state military leadership.

Milton immediately took steps to cope with both situations. His struggle with the friends of ex-Governor Perry has been detailed in a previous chapter, where it was made clear he was successful in coping with the radical element in the state military and political organizations. However, the struggle was not finally won until after the election in October, 1862.

*Notes to Chapter VII begin on page 230.

The dispute with the Confederacy was settled more rapidly. On December 9, 1861, Milton wrote to President Davis:

> The troops have been raised by authority of the War Department in disrespect to State authority and in disregard of States rights; and, in addition to the fact of vital ruin they are bringing upon the country, against which it is my duty to and I do solemnly protest, the tendency of the assumption and exercise of such power by the Confederate Government is to sap the very foundation of the rights of the States. . . . The worst feature of Black Republicanism was that it threatened to ignore State boundaries and the rights of States as free, sovereign, and independent parties to the compact known as the Constitution of the United States. . . . Yet the effect would not have been half so ruinous as is the policy pursued by the War Department in assuming to raise up armed bodies of men within the limits of a State in disregard of the constituted authorities of the State.[2]

These were strong words and the disagreement might have had grave consequences. Milton, however, was not a radical advocate of state rights and it seems that his anger at the system was aroused as much, if not more, by the fact that he, as governor, was not being treated with proper respect by Confederate officers. Seeming to sense this fact, General James H. Trapier, who became Confederate commander in Florida following General Grayson's death, began to work for a better understanding between the military and the state executive. His policy was successful and by a simple display of courtesy, he solved the entire dispute concerning the raising of troops. On December 12, 1861, he wrote a letter to Milton asking:

> May I ask of Your Excellency the favor to state whether the Confederate government has the sanction of Your Excellency to retain in service . . . troops already mustered, as also your consent to the mustering into the service of the Confederacy the two other companies now organized.

Milton seized the opportunity to restore harmony and answered the same day:

> It affords me pleasure to express the consent of the Executive of Florida, and to assure you, general, that to the utmost of my power any other requisition that may be made upon the State of Florida by the Confederate Government for forces shall be responded to promptly and cordially, and that you have and shall have the unreserved confidence and cooperation of the Executive of the State.[3]

Thus, within three days of his bitter denunciation of the war department to President Davis, Milton had pledged full cooperation.

As has been pointed out, Governor Milton fully expected a major attack against Florida's open coasts in an effort to drive the state from the war and thus raise northern morale.[4] To forestall this attack as well as to prepare the state for the position it must assume in the defense of the entire Confederacy, Milton appealed both to the Confederate government and to the state legislature. He sent a special message to the General Assembly on November 27, 1861, stating:

> The military organizations of this State are very imperfect, and these imperfections are attributable to the laws of the State, which are inconsistent . . . with any known system based upon the science of War . . . The militia system must be maintained . . . The result of the attempt to form voluntary companies . . . from the militia . . . is . . . that the number of fighting men has not been increased, but the number of officers doubled.[5]

Milton then informed President Davis that Florida was in no way prepared to meet the threatened attack and that when, as governor, he had appealed to the war department for arms and munitions of war, he had been instructed to requisition the supplies from the officer in command of the military department. Milton complained that there was no one in command at the time and that "under the circumstances to have referred me to the Emperor of China would have been almost as reasonable." "We need troops and munitions," he continued, "and, if not promptly aided, Florida may be lost."[6]

He was doomed to disappointment. His appeal to the General Assembly went unheeded and military events elsewhere assumed so critical a position that the Confederacy was unable to reinforce Florida.

Not only did the General Assembly refuse to grant Milton's request but his entire state militia system was dealt a death blow in January, 1862. In that month a special session of the convention was called to discuss remedies for the danger threatening the finances of the state. The convention remained in session for two weeks and passed several important ordinances. One of these, strongly opposed by the governor, required the transfer, on or before March 10, to the Confederate service all troops in the service of the state. Any troops failing or refusing to go into Confederate service were to be disbanded and sent home.

Milton strongly denounced this action before the next General Assembly and reported that the state militia laws were a "tissue of absurdities." He again urged their repeal. He desired the enactment of a law by which every man and boy between the ages of sixteen and sixty capable of bearing arms might be formed into an effective body of militia, and prepared for immediate service.[7]

The immediate military crisis was the defeat of Confederate forces in Tennessee. Because of the disaster, the Confederate government found it necessary to concentrate its troops, in order to check the advance of Union forces in that area. All troops defending the Florida seaboard were to be sent to Tennessee and placed under the command of General Albert Sidney Johnston. The only troops to be retained in Florida were those necessary to defend the mouth of the Apalachicola, some independent companies of cavalry, and a regiment to remain temporarily in observation before Jacksonville.[8]

To Milton this strategy was unbelievable; but as a Confederate nationalist, he allowed it to be carried out. He immediately communicated with the Secretary of War, saying:

> The effect of the order is to abandon Middle, East, and South Florida to the mercy or abuse of the Lincoln Government. . . . I cannot and will not believe that an order to have that effect would have been issued without previous notice to the executive of the State, that proper measures might have been advised for the protection of the lives, liberty and property of the citizens. . . .
>
> But Sir, if the sacrifice of Florida is necessary to secure the sacred rights claimed by the people of the Confederate States, then there is not a man, woman, or child, true to the cause of liberty in Florida, but what will say Amen, and in the midst of desolation, however fearful, advocate and cheer the progress of freedom to the South.[9]

In obedience to the orders, Fernandina was evacuated as previously described, and Confederate troops were also withdrawn from St. Augustine.

Governor Milton was insistent in his demand that Apalachicola be adequately defended now that the east coast had been left unprotected. However, this could not be accomplished as the state troops were to be disbanded, and the Confederacy did not have adequate troops in the area to garrison the town. As mentioned in a preceding chapter, a Federal landing party from the blockading squadron occupied the town temporarily.

But this comparatively small incident at Apalachicola was important because it alarmed the people of the lower Chattahoochee Valley, who demanded that the port of Apalachicola be blocked.[10] The city council of Columbus, Georgia, voted more funds for obstructing the Chattahoochee above Apalachicola as a defense for the whole valley. The Confederate War Department agreed to construct a submerged boom across the river.[11] Milton informed President Davis that he disapproved of the plan unless the Confederate government would promise to remove the boom at its own expense when the war was over. He stated further that the only reason he would not seek to prohibit the boom's construction was that he did not wish to cause a conflict with the Confederate government.[12]

Milton, though he had agreed to the proposal in the interest of harmony, looked upon the decision to block the Chattahoochee as a direct result of the influence of persons in Alabama who desired to supplant Apalachicola as the port for Columbus by obstructing the river and then diverting trade to Mobile by the way of railroads.

Milton also attempted to cooperate with the Confederate government in the raising of troops. When it became apparent that the war would be long and bitter, both the Union and the Confederacy instituted conscription as a means of raising troops. In the Confederacy, the Conscription Act of April 16, 1862, was one of the chief points of contention between the states and the general government. Milton made his first public reference to the Conscription Act in a proclamation on August 12, 1862. He said that nearly all the Florida militia who were subject to military duty had volunteered for Confederate service. However, he continued, there were some ex-militiamen who had not, and he appealed to these to volunteer before they were drafted.[13] He did not express an opinion upon the subject, nor did he seek to prejudice Floridians concerning the law.

Privately, however, Milton was disturbed for he saw that Florida might be entirely depleted of manpower capable of defending the state. This was a complex problem. He did not wish to cause a conflict with Confederate authorities and yet he wanted to keep as strong a state defense as he could. To solve this question as judiciously as possible, he depended upon the Florida congressional delegation, to which he wrote:

> Should the act of Congress relative to Conscripts be amended so as to embrace persons over the age of thirty-five years there should be a savings clause in the act to retain in this state for local defense such of our citizens as shall be made subject to the amendment. . . .

Allow me to suggest most respectfully that you should advocate such measures . . . without compromising the honor and dignity of the State in her obligation to her sister States for the maintenance of the war.[14]

Flaws began to appear soon after the Conscription Act had been placed in operation. Men who had been discharged from service because of disability and who were within the age limits of the draft were compelled to report to camps of instruction before they could be examined and declared unfit for duty. This, to Milton, was a tragic and shocking situation that should be remedied immediately. The Conscription Act allowed a person subject to its provisions to hire a substitute. This caused revulsion in many people, in Milton especially. He wrote the Florida congressional delegation protesting these evils. His attitude is best shown by his question, "Shall the sulking coward be favored by a legal exemption, while wounded and discharged soldiers shall be forced as conscripts into camps of instruction?"[15]

The citizenry of Florida was not as openminded on the subject. There were flagrant violations of the act; and, in fact, in many places direct refusal to abide by it. General Finegan, commanding the Eastern District of Florida, reported to the adjutant general that the state officers were neglecting to perform their duty in enrolling conscripts. The camp of instruction, he stated, had been open for over four months and yet less than two hundred men had been sent to it. Some counties had sent no men.[16]

Governor Milton, realizing this situation, informed President Davis that enforcement of the act had had an unhappy effect and that he had no idea over three hundred men could be obtained in Florida because of the heavy volunteer enlistment earlier in the war. He felt, however, that hostility to the act would be reduced if the government would allow able-bodied men to volunteer even though they had already been enrolled.[17]

Milton's next effort to allay hostility was to urge compliance with the law in his message to the General Assembly on November 17, 1862. He stated in part:

Many are calling the Conscript Act . . . Unconstitutional. . . . When notified by the Secretary of War of the passage of the Act, and when I read it, and reflected upon the causes which induced Congress to pass it . . . I did not consider it necessarily a question of political power between the Confederate and State Government.

. . . I consider it much more important, during the existence of the war, to watch and baffle the purposes of the enemy, than with skeptical apprehensions to criticize and defeat the purposes of the Government of our choice, administered by statesmen of our own selection. . . . God forbid! that you, or I should do, directly or indirectly, aught to impede the victory of our arms.[18]

This patriotic appeal did not change the attitude of the legislature, however, which felt that Florida had depleted itself of men because of the large number of volunteers. It demonstrated this sentiment in a resolution, signed by the governor on December 13, 1862, to be forwarded to President Davis. It asked that President Davis exempt all Florida citizens from conscription who would volunteer for service in the state.[19] Davis received the resolution but did not comply with its request.

As the war progressed into 1863, the Confederacy was desperately searching for manpower, and on May 1, it extended conscription to certain classes of overseers. This action was in direct conflict with a Florida law which stated that a white person, either owner or overseer, must live on the plantation where slaves resided. Milton considered this an infringement upon the state's police powers as well as a danger to the South's agricultural livelihood. He denounced this extension in no uncertain terms and called upon President Davis to reconsider his action.[20] In his letter to the President, Milton said:

I say overseers [to be exempt], not owners of slaves, because as a general rule slaves have been managed by overseers, and but few owners have manifested the industry, skill, and energy necessary to successful agriculture.[21]

The governor did not allow his dislike of the extension of the draft to change his policy of cooperation with the Confederacy. This attitude was manifested by his reaction to the Florida elections held in the fall of 1863, and his reluctance to grant certificates of exemption. Many people in Confederate service, or subject to conscription, were elected to minor offices such as county commissioner and justice of the peace. It was the duty of the governor, under state law, to issue commissions to those elected to office which would entitle them to leave service or be exempt from the draft. Milton wrote the Secretary of War that he was not going to issue a commission to any person who was already in service or subject to call unless notified by the Attorney General to do so. His action was upheld by the Confederate government, and many soldiers were kept in service who would otherwise have been discharged. Sustaining Milton's action, Secretary of War James A. Seddon took advantage of the opportunity to thank the governor for his cooperation in the war effort:

> The Department cannot close this letter without expressing its obligations to Your Excellency for the cordial support you have habitually given to all measures for the common defense which have been adopted by this Government.[22]

Well he might have complimented Milton, because the governor scrupulously kept able-bodied Florida men in the fighting ranks. No other governor could match him. A report of John S. Preston to the war department on November 23, 1864, which dealt with exemptions given by the governors of the various states, showed that Milton had granted only 109 certificates of exemption out of a total of 18,843![23]

Another problem that gave rise to friction between the states and the Confederate government was the enforcement of the Confederate Impressment Act and the collection of the Confederate tithe. In Florida, these acts were accompanied by friction between local and Confederate officials.[24] Governor Milton, in an attempt to remove the friction, interpreted loosely state legislation regulating impressment officers. The laws regulated confiscation of goods en route to market and compelled enforcing officials to register individually with the governor. Milton accepted a certified list of authorized officials in lieu of individual registration and permitted continued impressment of cattle in southern Florida.[25]

The governor, though he had cooperated to this extent, disliked impressment. This dislike turned to open hostility when he was informed that many officers in the Confederate service had exceeded their authority in securing supplies. This abuse of authority was brought about when, in the name of the district commissary, the officer offered the farmer a given price for his product. If this price was unsatisfactory to the farmer, the officer then invoked his authority to impress the goods and informed the farmer that any alteration of the product in any way would make necessary a forcible search of his premises and seizure of the goods.

When the General Assembly met in November, 1863, Governor Milton informed it of this situation and declared:

Is there any act of Congress which can justify such extraordinary measures? Has Congress the constitutional right to authorize such proceedings? If nay . . . Congress cannot rightfully exercise any power not granted by the Constitution. . . . It is painful to me to believe, and to express the opinion, that there exists a necessity for the interposition of State authority to protect the rights, lives, and liberty of citizens against the military orders of Confederate officers. . . . But I would be recreant to the high trust confided in me . . . if I were to hesitate a moment in defense of their rights.

I have unlimited confidence in the wisdom and integrity of the Confederate Government when justly administered; but at the same time can only be sensible of its appropriate influence in the maintenance of the sovereignty of the State. Better that Florida should be a waste of flowers, enriched with the blood of her brave citizens, than to be inhabited by them as slaves or willing to be slaves.[26]

Milton then informed the war department that the effect of impressment in West Florida was the desertion of a large number of men who desired to save their families from starvation. Many of these deserters went over to the enemy camp. Milton expected the wave of indignation concerning impressment to drive still greater numbers into the enemy camp if the evils of the system were not immediately corrected.[27] This challenge had the desired effect as Secretary of War Seddon promised an immediate investigation.[28]

The investigation did not settle the controversy, however. The most serious conflict was that arising from the seizure of property belonging to the Florida Railroad. In the spring of 1864, the Confederate War Department determined to complete railway connections between Central Florida and the Chattahoochee River. To accomplish this purpose, railroad iron was impressed in East Florida.

The railroad owners and their friends, led by ex-Senator Yulee, filed a bill in the court of Alachua County against Lieutenant Fairbanks, who had been ordered to seize the railroad iron. In response to the petition, the court granted an injunction against the defendants restraining them or their agents from removing the iron. The military ignored this injunction and removed the iron while working under armed escort. When the court saw that it could not enforce its decision, it dropped the case.

It is not in the realm of this story to discuss at length this court controversy. But since this was a clear case of civil authority opposing military authority, it is of interest to observe the position taken by Governor Milton. He favored the action of the military and, in fact, was responsible to a large degree for the decision. On July 20, 1863, he had written Secretary Seddon calling for the completion of the Central Florida rail link, and had asked the secretary, "Shall what is necessary to the defense of Florida be ordered or shall the State be left defenseless in compliment to Mr. Yulee?"[29] He regretted the conflict that arose in the courts but upheld the action of the military. In a letter to the judge of the Alachua court, he said:

> Nothing can justify a conflict between the State and Confederate Governments but an absolute necessity for the protection of civil liberty. . . . With regard to the propriety and necessity of removal and appropriation of iron from the Florida R.R., my opinions have undergone no change—that as a military necessity for the defense of the state the iron should be removed.[30]

In harmony with his loyalty to the Confederacy, Milton condemned private and state blockade-running. In this he differed with many southern leaders in his belief that the practice was detrimental to the cause of the Confederacy. He believed that it substantially relieved the pressure felt abroad by the loss of southern cotton, and that it invited retaliation by the federal government.[31]

Milton reported to the Secretary of War that a copartnership existed, formed by merchants in New Orleans, Havana, and New York for blockade trade. He stated that this trade was carried on with the knowledge of the blockading fleet, and that by such means "information prejudicial to our best interest is obtained, our slaves enticed away, and ignorant citizens corrupted by southern partners —men of northern birth or villainous Jews professing to supply the people of the South."[32]

The governor was forced to allow blockade-running to continue in Florida, however. He attempted to prohibit six vessels from leaving Apalachicola, but the Secretary of the Navy ordered their release, and the war department informed Milton that it had no authority to stop the export of cotton except to prevent it from falling into the hands of the enemy.[33] Nevertheless, Milton held steadfast in his belief that trade in nonmilitary articles should be abolished.

Governor Joseph E. Brown of Georgia invited Milton to join in a protest to be made by southern governors to the Confederate government, objecting to the policy of forbidding the states to export their own products in their own ships unless the government could occupy half the room for its own use. Milton refused:

My judgment . . . does not approve of any direct attempt by persuasion or otherwise to be made by the Governor of a State, or Governors of states, to influence the legislation of Congress. . . . The safety of the people and preservation of their rights under the Government of free, sovereign, and independent States confederated for mutual protection, demand the utmost confidence and generous support of the State governments to the maintenance of the Confederate Government in the execution of sacred trusts which have been confided to it. It is best, therefore, when it can be honorably done, to avoid all conflicts and competition between the state and Confederate authorities.[34]

No study of John Milton as a war leader and his attitude toward the conduct of the war would be complete without a glance at his attitude toward peace and his opinion of the abilities of President Davis. By the end of 1864 it had become apparent to many southern leaders that there was no chance for victory, and it was natural that there would be much talk concerning peace. Governor Milton, however, did not desire peace. In November, 1864, he told the General Assembly:

Another year of war has been added to the history of our country since you last assembled. . . . I had hoped to congratulate you at this time on the return of peace and the recognition of the independence of the Confederate States; but our enemy . . . still presses the vain hope of accomplishing our subjugation. . . . It is but natural that the miseries of a contest so long and severe should produce in the hearts of all a desire for peace. . . . But as earnestly as we desire peace, a dishonorable peace is not for a moment to be contemplated. . . . A peace which does not secure our independence would be an affliction at least as great as war itself. . . . The men who have slain our fathers, sons, and brothers, insulted our women and ravaged our country, cannot be again united with us by any tie under heaven. . . . Let us make up our minds to the stern conditions of the contest. We must place the enemy in a position in which they desire peace with us. . . . When this is done, there will be no difficulty about the method of arriving at peace.[35]

Milton had in the beginning, and kept to the end, the highest regard for and confidence in President Davis. Toward the end of the war, he declared that the "lofty character, noble virtues, and great abilities" of Jefferson Davis qualified him for his high office and that the President's enemies, "public or private," could never "shake him from the eminence that he holds so gloriously for himself and so fortunately for his country."[36]

This high esteem of President Davis was reciprocated. The President looked upon Governor Milton as a true patriot and praised his cooperation:

It is gratifying to me to be able to say to you that in this time of trouble, when so many are disposed to withhold from the Confederate Government the means of success, you should occupy the high standpoint of strengthening its hands by all the means in your powers, and of nobly disregarding all considerations except the common weal.[37]

This cordial attitude was retained until the cause for which both men had given so much disintegrated about them. For Davis the end meant prison; for Milton the end meant death. Milton, sick in mind and body, found the collapse of the Confederacy an unbearable reality. He left the capitol and returned to his home at Marianna. There, on April 1, 1865, he ended his life by his own hand.

VIII

SALTMAKING AND RAILROADING

WHEN FLORIDA SECEDED from the United States on January 10, 1861, there was little manufacturing in the state, although the widespread pine forests made lumbering almost universal. Many plantations had their own sawmills, and the towns of Pensacola, Gainesville, and Jacksonville were centers for commercial mills.[1] *

But with the exception of sawmilling, there was no industry that was general throughout the peninsula. Monticello in middle Florida, the only industrial center in the state not based on lumber milling, was the site of a small shoe factory, a small woolen factory, and the Bailey Cotton Mill, the only cloth mill in the state. The Bailey mill was located on the stage road to Alligator about a mile and a quarter east of Monticello. The mill building, made of brick and covered with tin, was three stories tall, seventy-five feet long, and forty feet wide. All material and labor for erecting the mill had been furnished locally, but it had been necessary to send north for the machinery and an experienced superintendent.

The mill, driven by a wood-burning thirty-five horsepower steam engine, was designed to manufacture both yard and cloth. Equipped with fifteen hundred spindles and fifty looms, the Bailey mill could manufacture 400,000 pounds of cotton into 600,000 yards of Osnaburg and 100,000 yards of yarn annually.

Florida did not adequately support its one cotton mill, however. The factory, completed in December, 1853, did not prosper and by 1858 was $20,000 in debt. In that year General William Bailey purchased the stock and continued to operate the mill at a loss until the war. In 1860, Bailey employed forty men and twenty-five women in the manufacture of products which had a value of $40,000.[2]

*Notes to Chapter VIII begin on page 231.

Madison, another Middle Florida town, was the location of the state's largest leather factory. The Madison Shoe Factory, ten miles west of town, employed twenty-six slaves in the manufacture of some eleven thousand pairs of shoes annually. The factory also manufactured wagon and buggy harness and other leather goods required on the plantations of the area. The products were of high quality and the entire output was sold in the state.[3]

Newport, on the Gulf below Tallahassee, had a small privately-owned iron foundry which serviced the surrounding area prior to the war. It was of very little value to the Confederacy, however, and the Federal blockading vessels allowed it to operate until it was destroyed on March 5, 1865, by Confederate skirmishers before the Battle of Natural Bridge.[4]

With the exception of these factories, there was very little manufacturing in Florida prior to the Civil War. Hence, secession, the formation of the Confederacy, and the beginning of hostilities did not create major industrial problems in the state. In fact, the only factory which the state, or the Confederacy, considered of any importance to the war effort was the Bailey Cotton Mill, known officially as the Jefferson Manufacturing Company.[5]

The mill, located in the heart of the Florida plantation area, had no difficulty during the war securing raw material.[6] Lack of manpower to operate the mill, however, began to present difficulties following the Confederate Conscription Act. The Florida legislature, recognizing the mill's value to the state and feeling that its operation would be impaired if the conscription act was enforced against Bailey's employees, requested the Florida representatives in the Confederate Congress to endeavor "to have exempted [from the draft] the workmen and persons employed in the Jefferson Manufacturing Company, their services being indispensable in conducting this useful and important work."[7]

The same legislature expressed the gratitude of the people of Florida to General Bailey for the "liberal and enlightened manner in which he is dispensing his means, and [the] zeal and efficiency with which he supports the [Confederate] cause."[8]

These requests and expressions of gratitude did not solve the manpower problem, however. The Confederate government refused to exempt workers liable for the draft but did assign several soldiers to work in the mill. By 1863 many disabled soldiers had been discharged from the service and these men plus those not subject to military service enabled the Bailey mill to remain in operation throughout the war.[9]

General Bailey's control of the mill was threatened in the summer of 1864, when the Commissary Department of the Confederate government proposed to commandeer it to supply Confederate troops. The mill was to be used for processing cotton which the Confederacy received in Florida from the tax in kind. This "tithe cotton" was to be manufactured exclusively into Osnaberg.[10]

Governor Milton, although a Confederate nationalist, insisted that the mill remain in Bailey's possession. Milton had been an exponent of a central supply system for the Confederacy but when other southern governors refused to cooperate in such an effort, he determined to keep the Bailey mill out of Confederate hands. Furthermore, he believed that the mill was operating as efficiently as possible and considered Bailey truly dedicated to the Confederate cause. The war department acquiesced and left the mill in local hands.[11]

The beginning of hostilities and subsequent shortages of basic supplies within the state and throughout the Confederacy brought several new industries into Florida. The shortage of yarn and cloth became critical within a year after hostilities had begun. With the state's only cotton mill busy supplying troops, production of cloth and yarn for civilian use rested to a large degree upon home industry. This home industry, in turn, rested upon the availability of spinning wheels, cards, and other materials necessary to the spinning of yarn and the weaving of cloth.

In 1862 the legislature voted $20,000 from which the governor was to purchase cotton and wool cards abroad.[12] These cards were to be distributed at no cost to families in need. The governor did not follow this plan, however, because he found them too expensive. Instead, he entered into a contract on behalf of the state with William Bailey, Joseph John Williams, John Cardy, and Edward Barnard, who agreed to form the Florida Card Manufacturing Company provided the state would subsidize it through contracts. The governor agreed to purchase 25,000 pairs of cotton cards and 500 pairs of wool cards at $6 per card. Furthermore, he agreed that on receipt of the first one thousand pairs of cards, the state would pay the company a bonus of $2,000 provided the cards were manufactured in Florida.[13]

The Florida Card Manufacturing Company began operations in the spring of 1863. By November 1 it had completed 547 pairs of wool cards and delivered them to the state. But when it shifted to manufacturing cotton cards, the company immediately encountered difficulty. It had to manufacture its own wire for the cards, and possessed no machinery adequate for the high-speed production of good wire. New machinery and more powerful engines were secured, and by November, 1863, the number of cotton cards produced was rising daily.

But new machinery and more powerful engines could not solve the problems of labor supply and raw materials. To help solve the former, the army began to detail soldiers to serve as factory laborers. The army, however, allowed the company to keep men on short detail only and, as a result, there was a rapid turnover. The production schedule rose and fell according to the number of trained men working in the factory and production remained erratic throughout the war.[14] To find raw materials, the company advertised in the newspapers of Middle Florida appealing for leather or skins. The advertisement explained the necessity for leather in making cotton cards and offered $1 each for usable leather strips which measured six by twenty-two inches. The company would also buy animal skins, with the exception of raccoon skins, of the same size at 50 cents each.[15]

The Florida Card Company remained in operation throughout the war. Its product was inferior, and was purchased primarily by the state for distribution to the poor. Floridians who bought their own cards preferred those brought through the blockade from Europe or the North even though they were much more expensive. "[Florida] factory cards are not worth buying," Mrs. Edward Bradford wrote, "[as] they don't understand tempering the wire, and northern cards sell for sixty dollars a pair."[16]

The largest industry to develop in Florida as a result of the Civil War was the production of salt by boiling ocean water. At the outbreak of the war three methods for producing salt were known and practiced: extracting the salt from saline artesian wells, boiling down sea water or water from inland salt lakes, and mining deposits of rock salt.[17] The method by which salt was secured from boiling sea water was the cheapest, as no wells or machinery were necessary.

When the blockade became effective and English salt could no longer reach the South, a desperate situation developed.[18] In the absence of a general system of refrigeration, salt was an absolute necessity for preserving all meat, fish, butter and other perishable foods. Salt was used also to preserve animal hides for making leather, and it was necessary for the diet of the work animals on the plantations and in the service of the Confederacy. And salt was, of course, a necessary part of the diet of all Southerners, both soldiers and civilians. In short, without salt the South could not survive for long.

The making of salt from sea water was not new to Florida. In the antebellum period when salt was needed on a plantation, the overseer often would go to a suitable location on the coast and with the aid of slaves make enough salt to last throughout the year. When salt became scarce, therefore, Floridians and other Southerners immediately turned to the sea. The immense seacoast with many secluded bays and inlets and the availability of pine forests for fuel overcame the disadvantages of poor transportation facilities and remoteness. Saltmaking was prevalent along the entire Atlantic and Gulf coasts of the Confederacy, but no state played so large a part in this enterprise as Florida.[19]

Saltmaking began in earnest in Florida during the fall of 1861. Small saltworks began to appear on both coasts of the peninsula, but the most favored location was the Gulf Coast between Choctawhatchee Bay and Tampa Bay with a majority of the works located on St. Andrews Bay and the coast of Taylor County.[20] These works were frequently established at the head of small inlets or bays, from one to five miles inland from the open Gulf or the deep water of a large bay, seeking thus to escape detection by blockading vessels and deep-draught gunboats which could not penetrate so far up the inlets.

Interest in the success and safety of the saltmaking enterprise was immediately manifest in Florida. The Tallahassee *Florida Sentinel,* one of the more influential newspapers of the state, began a campaign early in 1862 to enlarge salt production.[21] Four months later it called upon every able-bodied person to devote at least a part of his energies to salt manufacture. At the same time, the editor exhorted state and Confederate governments to recognize the importance of full-time saltworkers. "If these workers are not protected and allowed to remain at their important work," the editor concluded, "starvation will be the inevitable result."[22] The *Sentinel* was not satisfied with the results, however, and on July 15, 1862, a front page advertisement proclaimed:

> Special to Planters—Make Salt! Make Salt! Let all make Salt who never made before; those who have made now only make the more—your bread crop is now pretty sure of making—your next care should be to *save your bacon!*

Appeals by newspapers and state officials had some effect upon increasing salt production, but the principal cause of the rapid increase was the scarcity of the article. As the salt shortage spread throughout the South, many citizens of Georgia and Alabama entered Florida to establish saltworks. The exact number of these out-of-state saltworks and their production is unknown, but both were considerable. Governor Milton told the state legislature in 1862 that thousands of bushels of salt were being produced in Florida by citizens of other states.[23] The Florida General Assembly also took notice of these out-of-state salt manufacturers by legalizing their activity in Florida, and, at the same time, extended an invitation to all citizens of the Confederacy to make salt in Florida.[24]

The rapid increase in saltmakers caused many problems. The hundreds of wagon teams passing to and from the saltworks consumed increasing amounts of animal fodder in West and Central Florida, thus lessening the available supply for use by residents and consequently forcing up the price of hay, oats, corn, and other grasses and grains suitable for animal feed. The rise in prices aided those few farmers with grain to sell, but by 1862 most small farmers were purchasing much of their animal fodder. High grain prices and the resulting increased inflation hurt Floridians more than the increased price for their products aided them.

Another problem caused by the swift increase in the number of saltworks was that saltmaking fell more and more into the hands of speculators. In the spring of 1862 salt was selling in Florida at $3 per bushel, but by fall the price had risen to between $16 and $20 per bushel, according to its quality. Speculators added to the cupidity by refusing to receive Florida treasury notes in payment. Governor Milton, protesting against this refusal, proclaimed that nothing but the lowest form of humanity would "while deriving subsistence from the State, inflict injury upon its credit" by refusing to accept the Florida notes.[25] These men, the governor continued, were cowards,

> dodging from place to place to avoid being made conscripts, and say that they would rather die than to be disgraced by being made conscripts, and doubtless would as willingly be hung as traitors as [to] die in battle vindicating the rights of free men.[26]

The rapid rise of the salt industry also caused a problem because of the sudden increase in the price of land suitable for the works.

Speculators purchased large tracts of the most desirable coastal land and then leased or sold small portions at exorbitant prices. This swift rise in land manipulation deprived many individual Florida citizens as well as citizens of other states of the opportunity to manufacture their own salt supply. Governor Milton intervened by withdrawing all public lands suitable for saltworks from the market and allowed approved individuals free use of the locations.[27]

Defending the saltworks also became a problem as they increased in number. The Union blockading squadron did not molest the few small works during 1861. But as the number of works increased and their importance to the Confederacy grew, it became apparent that the installations would be a point of attack. In February, 1862, the *Florida Sentinel* appealed to the state government to recognize the danger of Union attacks upon the salt works and to provide a satisfactory defense for the most vital areas before such an attack took place. General Joseph Finegan, Confederate commander in Florida, heeded the appeal of the *Sentinel* and of public sentiment in general by stationing three companies of troops in the area adjacent to St. Andrews Bay.[28]

This public concern for the safety of the saltworkers soon changed. Under the Confederate Conscription Act they were not exempt from military service but because of the scarcity of the commodity, the law was interpreted loosely and saltworkers secured immunity from military service.[29] This, of course, caused much resentment among many individuals who were conscripted. Another cause of the change of attitude was the rise of speculation in salt. The *Florida Sentinel,* which had consistently urged greater salt production and had, at first, urged protection for the works, began to protest the special treatment for saltmakers. In an editorial of October 14, 1862, the newspaper upheld the right of all citizens to the protection of the laws and military forces of the Confederacy, but strongly opposed any special treatment for any segment of the population. The saltworkers, the editorial continued, used to have the respect and sympathy of the people but they had now lost it because of their speculative practices. The editorial concluded:

> We do not err when we say that the enormous profits of the saltmakers would enable them to hire a large force for their own defense. How, then, can such men ask or hope for protection at the hands of the very poor people upon whose dire necessities they are speculating.

A letter to the editor on the same day strongly protested the use of the militia to protect the saltmakers. The writer, who signed himself "Jeems," declared that the saltmakers were speculators and "conscript dodgers" who had no right to the protection of "patriotic" men.

These protests created a furor as very little military force was available to defend the entire population, much less a specific segment. The Florida General Assembly, meeting in the fall of 1862 and recognizing that the state militia could not adequately protect the saltworks, wisely made the defense of the salt industry the responsibility of those engaged in it, and thus appeased public opinion.

All saltworkers were organized into military companies enrolled and commanded by first lieutenants appointed by the governor. The state furnished arms and ammunition, and the companies became subject to the articles of war when engaged in repelling enemy attacks. They were not considered true military companies, however, and the legislation creating them specifically denied any individual enrolled the right to hold or place a claim against the state.[30]

The act of the legislature did not constitute an adequate defense, however. William Fisher, the enrolling agent appointed by Governor Milton, reported on January 9, 1863, that he had registered and organized all saltmakers on the coast between the St. Marks and Suwannee rivers. A total of 498 men had been enrolled, but Fisher had been able to secure only forty-three guns in good condition. Of the 498 men, 300 were under forty years of age and most of the younger men were deserters from the army.[31] The shortage of arms together with the questionable character of many of the saltmakers plagued the industry for the rest of the war. As a result, no saltworks owner was certain of the number of guns available for the defense of his establishment or of the zeal with which his workers would engage the enemy. It is small wonder, therefore, that Union raiding parties met with little armed resistance.

Nowhere else were Federal naval attacks so frequent, so persistent, and so exclusively directed against the salt industry as on the Gulf Coast of Florida.[32] By the fall of 1862 the production had become too important to escape the notice of the Federal government.[33]

The first important raids were made by the U.S.S. *Kingfisher* on September 8, 1862, directed against the saltworks on St. Josephs Bay, and by the *Sagamore* on St. Andrews Bay three days later. The commander of the *Kingfisher* sent notice of his intent to the saltmakers under a flag of truce and allowed the Confederates two hours' grace to leave the place. The works were evacuated within the time limit and there was no loss of life.

A second serious attempt followed very shortly afterwards when the marines from the United States gunboat *Somerset,* reinforced by the steamship *Tahoma,* raided the saltworks at Suwannee Bay near Cedar Key on October 4. The gunboat commander ran his vessel in as close as the depth of the water would permit, then fired shells into the saltworks. After a white flag appeared, he sent a landing crew ashore to destroy the supposedly abandoned works. The Union crew was fired upon, however, and after approximately one-half of their number had been wounded were forced to retire to the *Somerset.* The unexpected resistance had been provided by twenty-five saltworkers concealed at the works. Two days later a larger landing crew composed of men from both vessels landed and destroyed the saltworks with very little resistance.

The method pursued by the raiders on the successful second attack is worth recounting because it became the method of attack generally used when the raiders believed a saltworks would be defended. The armed saltworkers were first put to flight by shell fire from the vessels directed at the houses, woods, and underbrush. The landing party then came ashore with small arms. Approximately one-half of the landing party deployed as skirmishers on each flank of the area to be destroyed. The remainder served as a working party and tore up boilers, kettles, houses, and other implements and buildings of the saltwork. If heavy resistance was feared, or if the boilers and other implements proved too difficult to destroy by hand, howitzers were landed and used either for added protection or to fire point-blank into the object to be destroyed.[34]

On November 14, 1862, a Federal expedition departed from Pensacola for St. Andrews Bay under orders to destroy the saltworks between the two localities.[35] The expedition was composed of five boats, sixty marines, and a special working gang armed with sledge hammers and other necessary equipment.

The expedition arrived in St. Andrews Bay on November 24 and landed without opposition. Several saltmakers and an unknown number of slaves remained to watch the demolition of their equipment. One kettle was very thick and hard to break. After attempting for some time to smash it, the Federals turned to another. A Floridian, who had been standing by watching the futile attempt on the kettle, remarked, "Captain, you've got hold of Vicksburg this time."

The captain stopped his crew and dryly replied, "You seem disposed to make a row sir." The Floridian assured him that he was unarmed and wanted no trouble so the raiders returned to breaking up the kettles.[36] The raid was successful and the saltworks with a combined output of 360 bushels per day was destroyed.[37]

For about six months saltmakers enjoyed peace, but on June 14, 1863, four extensive establishments on Alligator Bay, totaling sixty-five kettles, were completely wrecked and burned to the ground by a landing party from the steamer *Somerset.*[38] Scattered raids continued throughout the summer of 1863 but no new large-scale destruction took place until December when the raiders again struck determined blows in the St. Andrews Bay area.

These raids of December, 1863, were the most costly to the Confederacy of any made during the war. At Lake Ocala, they destroyed six large steamboat boilers, improvised into kettles, two large flatboats, six oxcarts, and all other equipment of works which were producing one hundred and thirty bushels of salt a day. The raids on St. Andrews Bay on December 10 and 18 were even more annihilating. Five hundred works, containing thirty-three wagons, twelve flatboats, two sloops, six oxcarts, four thousand bushels of salt, seven hundred buildings, and a thousand kettles and iron boilers were destroyed. This destruction was compounded when the Confederates themselves broke up many works for fear they would be attacked. The works destroyed by both sides had a combined production capacity of 15,595 bushels of salt per day.[39]

These serious blows not only deprived the Confederacy of thousands of bushels of salt but destroyed $6,000,000 worth of government and private property.[40] But loss of production and investment did not deter the saltmakers. Salt manufacture was lucrative, but more important, it was indispensable. Incredible as it may seem, the Confederate government was able to muster money, men, and material to rebuild most of its works on St. Andrews Bay in less than two months after the devastating raids of late 1863. Hence the Federals returned to the bay on February 17, 1864 to destroy "the largest government saltworks ever created in Florida," works with a capacity of 2,418 bushels per day. During the same month two expeditions sent out from the *Tahoma* destroyed the Confederate works at St. Marks and Goose Creek which had a production capacity of 2,500 bushels per day and were valued at $4,000,000.[41]

Harassment continued throughout 1864. Landing parties broke up works on the east arm of St. Andrews Bay in April,[42] and on the bay proper during the summer and fall.[43] Tampa Bay was raided in July, 1864, and other minor manufacturing areas were attacked occasionally during the year.[44] The concluding raid against salt manufacturing in Florida came in February, 1865, in St. Andrews Bay. Even at this late date, on the West Bay alone, Union forces destroyed works with a boiling capacity of 13,615 gallons of water.[45]

Saltmaking plus cloth weaving at the Bailey mill constituted the only manufacturing in Florida during the Civil War. The importance of cloth to the Confederacy is doubtful but the importance of the salt industry was significant. Nowhere else in the South was the industry more persistently attacked. Faced with overwhelming opposition from the Federal navy, suffering severe production losses, and losing a minimum of $12 million in investment, the saltmaking industry still was never completely destroyed.

Another problem to be solved in Florida in 1860 was the almost total lack of transportation facilities. The state's numerous rivers, which were sufficently wide and deep to allow steamboat travel, flow primarily in a north-south direction. The Apalachicola River had regular steamboat traffic from the town of Apalachicola at the river's mouth into the area around Columbus, Georgia. But traffic on this river served only a limited portion of the western area of the state. In East Florida, some irregular steamboat traffic occurred on the St. Johns River, but because of sparse settlement very little benefit was derived by the interior regions. Regularly scheduled runs were made between Jacksonville and Savannah but this again benefited the interior only indirectly.[46]

Interior Florida was dependent upon wagon roads and a few railroads. Good roads were nonexistent. The principal towns were connected by little more than cleared passages for travel by horse or wagon and carriage. These were poorly kept, and travelers through the sandy region of Middle and South Florida were often delayed.[47]

Railroads were also few in Florida, there being only six in the state in 1860, with a combined mileage of 401.5 miles.[48] They possessed poor equipment and small quantities of rolling stock. The Florida Railroad, longest and best equipped in the state, had only two passenger cars, two baggage cars, fourteen box cars and twenty-one platform cars in good repair in 1860.[49] The two passenger cars were new, of the latest design, and accommodated sixty persons each.[50]

The state government recognized the need for more adequate rail transportation. The secession convention chartered four new lines in January and February, 1861. The Alachua County Railroad Company was to run from Waldo in East Florida to Newnansville,[51] and the Lake City and Blunt Ferry Railroad Company was to run from Lake City to the Georgia boundary at or near Blunt's Ferry.[52] Two lines were chartered for West Florida. The Pensacola and Mobile Railroad was to begin at some point on the Florida, Alabama, and Georgia Railroad within twenty miles of Pensacola and run to the Perdido River at or near Hall's Bridge.[53] The Western Railroad was to run between St. Andrews Bay and the Apalachicola River by way of Marianna.[54]

Other railroad companies received charters for proposed construction after the beginning of the war. The Monticello and Thomasville Railroad Company was granted permission to construct a line between Monticello and the Georgia line near Thomasville.[55] Pensacola was authorized to aid, not in excess of $500,000, any company which would construct a line from the city to the Apalachicola River, or which would connect the Florida, Alabama, and Georgia Railroad with Selma, Alabama.[56]

Merely chartering new railroad companies did not solve Florida's transportation problem. The Federal blockade and the subsequent shortage of railroad equipment throughout the Confederacy halted all construction of new lines, except those in vital military areas. Hence not one of these proposed lines in Florida was actually constructed. In fact, the only rail construction which occurred in Florida during the entire war was the extension of the Pensacola and Georgia railroad from Tallahassee to Gee's Turnout, four miles from Quincy, which was opened on December 8, 1862,[57] and a military line from Live Oak to a point near the Georgia border, a distance of twenty-one miles.[58]

Another problem which confronted the convention was the desire of several of its members to link the rail lines of Florida to those of Georgia. The proponents contended that in the event of war such a connection would greatly facilitate the movement of troops and supplies. The Committee on Internal Improvements opposed such action and cautioned the convention that the primary object of the state had been to perfect and complete the railroads "within her own borders, independent of, and without regard to those of adjoining States. . . . [and that] Great care and caution should be exercised on our part in allowing connections with our system to be made with those of Georgia."[59] The convention accepted the committee's recommendation and no Florida railroad was connected to the rail systems of any other state during the existence of the Confederacy.[60]

Secession, hostilities, and the subsequent blockade caused Florida railroads many difficulties. Not only were they deprived of the iron needed to extend their mileage and to make necessary repairs but they were also unable to increase their rolling stock.

The Florida Railroad Company, the only cross-state line, was severely hurt by secession. On August 27, 1860, the Post Office Department at Washington, D. C., accepted a bid of $160,000 a year for conveying the mail on Route 5629 between Charleston and New Orleans via the Florida Railroad. Arrangements had also been completed for steamship lines operating from New York to southern ports and Havana to make regular stops at Fernandina, the Atlantic terminus of the railway. Steamship lines operating in the Gulf were to use the Gulf terminus of the line at Cedar Key. Thus the Florida Railroad had expectations of becoming a very successful commercial road almost immediately. The contracts were to go into effect on February 1, 1861, but of course Florida's secession canceled the contracts and ruined the railway's hope for immediate financial success.[61]

The Union blockade had an immediate effect upon all Florida railroads. Before the end of 1861 the board of directors of the Tallahassee Railway and the Pensacola and Georgia Railway requested that the Florida Senate appoint a committee to confer with them on the possibility of transferring the two railroads and all their equipment to the state for operation during the remainder of the blockade. "Without state assistance," the directors stated, "it will be almost impossible to continue to operate the roads much longer."[62]

The state government refused to assume control, but granted financial assistance during the crisis of early 1862. The Pensacola and Georgia Railroad was the principal road running east and west through West Florida and was badly needed to transport troops and supplies to Fernandina. During the period of expected attack on that city, the Pensacola and Georgia lost by fire its foundry, machine shops, one locomotive, "and all the oils and other material necessary to the operation of the road." The railroad's president, Edward Houstoun, informed Governor Milton that the Pensacola and Georgia was unable financially to replace the loss and that it could no longer meet its obligations to the military. Governor Milton, without hesitation, advanced the road $5,000 as a loan from the general funds of the state because he deemed the road vital to Fernandina's defense.[63]

The loss of Fernandina to the enemy on March 2, 1862, also occasioned the first loss of equipment by a Florida railroad to Union troops. The Florida Railroad which used Fernandina as its Atlantic terminus was unable to evacuate much of its equipment. Besides the station and other terminal apparatus, the company lost five locomotives and a number of cars to Union troops.[64]

Union depredations against Florida railroads never reached serious proportions except at Fernandina and in the area of Jacksonville and Baldwin, which occurred while the Union forces were occupying Jacksonville. The Florida Railroad suffered most from enemy action, but it lost only three freight depots, the Fernandina, the Baldwin, and the Cedar Key stations, to Federal raiders.[65]

Although Florida railroads were not seriously hampered by the enemy, they were unable to operate with efficiency. In 1862, it took two and one-half days to travel from Waldo, near Gainesville, to Tallahassee, a distance of less than 150 miles. On that particular trip travelers had to spend one night each at Lake City and at Madison. Florida citizens considered such practices outrageous and demanded better schedules.[66] Soldiers on furlough were even more outspoken because five days of their leave were spent traveling such a short distance. "It is an outrage on decency, common sense, and a soldier's furlough," wrote Private John Cromartie, "that it takes two and [a] half days to get to Tallahassee."[67]

Citizens also constantly complained of mismanagement by the railroads. Governor Milton reminded railroad officials that they had been "liberally aided" by the government of Florida, and called upon the legislature to see that the people received safe, prompt, and courteous service from the roads.[68] The legislature did nothing, however, until 1864 when public pressure forced an investigation of rail rates. The legislative committee held hearings and received many complaints by individuals that rates were exorbitant. On the other hand, the railroads contended that with the existing rates they could not meet expenses, pay the Confederate tax, and have a 10 per cent profit. The committee could reach no decision but recommended that the Internal Improvement Board continue investigations and report to the legislature in November, 1865.[69] The war having ended, the board never reported, and no adjustment of rates was made.

The railroads also had difficulties in their relationship with the Confederate government. The first conflict began in March, 1861. The Pensacola and Georgia Railroad had ordered a shipment of iron rails from England. Upon their arrival at St. Marks the railroad was unable to pay the 24 per cent import duty. Albert B. Noyes, collector of customs at the port, refused to allow the company to remove the iron until the duty was paid. Governor Perry entered the conflict on behalf of the railroad. He assured Noyes that the state would pay the duty if the Pensacola and Georgia did not. He also assured Noyes of his commission of $358.76.[70]

Noyes contacted Christopher G. Memminger, Confederate Secretary of the Treasury, about the Perry proposal and informed Memminger that the Florida legislature had taken matters into its own hands by passing a bill relieving the railroad of the import duties. Memminger held the Florida act inconsistent with the legislation of the Confederate Congress and ruled that the state could not interfere with collecting the duty from the railroad.[71]

Governor Perry ignored Memminger's ruling and granted the railroad permission to remove the iron from St. Marks. This was done. The Confederate government immediately instructed the Confederate States' District Attorney to take all legal steps necessary not only to collect the duty but to recover the iron.[72] The railroad refused to return the iron, and the governor remained steadfast in upholding the right of Florida to act in the dispute. The Confederate government never collected the duty on the iron. Ironically, it officially charged Noyes with nonperformance of duty for not collecting the import tax but did not force him to pay it personally because of Memminger's intervention.[73]

The railroads with which David Levy Yulee was connected had the most difficulty with the central government. The Atlantic and Gulf Central Railroad, in which Yulee was a stockholder, was the first Florida road to suffer confiscation of rail iron. On or about August 19, 1862, the Confederate government impressed 636 tons of iron rails from the road. Yulee negotiated with the government and was able to secure a written contract with the war department on April 6, 1864, which provided that an equal amount of new rails be given the road within six months after the end of hostilities, or the railroad was to receive $80 per ton for the iron removed.[74]

The Florida Railroad, of which Yulee was president, became involved in the most prolonged conflict with the war department. In fact, the issue of removal of iron from this railroad is the best example of a conflict between civil and military authorities in Florida during the Civil War. Governor Milton and the Confederate government ignored an order of Judge John Hawkins of the Florida Suwannee Circuit and allowed the government to remove, under armed guard, twenty-four miles of rails from the eastern end of the Florida Railroad. These rails were subsequently used to construct the line from Lake City to the Georgia border.[75]

The Florida Railroad also suffered more from the hands of the enemy during the Civil War than any road in the state. Because of the impossibility of procuring laborers the track from Gainesville to Cedar Key deteriorated as decayed crossties were not replaced, but the section from Gainesville to Baldwin was kept in good condition. Richard Meader, railroad superintendent, estimated in November, 1865, that if the twenty-four miles of rails lost to the Lake City line could be regained, the road could be returned to an operating condition, including rebuilding the three freight stations, for $17,500.[76]

Transportation was never a major or a decisive factor in Florida during the Civil War. Rates were high and service irregular and irritating, but the roads did manage to transport troops and supplies at crucial times. Florida was never a major combat area and few transportation facilities were developed during hostilities.

IX

PLANTER AND SLAVE DURING WARTIME

THE IMPORTANCE of the plantation slavery regime in antebellum Florida's settlement and development has been assessed by all the chroniclers of the period's history. The plantation system provided the principal economy, and the agrarian society furnished the dominant political and social leadership of the state. By 1860 the most populous as well as the wealthiest areas of the state were those in which the plantation regime prospered.[1*] Middle Florida, from the Suwannee to the Apalachicola, was the most prosperous of the three main geographic sections of the state. The dominant position of the area in the state economy was shown by the fact that over one-half of Florida's 61,745 slaves in 1860 were concentrated in the counties of Jackson, Gadsden, Leon, Jefferson, Alachua, and Marion.[2]

In the decade from 1850 to 1860 the number of slaveholders owning more than 15 slaves grew from 217 to 1,177.[3] This increase in larger slaveholders was caused primarily by the agricultural prosperity of the 1850's and by the extension of the plantation system into the North Central and Tampa Bay areas. In 1860 the planter aristocracy (those owning establishments of 1,000 acres or more) was limited to 77 members, 75 of whom were in the black belt of Middle Florida. But even in these "cotton counties" the farms of 50 to 500 acres greatly exceeded the number of plantations. Outside of the black belt the predominant farm holding was less than 50 acres, and even in counties with large slave populations small farmers outnumbered the planters. The large majority of Florida planters owned less than 11 slaves; 116 slaveowners held 50 but less than 70 slaves; 42 owned 70-100; 45 owned 100-200; and but 2 owned over 200 slaves.[4]

*Notes to Chapter IX begin on page 233.

These great planting counties of Middle Florida also contained over half of the state's wealth. The seven counties of Alachua, Marion, Madison, Jefferson, Leon, Gadsden, and Jackson held farms valued at $11,662,244 in 1860 whereas the entire farm valuation within the state amounted to only $16,435,727.[5]

While the plantation slavery regime supplied the paramount influence in all aspects of life in antebellum Florida, the overwhelming majority of the white population of the state did not own a single slave; of 77,747 whites only 5,152 were slaveowners.[6] Nevertheless, the pattern of life revolved around the plantation slavery regime. The idealization of the plantation way of life and the hope of some day attaining planter status, plus the planters' leadership ability and economic power, largely account for the general acceptance of planter leadership and policies by the farmers who so far outnumbered them.[7]

The plantation regime was based upon cotton, which prior to the war dominated the state's economic life. After the war began, however, the South began to realize that cotton must be subordinated to food crops. England's nonintervention on the side of the Confederacy and the tightening Federal blockade caused many Southerners to begin agitation for an immediate transition from staple crops to food crops. Planters in Florida voluntarily reduced their cotton acreage and increased their food production during the spring and summer of 1861. Many were not acting through purely patriotic motives but were reacting to the economic fact that cotton could not be sold in any quantity, and that foodstuffs, especially corn, had a ready sale at a good profit. This voluntary action was not sufficiently broad to satisfy the advocates of the agricultural transition, however. One correspondent to the Tallahassee *Florida Sentinel* complained that planters with large holdings "are offering aid and encouragement to the enemy by planting the usual amount of cotton . . . while the poor farmer whose family is dependent upon . . . the labor of his strong arm for the actual necessaries of life, has freely cooperated to grow foodstuffs and has freely volunteered to fight the battles of our country." If this policy were not stopped, the correspondent continued, he would advise all his fellow citizens in like condition to leave the defense of the state, as he would do, to "these patriotic citizens who prefer planting cotton to a provision crop and move from the State to an area where there is a probability of . . . getting enough food . . . while we serve our country."[8]

The *Sentinel* itself was dissatisfied with the Florida planters' actions. In an editorial the paper called upon them to realize the true situation: that the area once looked upon to supply the Confederacy with foodstuffs was either already lost or rapidly growing smaller. The editor candidly pointed out that Kentucky was lost to the South and that conditions in Tennessee were so unstable that the state could not even support the army sent to defend it. He then pointed out that Arkansas was lost and that Louisiana and Texas were cut off from the rest of the South. Virginia and North Carolina were subject to enemy action and could not, therefore, be depended upon for large quantities of food supplies. The true situation, he concluded, was that if South Carolina, Georgia, Alabama, Mississippi, and Florida did not turn to the production of food the Confederacy might well be starved into submission.[9]

The editor of the *Sentinel* not only wanted more corn to be grown but also that the planters sell corn to those who needed it. He quoted for the planters' benefit the twenty-sixth verse of the eleventh chapter of Proverbs, which says: "He that withholdeth grain, the people shall curse him; but blessings shall be upon the head of him that selleth it."[10]

These appeals of individuals and newspapers, plus the ready market, brought about a great increase in corn production during the summer of 1862.[11] Before the planting season of 1863, however, a definite change in the attitude of Florida planters had taken place. Optimism that an early end to the war was possible began to sweep through the planting counties. This optimism, based on rumors of English intervention on behalf of the Confederacy, caused many planters to begin preparing for a return to planting cotton instead of provision crops. This attitude on the planters' part might have had serious effects upon the amount of food produced, but fortunately the change was detected early in the winter, and those forces in the state which opposed a slackening of the war effort were able to organize a concerted drive to convince the planters that foodstuffs were still desperately needed.

The state press began an editorial campaign against optimism concerning the end of the war. The Tallahassee *Florida Sentinel* frankly stated that many planters were abandoning plans to grow food crops because of belief in an early peace. The editor strongly condemned this belief as extremely dangerous. "All we know about it," he warned, "is that the present war must terminate sooner or later . . . and we simply know that we are nearly two years nearer [the end] than when the fight commenced."[12]

Governor Milton also sought to fight the trend away from growing food products and back to cotton. On February 24, 1863, he issued a special appeal to the planters asking them to produce even more food than during the summer of 1862. The chief dependence of the Confederacy for food, the governor warned, must now be placed in Mississippi, Alabama, Georgia, South Carolina, and Florida. Milton closed his appeal by denouncing the belief that the war was almost over and by pointing out that Florida was the only Confederate state which had not limited cotton acreage by legislation. He appealed to the planter to so conduct himself that such legislation would be unnecessary.[13]

Individuals also entered the campaign to persuade the planters to raise edible crops. One soldier, "Occasional," wrote to the *Sentinel* on March 17, 1863, from Hamilton's Crossing, near Fredericksburg, Virginia, telling of the impending battle and the loyalty of Florida troops to the Confederate cause. "Occasional" emphasized that the Florida troops would stay in the fight until the war was over, even if it meant being away from home for five years. "But this they will not do," he warned, "if their friends—friends did I say? —enemies I mean, plant cotton and starve the army in the field and their families at home."[14]

The climax to the anticotton campaign was a public meeting held at the capitol in Tallahassee on March 11, 1863. General Howell Cobb was the principal speaker. Following his appeal for more food crops, the meeting adopted a resolution condemning the planting of cotton. The *Sentinel* reported that the effect of the meeting was strongly felt throughout the planting counties. It summed up the reaction with a quotation from a nine-year-old boy, who, upon returning home, said, "O! Mother, who can have the heart to plant cotton after hearing General Cobb speak."[15]

Some were not so optimistic. Governor Joseph Emerson Brown of Georgia, having succeeded in getting the Georgia General Assembly to pass restrictive legislation concerning planting cotton, asked Governor Milton to do likewise. Pressure was also exerted on Milton to call the state legislature into special session. Public meetings in several Florida counties petitioned the governor to call the General Assembly together to pass legislation controlling the planting of cotton.

Milton answered by steadfastly refusing to convene the legislature. He contended that the legislature of 1862 had discussed at length the problem of legislating against cotton planting and had defeated a proposal for that purpose. The governor also contended that, even if he convened the General Assembly, it would be too late to stop those planters who were determined to plant cotton because of Florida's early planting season.

Milton further expressed serious doubt as to the legality of any government prescribing what shall and what shall not be planted. He maintained that the idea of reducing the amount of cotton by prohibiting its cultivation by slave labor was extremely dangerous, for it would encourage abolitionist sentiments throughout the world. Such a policy would remove one of the strongest defenses of the slave labor system.[16]

The campaign in the press and among individuals, plus the moral persuasion of the governor, turned out to be sufficient. Foodstuffs were planted, in most instances, rather than cotton. The growing season was good and as a result the plantations and farms produced a near record volume of farm produce.[17]

But state-wide discussion and the action of other Southern states ultimately caused a change in the attitude of the Florida legislature. It met in 1863 determined not to leave food production to chance. With very little debate, it passed an act that made it unlawful "to plant and cultivate . . . a greater number of acres . . . in cotton than one acre for each hand owned or employed . . . between the ages of fifteen and sixty." If a person employed hands over sixty and under seventy, and over nine and under fifteen, one-half acre of cotton could be planted for each hand. Any persons who agreed to manufacture, themselves, all of the cotton they grew, or to sell their cotton to other citizens of Florida at a price under the existing prices, would be exempted from the act. Tobacco was limited to one-quarter of an acre per hand regardless of worker's age.

A violator was to be fined $1,000 for each acre above his rightful planting. If information furnished by an informer led to the arrest and conviction of the violator, half the fine went to the informer and the other half to the county to aid the indigent families of soldiers. In cases where there was no informer, all the fine was to be used by the county for aid to the indigents.[18]

This legislation together with the general knowledge of Florida's importance as a source of food for the entire Confederacy ended all efforts at large-scale cotton planting within the state. Most planters and farmers planted less than their legal acreage in 1864, and used their lands and hands to raise provisions for themselves, their neighbors, and the Confederacy.[19] In fact, General John Keith Jackson, Commander of the Military District of Florida in 1864, appealed for reinforcements for the state solely on the basis of defending a vital supply area. He stated that Florida was indispensable to the Confederate Army because it was producing annually for the army 25,000 head of cattle, 1,000 hogsheads of sugar, 100,000 gallons of syrup, 10,000 head of hogs, 50,000 sides of leather, and 100,000 barrels of fish, plus oranges, lemons, limes, arrowroot, and, of course, large quantities of salt. General Jackson ended his appeal by reminding Confederate authorities that the meat annually produced by Florida for the army was equal to the supply for 250,000 men for 180 days.[20]

Food supplies were, of course, not produced without difficulty. One difficulty was the shortage of overseers. In the first great patriotic fervor which swept the state, a large percentage of the planters and overseers volunteered for Confederate service. This left many of the smaller plantations without a white male adult and gave rise to fears of slave insurrections or, at least, of poor harvests because the slaves lacked supervision.

The *Florida Sentinel* in an effort to halt the indiscriminate volunteering of planters and overseers editorialized on true patriotism. The editor cautioned that many men could serve the Confederacy better out of military service than in it, and that it was a mistake for planters and overseers to desert their plantations. The governor, the editor continued, should take immediate steps to see that at least one white adult male was left on each plantation so that the crops could be properly harvested and the slaves properly supervised.[21]

Governor Milton was not unaware of the situation developing on the plantations. He took no direct action, however, until after the act of the Confederate Congress of May 1, 1863, which greatly reduced the number of overseers exempt from conscription. The governor protested this act strongly in a long letter to President Davis. He argued that it not only could weaken the Confederate armies by a reduction of their food supply but was also in direct conflict with a Florida law which required at least one white adult male, either owner or overseer, to reside on any plantation where slaves lived.

The governor also attacked the Confederate Conscription Act upon the ground that it erred in its basic assumption. Milton stated to Davis that it was generally assumed by Congress that enough able men over forty-five years of age could be found to replace the conscripted overseers. The governor took issue with this assumption and pointed out that in Florida most competent men over forty-five who were hired as overseers had already entered Confederate service either as volunteers or as substitutes for younger men. The reason for this action, Milton continued, was that as an overseer the individual received from $200 to $600 per year, but as a substitute in the army the same individual would receive from $500 to $5,000. Hence, the lure of money and the belief in a short war had caused most capable older men to enter military service. The governor concluded his protest by assuring the President that the overseers in Florida were not members of rich families attempting to avoid conscription but were "poor men who have distinguished themselves for their industry and integrity."[22] The Confederate Congress did not repeal the legislation, however, and the shortage of white adult males on the plantations remained a concern for the duration of the war.

As the war progressed into its second and third years, the repair of equipment and buildings also became a major farm problem. Plantations began to disintegrate. Fences fell, gates rotted from their hinges, and livestock roamed almost at will. Equipment broke down, but the demands of the armed forces caused a severe shortage of iron and other articles necessary for the repair of even the simplest of farm tools.[23]

The occupation of the St. Johns River valley also created difficulties for Florida planters. The nearness of the enemy to the interior of the state made Federal raids a distinct danger to any planter from Lake City to the southern extremity of the plantation district. If a Federal raid did not occur, the planter still had the problem of keeping his slaves loyal and preventing their escape into the nearby enemy lines.

Individual planters reacted in different ways. Some allowed the general confusion of the time to sweep them into a state of inactivity and indecision.[24] Others sent all their slaves to the safety of the interior, and cultivated a few acres with the labor of their families. This latter action, of course, brought about a great change in the life of the plantation family. A daughter of such a planter wrote:

"We have some funny experiences, and cut, burnt and sore fingers enough. However . . . it is impossible to keep negroes on the river now, so father determined it was better to have a home without servants than servants without a home. So we stay here living on cornbread and hope."[25]

Other planters evacuated their coastal plantations and fled to the interior. Here they still did not feel secure for it was obvious that the Confederacy would not make a major effort to defend Florida. As a result, these planters fled and became refugees in other Confederate states.[26] Some actually fled to Virginia because they realized that there the interior must be defended at all costs.[27]

Other planters fled before the Union forces, but remained in Florida and continued to plant crops for their own use and for the Confederacy. They either owned two plantations, one of which was inland, or they rented land. Some of them who rented land settled in the Lake City vicinity where they paid $3 per acre rent on all land which they planted and $30 per year rent for the small farmhouses they used for residences. These refugee planters were usually unhappy with their situation. Most of the land available for rent had been cultivated for fifteen to twenty years with little or no rest. As a result, the yield per acre was less than one-half of the yield on the planter's own land.[28] In fact, the refugee planter often became little more than a subsistence farmer forced to survive as much by his wits as by his means; hence, he suffered a great loss of morale.

A constant source of concern was the Negro. The plantation regime was built upon the concept of slave labor, and any event in the course of affairs which affected the slave in any manner was of great concern to the planter and to the other citizens. When the war began, Florida, as all other Southern states, controlled the Negroes within her boundaries by means of a state slave code. One of the code's central features was the county patrol which periodically patrolled county roads and visited the slave quarters of the plantations in the county. These patrols, composed of white men, were primarily concerned with controlling the movement of slaves by making sure they had permission to be absent from the plantations. The patrol also searched Negroes and their quarters for whiskey, firearms, and other forbidden possessions. It was quite natural, therefore, that with the outbreak of war Floridians wanted a more rigid enforcement of any legislation which would protect them from the slaves and at the same time protect their investment in the slaves.

One of the first acts of the state legislature in the fall of 1861 was to provide for an organized and consolidated county patrol system. According to the new legislation, the county commissioners at their first meeting in April of each year were to appoint a patrol committee of three persons from each justice of the peace district. Committee members were to serve for one year, and were to exercise complete control over the patrol in the district. All persons who were subject to militia duty were made liable for patrol duty, and a detailed and somewhat complex schedule of patrols was established.

All assemblies and congregations of slaves or free persons of color, or both, consisting of four or more meeting together in a "confined or secret place" were declared unlawful. Slaves were also forbidden to be away from the plantation without a pass, trade with other persons without permission, possess firearms or liquor, and many other actions deemed a threat to the white population.

Patrol members could administer punishment not in excess of thirty-nine lashes but were liable to a suit for damages if unnecessary violence was committed under the guise of performance of duty. The legislation also provided that all incorporated cities, towns, and villages could form their own patrols with rights and privileges similar to those of the county patrol.[29] This legislation remained the basic patrol law throughout the war, except that the act was amended in 1863 to make all white males between the ages of sixteen and sixty liable for duty with their local patrol unit.[30]

The disposition of a slave charged with a capital crime was not left to the discretion of the county patrol. The twenty-seventh section of Article Four of the Florida Constitution as adopted in 1861 provided for the organization of a court for the trial of slaves, free Negroes, and mulattoes charged with criminal offenses. This court, composed of two justices of the peace and twelve citizens, was to hear the testimony and render a verdict.

Governor Milton was dissatisfied with these special courts and desired a change. He attacked the courts on the ground that the Constitution established them on a temporary basis until the General Assembly could provide a better procedure. Further, he argued, any fourteen-man court was slow and unwieldy at best, and experience had shown that often none of the twelve citizens on the court was familiar with the state laws or with court procedure.[31]

The legislature did not share the governor's apprehension and took no action. Nor were the newspapers unduly concerned, as the following account of a trial shows. "Alic, belonging to Mr. McLeod, and London and Paul, belonging to Mr. Hicks were tried at Waldo . . . before Justices Earl and McRae, and twelve citizens, on the charge of murder. . . . The negroes were acquitted."[32]

As the war progressed, however, evidence disclosed that the slave courts experienced difficulties. Consequently, the legislature in 1864 enacted specific legislation concerning the procedure of these courts. Under the new legislation, any "citizen of good repute" could swear under oath to a justice of the peace that a slave, free Negro, or mulatto had committed a capital crime. The accused was then imprisoned and another justice informed that he was to aid in the trial. The two justices met and chose the twelve jurors, who were summoned to the county seat on a day not exceeding the fifth day from the summons for the trial. Any absent juror was replaced by a substitute from the vicinity. All were sworn to be fair and impartial, and rendered their decision without conferring with the justices. In order to convict, the verdict had to be unanimous, and each juror was required to sign it.

The new legislation provided for an appeal to the local circuit court on order of the judge. The appeal, however, could only operate as supersedeas for no proceedings of the slave court could be annulled or impeded because of an error of form.[33]

The legal status of the Negro was a vexing problem during the first eighteen months of the war for officers of the Union Army in Florida. The first Federal Confiscation Act, August 6, 1861, made it the duty of the President of the United States to confiscate all property used in "aiding, abetting or promoting" the war against the Union.[34] Slaves employed in any military or naval service against the Union were declared contraband of war, but the slave of a master who remained loyal to the United States remained unaffected by the legislation.

It was the duty of the Federal officer in the field to determine the status of a slave who had not been used directly to oppose the Union, but whose owner was in Confederate service. What, for instance, should be done with a fugitive slave who voluntarily entered the Federal lines? Should he be returned? Also unanswered was the question of whether or not slaves should be taken during raids along the seacoast or into the interior. Both army and navy commanders seized slaves along the Florida coasts under the first confiscation act, but some of the officers desired specific instructions.[35]

Lieutenant Colonel Louis Bell, Union commander at St. Augustine, wrote to his commanding officer on April 15, 1862, asking for instructions on the matter of slaves belonging to disloyal Floridians, stating that until such instructions were received he would continue to hold such slaves, "furnishing them with food and compelling them to work, and simply excluding other slaves from the fort."[36] As a result of the confusion a Negro slave who belonged to a "disloyal" master was fed by the Federal forces while the slave of the "loyal" master was excluded.[37]

Major General David Hunter, Federal Commander of the Department of the South, in an effort to simplify the situation as well as to please northern abolitionists, ordered that all slaves in South Carolina, Georgia, and Florida be freed immediately.[38] President Lincoln repudiated Hunter's action and denied that any officer of the United States armed forces had the authority, either real or implied, to free a slave.[39] Thus the status of slaves was more confused than ever.

The second Federal Confiscation Act, July 17, 1862, attempted to remove the confusion. By this legislation all slaves of "disloyal" masters who entered Federal lines were deemed captives of war and "forever free from their servitude."[40] Thus Negroes belonging to "loyal" masters remained slaves while Negroes belonging to "disloyal" masters became "Free Captives of War."

These various statutes and orders respecting slaves did not immediately affect the vast majority of Florida Negroes, for few of them were within Federal lines.[41] Most Florida slaves were busily engaged in producing food and performing the other tasks of plantation life with little or no comprehension of the importance of the events taking place so near at hand.

When hostilities began, and overseers and other white males went off to war, the supervision of many Florida plantations became the responsibility of women, or elderly, and often infirm, males. The manner in which the Florida Negro would react to this new circumstance became, therefore, extremely important not only for the state but also for the entire Confederacy. Florida slaves generally remained loyal. They raised the crops, operated sawmills, shingle mills, and grist mills, made bricks and salt, tended livestock, and did all the other innumerable jobs which had to be done; and they generally did them well.[42]

The Florida slave also contributed directly to the Confederate war effort. The December, 1862, session of the legislature granted the governor authority to request from the slaveholders a sufficient number of slaves to complete any construction task which the Confederate government might deem necessary. If the slaveowner did not grant the request, the governor was empowered to impress the needed slaves.[43]

From time to time the authority was exercised. In the spring of 1863 the governor impressed slaves in West Florida to construct defenses along the Apalachicola River. The majority of the workers were kept in Confederate employment for five months from February through June.[44]

A larger impressment of slaves occurred in East Florida during the spring of 1864. Major General Patton Anderson, Confederate commander in Florida, issued an order calling for the impressment of seven hundred slaves to construct defenses against the Union troops in the Jacksonville vicinity. These slaves were to be impressed from the area east of the Suwannee River, and not more than one-fourth of the able-bodied Negroes of any owner were to be taken.[45] The impressed slaves, ranging in age from seventeen to forty, were divided into work gangs of thirty-five each.[46]

Some Florida Negroes were impressed into direct Confederate service. The Confederate Congress provided on February 17, 1864, for the impressment by states of twenty thousand free Negroes and slaves for menial service in the Confederate Army. The war department fixed Florida's quota at five hundred.[47]

Free Negro laborers were conscripted first. The exact number is unknown but free Negroes were sent to Camp Lay, near Madison, in the fall of 1864. At the camp they were clothed, given a physical examination, then sent to work details.[48]

The impressment of slaves began in December, 1864. The state legislature amended the state impressment act to conform with Confederate legislation and provided that slave impressment in Florida would be conducted by the county sheriff.[49]

The slave's owner received a receipt which gave the age, description, and appraised value of the slave. The appraisal was made by the impressing agent and one other person designated by the owner. Upon arrival at the camp of instruction, the slave received a physical examination and the owner was informed, in writing, as to his physical condition. The slave then entered Confederate service at a pay not to exceed $25 per month.[50]

Not all Florida slaves worked faithfully on the plantation, or quietly and loyally entered Confederate service. As soon as Union operations began along the Florida coasts, they began to enter Union lines, or to join the blockading vessels along the coast. This, of course, gave rise to the fear that slave disloyalty would spread.

The great fear was that disloyalty, if it spread, would turn to violence. Florida soldiers fighting in other parts of the Confederacy became concerned over the safety of their families as early as the spring of 1862. Letters expressing anxiety and counselling caution in dealing with slaves were dispatched to wives and children. They urged that unknown Negroes be reported to the authorities at once and that no food be left in the open where it might tempt a runaway slave to enter the house. Doors should be locked at night and firearms kept near the family sleeping quarters.[51]

Floridians at home also showed concern. The Tallahassee *Florida Sentinel* warned on August 5, 1862, that the town was in the midst of a wave of robberies carried out by Negroes from both the city and the county. It concluded that, "There was a time when a man might go to sleep and leave his house open with impunity in this city, but we fear that time has passed away."

Floridians not only feared the runaway slaves; they also feared the outwardly loyal slave. Mrs. David Levy Yulee distrusted her husband's personal slave to such an extent that she wrote:

> *Sell Tom,* I am not happy with the thoughts of your being alone with him. . . . He will never abandon the hope of freedom, and if your life should stand in his way, you are not safe. . . . I would not have you between him and freedom for the wealth of the world. Tom must go out of our household.[52]

As the war progressed without any serious slave uprising, the fear gradually subsided. After the fall of 1862, the concern of most Floridians was the possible loss of their slaves to the enemy.

Brigadier General Rufus Saxton, Union commander of the Department of the South, did little to allay this concern. A firm advocate of using the ex-slave in any capacity which would aid the Union cause, General Saxton began early in the war to use Negroes as guides for the coastal raiding parties.[53] Next, he requested and received permission to enlist, arm, and equip up to 5,000 Negroes for service under his command.[54]

Confederate authorities in Florida reacted to this plan to use colored troops by removing all slaves who had no owners with them and all free Negroes from the St. Johns River into the interior. There they were placed under the direction of a white person; the free Negroes were left to their own charge, subject to state law.[55]

The first Negro troops used in Florida by the United States were the First and Second South Carolina Volunteers. These regiments had been organized at Beaufort, South Carolina, and their first large-scale action was against Jacksonville in March, 1863. The purpose of the expedition was to occupy the town, make it a base of operations for training the Negroes, and then capture the entire state by the use of colored troops. The occupation of Jacksonville was a success and Union forces ranged almost at will up the St. Johns River.[56] No large number of slaves was captured, however, because of their previous removal. As a result, and because of military necessities elsewhere, Union forces abandoned their Negro-hunting expedition. Jacksonville was put to the torch and evacuated on March 31, 1863.[57] Union forces returned in 1864 primarily because of political factors which will be discussed in another chapter. They retained possession of the city for the remainder of the war, but the area never became a rallying point for a large number of disloyal slaves.

The record of the Florida slave during the war was generally excellent. There was no slave revolt and a very small number ran away. In fact, 1,290 white Floridians joined the Union Army while only 1,044 Negroes joined.[58] Florida furnished fewer Negroes to the Union forces than any Confederate state except Texas.

X

A HINT OF TREASON

THERE WERE FEW Union sympathizers in Florida after secession. During the election campaign of 1860, public opinion had been divided into the three groups of pro-Union, anti-Union if a Republican president was elected, and "cooperative thinking." The latter was composed of those who took a wait-and-see attitude. Secession destroyed the position of the cooperative group and there remained in Florida only Unionists and Confederates.[1] *

It has been shown earlier in this work that most Florida Unionists became loyal to the cause of their state following secession. The opinion among most of those in the interior was succinctly phrased by Ellen Call Long when, after deploring secession, she said, "We must all sink or swim together now—individual opinion is of no consequence."[2] Other Unionists cooperated so that the Secessionists could "carry out their plans, without a chance to blame *us* for the awful responsibility they have assumed."[3]

In 1861 probably not more than four thousand men and women in Florida were Union sympathizers. By 1865 the number had doubled. The proportion, therefore, of Unionists among the 78,679 free inhabitants varied between 5 and 10 per cent. It is also apparent that most of the Unionists were from the northern-born or foreign-born citizens and the native Southerners of the poor white class. The size of the poor white class cooperating with the Union increased rapidly as the war progressed because of the Confederate Conscription Act and heavy Confederate taxes.[4] But Unionism on the Florida mainland was not an important factor until the beginning of Federal invasions of East Florida in March, 1862.

This was not the situation on the island of Key West, however.

*Notes to Chapter X begin on page 235.

There, far removed from the heavily populated middle and western areas of the state, Unionism was an immediate problem. When Florida left the Union, the Federal government had a gunboat and two companies of artillery at the Key West Naval Base, sufficient to enforce beyond question United States authority on the island. But the soldiers could not control sentiment, and the people were soon divided into pro-Secessionists and pro-Unionists.

The only United States civil officials at Key West who did not resign their offices after Florida seceded were District Judge William Marvin and Charles Howe, Collector of Customs. Neither the state nor the Confederate government recognized the authority of Judge Marvin or Collector Howe. Early in May, 1861, McQueen McIntosh, a secession leader, was sent to Key West as the new state appointee to the bench occupied by Marvin. McIntosh demanded that Marvin relinquish the office and surrender all records and papers pertaining to the post of district judge. Judge Marvin refused, but his personal intervention with the Union officers kept McIntosh from being arrested. Instead, McIntosh was allowed to leave the island. The last hope of the Confederacy to assert peaceably its authority at Key West was now gone, and because the island was never invaded by the Confederacy it remained Union territory throughout the war.

The departure of McQueen McIntosh from Key West might have signified the end of Confederate hopes for peaceable control, but it did not settle the many issues facing the island's citizens. Confederate sympathizers comprised at least 80 per cent of the population and controlled the only newspaper.[5] This situation was summarily dealt with by the Union garrison. Martial law was declared on May 10, 1861,[6] and all persons were ordered to take the oath of allegiance to the United States or leave the island at once.[7] The Secessionist newspaper, *Key of the Gulf*, was suppressed and in its place rose a "loyal" press appropriately named *The New Era*, which had as its aim: "to add our mite toward the spread of true Republicanism. . . . We believe in . . . no compromise but a vigorous prosecution of the war, until every traitor shall have laid down his arms."[8]

The intention of the Federal government was manifestly clear. Robert Watson, a cabinet maker, when asked why he was leaving Key West, understood the situation correctly because he answered, "I deem it unsafe for a southern man to live here."[9]

The exact number of persons who chose to leave rather than take the oath of allegiance is unknown. It most certainly was a small percentage of the population. Enough left, however, to cause a minor refugee problem at Tampa. Governor Milton appealed to the citizens of the state to aid these victims of "Lincoln's Vandals" by generous donations of food, clothing, and money.[10] A company of soldiers, known as the "Key West Avengers," was recruited from among the refugees in January, 1862, and immediately accepted into Confederate service.[11]

The Key West citizens who remained on the island presented a greater problem for Florida than the refugees. Most of them made their livelihood either by "wrecking"[12] or by fishing. The wrecker remained on the island or very close to the Florida Keys and presented no problem. The fishermen, however, were a source of concern as their boats left United States soil, fished along the Florida coasts, and returned with their cargoes to a Union port. As a result, Florida officials began seizing the boats under the authority of the third section of the Third Article of the Confederate Constitution. This section defined treason against the Confederacy and included adhering to or giving aid and comfort to an enemy of the Confederacy. Florida authorities contended that any person who took the oath of allegiance to the United States or sold a cargo of fish to the Union garrison, regardless of the circumstances, was committing a treasonable act, hence his property was subject to seizure.

The citizens of Key West protested against this interpretation of their actions. Petitions were sent to Tallahassee denying treason against the Confederate States of America and appealing for an understanding of the awkward position in which the pro-southern inhabitants of the island found themselves.[13] The General Assembly discussed these petitions at length and passed a resolution urging the governor to release all boats belonging to "loyal southerners whenever in his judgment it can be done without injury to the state or the Confederate States of America."[14] The governor, of course, found it very difficult to determine the true sentiments of the owners of seized vessels. Very few vessels were ordered released but the situation was solved by the rising supremacy of the United States Navy in the Gulf. After 1861 the Key West boats fished in the areas the navy controlled.

Unionism on the mainland was chiefly confined to East Florida during the first stages of the war. The situation of the "Union man" in this area was much like the position of the "Southern man" at Key West. At the beginning of the war, the area was controlled by Confederate forces and to oppose the southern cause openly was foolhardy.

Confederate East Floridians knew that there were those among them who were not to be trusted. As early as May 7, 1861, the Jacksonville *St. Johns Mirror* was editorializing on the Union men, advocating that "as a prudent measure of safety . . . it might not be amiss to adopt some plan by which every man's true sentiment may be ascertained and put upon record." The editor suggested that the best method would be an oath to uphold the Confederate Constitution taken before some judicial officer. The editor of the nearby *St. Augustine Examiner* agreed wholeheartedly and suggested that the oath-taking begin in Jacksonville because of the large number of Northerners residing there.[15]

No oath of allegiance such as the two editors envisioned was ever administered. However, the same end was achieved by the passage and enforcement of the Confederate Sequestration Act of August 30, 1861, which in its original and amended form had the effect of confiscating the property of enemy aliens.[16] True Unionists were forced, therefore, to become outward supporters of the Confederacy.

A crisis soon arose for these Unionists. In March, 1862, Federal forces began invasions along the east coast of Florida. The problem of the Unionist rapidly became the simple proposition of whether or not to admit openly his Unionism and remain in the path of the United States Army. To do so might endanger his life and his property as the irregular bands of Floridians known as Regulators were active in the St. Johns River area. These Regulators had killed Unionists and burned the property of several well-known Union sympathizers and any Union man was in grave danger. If, however, the Unionist declared himself and could remain within the protection of the Union lines, he could live openly under his chosen political system and at the same time save his property from seizure by Union officials under the Federal Confiscation Act. He was forced to make a choice, as indecision could be dangerous. But the wrong choice could be disastrous. At Jacksonville, several hundred men, women, and children decided to remain, for various reasons, to greet the Union troops.

The occupation of Jacksonville had not been intended by the Union forces. The expedition up the St. Johns had as its only purpose the recovery of some guns which the Confederates had removed from Fernandina before it had been evacuated.[17] When the Unionists at Jacksonville learned this, they immediately protested to the Union officers that to evacuate the city would cost them not only their property but also their lives. Upon learning of this protest, Brigadier General Thomas W. Sherman, commander of the Federal troops in action against Florida, visited the town and conferred personally with its citizens. Following the conference, General Sherman decided not only to keep the troops at Jacksonville but to increase their number.

Encouraged and stimulated by the presence of a friendly army and the belief that it would remain in the area, East Florida Unionists attempted political organization. On March 20, 1862, the day following the interview with General Sherman, a meeting was held in the courthouse. About one hundred Union men were present. Philip Fraser, a one-time citizen of New Jersey, opened the meeting by reminding those present of their loyalty to the United States. "I take it," he concluded, "that no one is here, who is not prepared to acknowledge his allegiance to the Union." He was correct. The meeting adopted resolutions which declared the Ordinance of Secession null and void and held that the state of Florida "is an integral part of the United States." Other resolutions condemned the treatment Union men had received at the hands of Floridians, and called upon

> the citizens of the State who hold to their allegiance to the United States to raise up a State government according to those provisions . . . which are not in conflict with or repugnant to the provisions of the United States.

On the same day, but only after the resolutions of loyalty had been presented to him, General Sherman issued a proclamation to the "People of East Florida." The General assured the people that the Union army would protect the loyal citizens from further molestation by the Regulators and recommended that "in every city, town, and precinct you . . . throw off that sham government which has been forced upon you . . . and organize your government and elect your officers in the good old ways of the past."[18]

At another meeting four days later, the Jacksonville Unionists decided to form a new and loyal state government at a convention to be held at Jacksonville on April 10. This government was to consist of ordinary state and Federal officials. Any locality in Florida could send delegates, but a special request for participation was sent to St. Johns, Nassau, Putnam, Clay, Volusia, Orange, and Brevard counties. Delegates to the convention were to be elected on April 7. The meeting was so confident of the successful launching of a new political future for East Florida that it adjourned sine die.[19] General Sherman, also, was optimistic. "I have the sanguine hope," he reported to the war department, "that Florida will soon be regenerated."[20]

These hopes were ill founded. On March 31 Brigadier General Horatio G. Wright, Union commander at Jacksonville, reported to his superiors that he had information to the effect that the Confederates were preparing an attempt to recapture the town. While assuring those at Department of the South headquarters that he would fight to hold the town, he warned them that without immediate reinforcements the fight would be in vain. The order to evacuate Jacksonville reached him on April 6, and he made preparations to comply. The orderly withdrawal was completed on April 9. News of the proposed evacuation aroused consternation and disbelief among the Unionists. Thoughts of a reconstructed Florida were replaced by the desire for survival. Accordingly, approximately one hundred families fled on Union transports.[21] Thus the first attempt at Unionist politics in Florida ended in flight.

But the dream of a pro-Union government in Florida did not die. It was revived during the brief Federal occupation of Jacksonville in the spring of 1863 and was developed into a grandiose scheme of conquest and political intrigue in 1864 which ended with the Battle of Olustee.

Unionism, while a constant threat, never alone endangered the lives and property of the majority of Floridians. Unionists, however, combined with Confederate deserters and Florida men who refused to be conscripted, constituted a real hazard. After the passage of the Confederate Conscription Act in April, 1862, opposition encountered by Confederate enrolling officers increased. Governor Milton, greatly disturbed by the events, complained to the Confederate authorities, "The opposition to the Conscript Act and the attempts to enforce it have produced much dissatisfaction and I am informed that some men of influence . . . have taken advantage of circumstances to array a feeling of hostility against the Confederate Government."[22]

Many who had not volunteered for Confederate service by the time the Conscription Act became operative in 1862 had no intention of entering service by compulsion or otherwise. They preferred to "lay out"—that is, to secret themselves near their homes, if possible, and if not, in some other area of the state, in order to escape military service. The controlling motive for these men was not love for the Union. They were actuated almost entirely by the desire to remain out of Confederate service. To do this they were willing to be classified as traitors. Usually they were poor and illiterate. The following letter, written by such a person who had entered service from Madison County, illustrates sentiments of this class of individuals.

December 4, 1863

Dear Mother

Seat my Self this Morning to inform you that I am Well and we have got orders to leave here But I do not know wher we are going to but out west I will wright to you as soon as I git to my Journey end. . . . Wright to me [if] Brother Ben is gone back to Virginia and Tell Him If He Haint Gone Not Go Take the Woods First.[23]

Another factor which contributed to desertion or "laying-out" in Florida was the concern over the welfare of the individual's family. Letters to soldiers often described hardships at home and led to a growing discontent with army life. One Florida deserter, who was captured and executed, had been led to desert by his wife who had deceived him as to the severity of her hardship. "Soldiers' wives," the newspaper account of this unfortunate situation concluded, "cannot be too cautious in their letters to their husbands. They should not make them believe they are suffering when really they are not. Such letters cause more than half of the desertions in the army."[24]

Most cases of extreme hardship were not fictional. As has already been pointed out in the discussion of state finances, one of the ever-increasing expenses of state government was aid to needy families of soldiers. The situation became so critical in Taylor County that on August 11, 1862, a petition was sent to Jefferson Davis, signed by the county officials, asking that all males between the ages of eighteen and forty-five in the county be exempt from conscription. The reason for the request, the officials stated, was that if any more men were removed from the county widespread starvation would occur among the women and children.[25]

Florida also became a haven for deserters and "lay-outs" from other Confederate states. The numerous swamps and the sparse population made the area an excellent place to hide. The influx of these undesirables from other states added to the hardships and dangers inflicted upon the Floridians. Governor Milton was cognizant of this condition and appealed to the Confederate War Department for assistance in combating the rising influence of the deserters over citizens of the more remote sections.[26]

The deserters and the "lay-out" made no distinction between themselves. Because both were seeking to avoid capture and therefore shared common dangers, they soon joined together in armed bands. These organized bands were especially strong in Lafayette, Walton, Taylor, Levy, and Washington counties in West Florida, and in the part of Southwest Florida from Tampa Bay south to Fort Myers.[27] Other counties, of course, had difficulty with armed bands of deserters, but depredations by such groups were temporary. On the East Coast, Volusia County suffered at the hands of the raiders more than any other county except Duval, Putnam, and St. Johns. These three counties were occupied by both Union and Confederate forces and this, naturally, led to raids and counterraids by both regular and irregular forces.[28]

Federal naval and military authorities in Florida encouraged and supplied the deserter groups. As early as December 6, 1861, Federal commanders agreed to accept into Union service any men who recruited according to the rules and regulations of the United States pertaining to the volunteer system.[29] This recruiting drive did not succeed because of close Confederate control over the area in the early stages of the war. On October 8, 1863, Brigadier General Alexander Asboth became Federal commander in West Florida. He was ordered to resume recruiting in an attempt to raise a company of cavalry.[30] General Asboth was able to report partial success but complained of being unable to reach the deserters because of the inaccessibility of their hiding places. He concluded his report by appealing for a Union policy of financial aid to the "refugees." He knew of no better way to secure their loyalty because of "the destitution of the people."[31]

The deserter as a rule had not left one army to enter another, and recruiting went very slowly. On June 6, 1864, in line with Unionist political ambitions in Florida and because of the poor record of volunteering for Federal service, Major General John G.

Foster, commanding the Department of the South, ordered full-scale recruiting within the state. Every white male between eighteen and fifty within Union lines was to register and be organized into militia companies. The companies were to drill two hours each week and could be used to defend their area or for garrison duty. If any white male desired to enter regular Union service, he was to be placed in a company for service within Florida and treated as any other United States volunteer. Deserters were wisely exempted from the provisions of the decree.[32] Evidently this order failed to have the desired effect. On September 19, 1864, the *Jacksonville Union*, the newspaper of occupied Jacksonville, ran a notice declaring:

> The First Regiment of Florida Cavalry is now being raised. Union men desirous of assisting in giving the final blow to the rebellion are informed that now is the time for them to step forward and join.

Union men and deserters did not join in the desired numbers, and the newspaper again issued the call for volunteers on February 11, 1865. It closed by reminding the reader that each recruit would receive six hundred dollars as a bounty.

Federal authorities in Florida had much greater success with the deserter when he was allowed to use Federal arms and seek his own vengeance on the Confederacy. In most instances the larger deserter bands became very powerful. In late 1863 and early 1864, one such group in Taylor County formed an organized company called the "Independent Union Rangers." These Union Rangers drew up a document which served as their constitution and which was signed by the thirty-five original members of the company. Among the provisions were: "true allegiance to the United States of America"; absolute obedience to their officers; execution of "proven spies"; just division of all spoils; complete secrecy concerning the Rangers; and the death penalty for any member who deserted the band.[33]

Deserter bands became aggressively hostile as the war progressed. Early in the war they had contented themselves with leading an occasional ambush of Confederate patrols, stealing what arms and provisions they needed from nearby plantations, and providing Union blockaders with any information of military importance they might possess.[34] By the spring of 1864, however, these bands were terrorizing entire areas of the state. The stealing of Negroes had become so prevalent in coastal areas by 1864 that planters were forced to move their slaves to the interior. The *Gainesville Cotton States* on

June 18 saw in the increased stealing of Negroes proof that "the deserters are now carrying on an organized attempt to steal every negro they can in an effort to ruin the County." The editor warned that the only hope for the people east of the Suwannee River was to organize and fight back. "East Florida," he declared, "must make up its mind whether to *Fight* or submit to the deserters."

The deserters in Southwest Florida also were guilty of thievery. This region was sparsely settled and had relatively few slaves, but by 1864 it had become a principal source of meat for the Confederate forces. In an effort to halt this movement of beef, deserters began a systematic attempt to steal or slaughter all the cattle possible. The stolen cattle were driven southward to the vicinity of the Union stronghold at Fort Myers where they were used to feed the families of deserters as well as the Union garrison. Slaughtered cattle not needed immediately as food by the raiding group were left where they fell.[35]

Confederate authorities reacted sharply to this campaign of theft and slaughter. Major Pleasant W. White, Chief Commissary of Florida, wrote General Patton Anderson pointing out the value of the cattle in South Florida to the Confederacy and requested immediate military action against the deserters. General Anderson agreed to send troops as soon as possible, but he determined they would be Confederate regulars and not armed local irregulars. Fifty-seven of the last eighty irregulars supplied with Confederate arms had immediately deserted to the enemy.[36] In April, 1864, Lieutenant Colonel T. W. Brevard, commanding the Sixty-fourth Georgia Regiment, was ordered to the Fort Meade area to operate against the deserters. He was to seize Fort Myers if in his opinion it could be taken, but he was primarily to protect the cattle supply from further depredation.[37] The campaign of the Sixty-fourth Georgia Regiment was a failure. The deserters refused open combat and moved from place to place in order to avoid contact. Many of them retired to the coastal islands where they were protected by the Federal blockading squadron.[38] After the Confederate campaign failed, Southwest Florida fell under the influence of the deserters to an ever-increasing degree until the end of the war.[39]

The deserters did not confine their campaigns to stealing slaves and cattle. The bands, growing even braver as the inability of the authorities to retaliate against them became more and more apparent, began to steal Confederate supplies and to rob the mails. In

February, 1864, Captain John Rodger Adams, commanding officer of the commissary warehouse at Gainesville, organized a wagon train to transport supplies to South Florida. Upon reaching Flat Ford on the Hillsborough River, the wagon train was surprised and captured by a band of deserters who burned the wagons and destroyed the supplies.[40] Attacks upon the Confederate mails became so frequent that mail service, in the last year of the war, became very irregular in Florida.[41] In West Florida, the most frequent attacks upon the postman occurred in the area adjacent to the Choctawhatchee River and Bay. These attacks usually consisted of seizing the postman at some lonely location along his route and holding him prisoner while other members of the gang rifled the mail bags, taking what they thought might be of use to them.[42] Deserter bands also destroyed railroad trestles, burned bridges, cut telegraph lines, and in general attempted to disrupt communications both within the state and between Florida and other Confederate states.[43]

As the armed groups increased the area over which they operated, their influence grew proportionately. Local government was often seriously hampered or totally disrupted in the counties which contained a large and well-organized deserter group. The disruption of local government manifested itself by the desertion to the enemy of some local officials and by the intimidation of those officials who remained loyal to the Confederacy. The sheriff of Washington County along with others defected to the Federals in January, 1864,[44] and in February Edward Jordon, sheriff of Taylor County, reported:

> It is with a great deal of displeasure I am driven to the necessity of informing you that I am compelled to stop collecting, or assessing Taxes for the present, in Consequence of The Enemy . . . and having rece'd a message from a Squad of Persons that call themselves *Union men.* I have thought it best to desist . . . until there is a force in the County to check them if not I shall have to leave I cannot say how soon for safety for, I have rece'd orders to join them or I cannot stay in the County.[45]

The sheriff of Manatee County, J. J. Addison, experienced similar difficulties, and reported, "There is over half the Tax payers of this County gone to the Yankees . . . one of our County commissioners has gone to the Yankees two of the outhers taken and Prisiners."[46] Even the governor was not immune from the audacious plans of the deserters. On February 3, 1864, Governor Milton was informed that they had learned of his travel plans and approximately one hundred of them had organized in an effort to capture him.[47] The governor remained in Tallahassee to avoid the possibility of becoming a prisoner or a casualty.[48]

The Confederate and state governments were, of course, aroused by the behavior of the deserters, whose activities were an insidious form of invasion as they were effectively reducing Florida's war potential. On the coastal fringes of the state, many of their raids were coordinated with activities of Federal troops.[49] Action by the Confederacy was mandatory as such a situation could not go unnoticed. However, no consistent policy toward the deserter was ever adopted by the state or the Confederate government. Prior to 1864, about the only action was the publishing of newspaper appeals for all Florida men who were "Absent Without Leave" to join their companies before they were classified as deserters and "proceeded against accordingly."[50] By 1864, however, almost every newspaper in the state was carrying notices of rewards for information which could lead to the capture of deserters.[51] These newspaper notices brought in very few men. More drastic measures were needed and the Confederacy began military campaigns against them in the spring of 1864.

A systematic and merciless campaign was carried out against the deserters in Lafayette and Taylor counties just southeast of Tallahassee. The bands there had been augmented by many others from South Georgia. Taylor County, especially, had extensive swamps which provided an excellent hiding place. As a result, the deserters had been able to raid the nearby rich planting area with considerable success at a minimum risk to themselves.[52]

In March the Confederate government assigned Lieutenant Colonel Henry D. Capers the task of driving them from the Lafayette and Taylor county swamps. He was given a detachment of cavalry, commanded by Major Charles H. Camfield, and the Twelfth Battalion of Georgia Infantry. Intelligence reports to Capers placed the deserters' camp on Snyder's Island on the east side of the Econfina River, near its mouth, and surrounded by nearly impassable tidewater flats. To seize the location, Colonel Capers ordered the cavalry to proceed along the east bank of the river while he led the infantry through the coastal swamps from the Aucilla River. The location of the supposed camp was reached on the morning of

March 24, but nothing was found except deserted huts. Conditions indicated that the camp was used irregularly by the deserters. This caused Colonel Capers to conclude that they did not maintain an organized encampment but remained concealed in the vicinity of their homes. Capers, therefore, ordered their homes destroyed and their wives and children seized. The raid ended in utter failure except for the capture of two deserters and the seizure of sixteen women and their children. It caused the colonel to conclude that the only effective way of hunting deserters in Taylor County would be "with dogs and mounted men under the command of an experienced woodsman who is familiar with the country." The experience of the Seminole War, he felt, "will fully establish this fact." Colonel Capers, in an effort to induce some or all of the group to return to Confederate authority, left a proclamation offering a full pardon to any deserter who would agree to rejoin his command and who would report to Camp Lay at Madison on or before April 5. Those refusing this offer of pardon were to be hunted down and, if armed when captured, shot.

The leader of the deserters, William W. Strickland, who had now changed the group's name from the "Independent Union Rangers" to the "Florida Royals," answered the proclamation for the group. In a letter to Colonel Capers he stated:

I got your letter [the proclamation] that you left. . . . I am anxious to hear from you, and you from me, for I cannot controle my men since they saw you fire our house. . . . I ain't accountable for what they do now. As for myself, I will do anything that any half white man ever done, only to go into the Confederate war any more, though when I was in it I done my duty, I reckon. Ask Colonel Smith, if I was not as good a soldier as long as he was captain, and would have been yet if Mr. Smith had of staid captain, but now I have went on the other side and tried what we call United States of Taylor, but I find it is like the Confederate man —more wind than work. . . . If you will send and get me an exemption and my men that have taken the oath [to the Union] to stay in Taylor and raise stock for you they will do so, but they will not go into war if you had as many again men and dogs, for our title is Florida Royals, and if we can't get a furlough from Mr. Jeff. Davis during the war you will find our title right for awhile; so I remain a flea until I get a furlough from headquarters. . . . I give you my respects for the good attentions you paid to my wife, for it was not her notion for me to do as I was doing. Just set me and my men free from the war. . . . If not, you can go to moving steers out of the adjoining three counties. So here is my love for the good attentions for my wife and child. If the war lasts long enough and you will raise him to be a soldier he will show the spunk of his daddy.

So I remain,

W. W. Strickland,
Florida Royals.[53]

The women and children seized by Colonel Capers were transported to Camp Smith, six miles south of Tallahassee, where they were housed in nine especially constructed houses. These houses had been built by local planters, at government request. No one knew their purpose until the women arrived. Many of the women were sulky and "used the worst language possible to imagine and made dire threats of what their men would do." These threats did not trouble Tallahassee residents, and when no rescue attempts were made they began taking food to the deserters' families. The women were well treated but an armed guard was kept around the camp.[54]

Governor Milton, learning of Colonel Capers' seizure of the women and children, was greatly displeased. On May 5, 1864, he expressed his displeasure in a letter to General J. Patton Anderson, Confederate commander in Florida. He reminded General Anderson that some of the seized women were the mothers or sisters of loyal Florida troops serving in the armies of Virginia and the West and that as governor he could not tolerate such action. Milton then requested that Anderson issue an order forbidding a recurrence of the incident. Milton explained he did not feel any mercy toward the deserters, but "I cannot," he concluded, "approve of a warfare on women and children."[55]

The women at Camp Smith, despairing of rescue, petitioned Governor Milton to allow them to be sent to Union blockading vessels. The petition explained that however wrong the actions of the men had been, the women "as their wives and daughters are eternally united with them, and situated as we are, we prefer to follow their fortunes."[56] Milton ordered their release and had them escorted to the Union blockading vessel off St. Marks on July 19, 1864, bringing to a conclusion one of the cruelest incidents of the war in Florida.[57]

The armed assaults upon the deserters had failed and, as a result, by August, 1864, Brigadier General John K. Jackson, then commanding Confederate forces in Florida, openly called for less severe measures. He instituted a policy of dealing with the deserters harshly whenever they were captured while raiding the interior, but otherwise, holding out the promise of a pardon for any who surrendered voluntarily.[58]

The governor objected to the policy of leniency and ordered the newly formed state militia not only to arrest deserters, but "all persons [male] who harbor deserters or encourage desertion." The militia was able to make some arrests and these captives served as a boon to the state's sagging morale.[59] The arrests were of individual deserters, however, and the state militia was no more effective against the organized bands than had been the Confederate troops.

The last effort to deal with the deserter in Florida was a part of the general policy of the Confederacy. On February 11, 1865, General Robert E. Lee issued an amnesty proclamation to all deserters. The proclamation allowed all men absent without leave to return without punishment, provided they returned within twenty days. The offer excluded any person who deserted after the date of the proclamation, persons who had deserted twice, or any person who had sworn allegiance to the United States after desertion. The Florida press gave the proclamation wide coverage and advised the deserters to take the opportunity to "redeem their honor and their country from peril."[60]

This appeal was no more successful than the proclamations issued during the earlier stages of the war. In fact, as the end of the war approached, the exodus to the enemy became a steady stream. Families deserted en masse to Jacksonville. The situation became so acute that the Confederate and Union commanders in the Jacksonville and Waldo areas adopted a system whereby these individuals entered the Union lines under a flag of truce. It also became accepted procedure that the families' baggage would be limited to "one or two trunks and a bed or two." The editor of the *Gainesville Cotton States* declared that as many as forty-nine people a day were passing into the enemy lines. "This is wrong," the editor declared, "as it invites a soldier to desert as it seems to say—'Go over to the Federals and we will send your family.' "[61]

This exodus to the enemy was an obvious indication of the internal disintegration of Confederate Florida in the last months of the war. The necessities of life were becoming scarce. Law and order were breaking down in the fringe areas. Lives and property were no longer safe in those areas. The inhabitants of central Florida were comparatively safe and desertion to the enemy did not become a problem for the authorities. As a result, no more than 15 per cent of the white male population of the state became involved in Unionism or desertion even during the last days of the war. The surprising fact is that the exodus to the enemy did not become a migration.

XI

THE HOME FRONT

WHENEVER A NATION goes to war the life of the people is drastically changed. Men enter service and adopt a new and regimented concept of life. But many more citizens remain at home than enter the military service; hence, the home front becomes as important as the battle front in modern warfare. The Confederate home front was no exception; Florida was no exception among the Confederate states.

When Florida seceded from the United States on January 10, 1861, and subsequently joined the Confederate States of America, very few of her citizens had the remotest concept of how warfare would affect the lives of the noncombatants. The hope of early victory, if war should come, made the political proceedings assume a festive air. But as the speeches of politicians gave way to the noise of cannon, civilians in Florida were faced with the terrible realities of war and its effect upon their way of life. The women, of course, were immediately affected. In Florida, as elsewhere, they responded with great enthusiasm at first, which turned to grim determination as the war dragged on.[1*]

A problem facing the whole state was the need of clothing. The people were almost entirely dependent upon imported cloth. Prior to hostilities it had come from northern or English mills, but the state was now severed from both these sources of supply by war and the subsequent blockade. Domestic production was the only answer.

On most of the large plantations spinning wheels and in some cases looms had been kept as mementos of the past. These had been handed down from previous generations and many old Negroes knew how to use them. "In nearly every 'quarters,'" wrote a con-

*Notes to Chapter XI begin on page 236.

temporary, "some old woman could be found and employed with the spinning of either cotton or wool into knitting yarn." And elderly slaves, unable to work in the fields, knitted socks and stockings for the plantation families and the soldiers. As the seriousness of the situation became apparent carpenters were called in and new looms were patterned after the old ones. Wood was the universal material, as no iron could be spared for such projects. Spinning wheels and looms became important fixtures in the homes of those who could acquire them. Older Negroes taught the younger ones the art of spinning, and as the war progressed white women took up the work. By 1862, one diary stated, "the whirl of the wheel and the noise of the baton could be heard in almost every house."[2]

Sewing societies became the outlet for much patriotic fervor, and also met a direct need. Members assembled in the homes and sewed most of the day. These societies often met three or four days each week, sewing two or three days for the soldiers and one for themselves. Special drives for clothing, of course, meant extra days of sewing. Old members taught new ones until all became proficient in the work. "No moment is idle," one society member recorded, "in the cars traveling, visiting, in the dark, in the light, the . . . needle is going perpetually to clothe . . . our soldiers."[3]

The sewing societies received official recognition from the state government. On December 17, 1861, the legislature appropriated $10,000 to buy material for conversion into clothing for Florida soldiers by the Ladies Military Aid and other patriotic societies.[4] In December, 1862, Governor Milton noted a lack of clothing for the troops but paid tribute to the efforts of the women to supply it. "The women of Florida, 'God Bless Them,' have signalized themselves and our noble cause by their generous, patriotic and untiring efforts to . . . clothe our gallant soldiers."[5]

Clothing for the troops remained scarce, and the legislature appropriated $75,000 in 1863 to purchase the necessary materials for shoes and uniforms and to pay for having the material manufactured for use by Florida forces.[6] The ladies' societies aided in the preparation of these uniforms. In his report to the legislature in December, 1864, Milton again thanked the ladies for their devotion and patriotism but called for a change in the policy of acquiring clothing for the troops. It was expedient, Milton said, to leave it "almost entirely" to the Confederate government. The Confederate quartermaster could do it at less expense and with better material.

At the same time, he explained, the state would remove itself from an area in which some citizens felt partiality had been practiced.[7] The ladies' societies continued to sew, but primarily for friends, relatives, and loved ones.

The shortage of medicines also attracted the attention of women's societies. Some were formed for the specific purpose of aiding both military and civilian sick, wounded, and infirm. These societies, local in nature and usually named for a local hero, made bandages, collected linen and other articles needed for bandages, gave money, and in general did whatever was deemed of aid to the Confederate, state, or local authorities charged with responsibility for the sick and wounded. Many members of these groups literally gave all they had to give: blankets, linens, tablecloths, napkins—not a linen sheet, tablecloth, or napkin was left in many circles.[8]

Some societies concentrated on other phases of aid for the sick or wounded. The Soldier's Friend Society of Leon County stressed the need for proper nourishment for the wounded. Drives were held for foods to supplement the diet of the soldiers in the Tallahassee hospital. Chickens, eggs, butter, honey, syrup, and citrus fruits were most often requested.[9] Several organizations established wayside homes for the traveling soldier. Fatigued, ill, or in need of board and lodging, the soldier was welcome. Tallahassee and Monticello had the largest and most popular of the homes. The one at Monticello under the direction of Mrs. H. Louisa Guardian became so important that the governor used state funds to aid it.[10] Preparing packages for the soldiers both at the front and in the hospitals was a common practice of the aid groups. A plan was evolved whereby a state agent accompanied the packages and assumed responsibility for their delivery. Samuel Pauleston, the agent, would announce in the press that he would make a trip on a certain date to one of the areas where Florida troops were located. Packages destined for soldiers on that particular front were then forwarded to the address given by the agent, who would take them to the front. Upon his return, he would gather packages for another fighting front. The procedure was repeated until he had visited all fronts where Florida soldiers were engaged.[11]

Many women entered hospitals or sick rooms to nurse the ill or wounded. These women were, of course, invaluable but not necessarily competent. Many good-natured anecdotes circulated throughout the state about the "volunteer nurse." Most of them portrayed the volunteer who, in an effort to aid, actually only overnursed or angered the patient. One such story tells of a volunteer dressing a blister for a soldier when a bouquet was presented to him by a very beautiful young woman. The volunteer, who was rather unattractive, in an effort to please him exclaimed at length how lovely the flowers would look in the room. The soldier answered disgustedly, "Oh! dress my blister; you are the only woman in the world that can interest me at the present time."[12] These stories did not deter the volunteers and much of the nursing within the state was done by them.[13]

The ladies aid societies also undertook to entertain the sick and wounded. They sponsored concerts by bands from the various Florida regiments and used the proceeds to aid the project of the sponsoring group. Often the ladies held suppers with the band concert in an effort to increase both the attendance and the evening's profit.[14] Minstrel shows were also extremely popular with Floridians. Staged by the young men of the community, these became weekly or biweekly projects for societies in towns like Tallahassee.[15]

Theatrical productions were popular throughout the war and were effectively used to raise funds. On June 2 and 3, 1863, for instance, women from Jefferson and Madison counties, aided by friends in Tallahassee, presented an evening of thespian entertainment for the benefit of soldiers' families. The program consisted of an adaptation of Shakespeare's *King Lear*, and *Tampa*, an original melodrama founded on incidents of early Florida history. The Tallahassee press gave the event adequate publicity:[16] "The melodrama *Tampa* was the best received," the *Sentinel* reported, "as it was more fully understood."[17] The affair was a great success both theatrically and financially, as the spectators contributed over $800. *Dombey and Son* was another theatrical success of the Tallahassee group.[18]

Musical concerts were the most popular of the arts in Florida during the war. The citizens of Quincy raised $2,320 at two concerts.[19] A Tallahassee audience attended one in the chamber of the House of Representatives on the evening of April 9, 1865, not knowing that General Robert E. Lee had surrendered. The chamber was filled to capacity. The program consisted of such selections as "Une Pluie du Perle," "Sleeping I Dreamed Love," "The Southern Marseillaise," and, of course, "Dixie," as well as old-time airs and operatic music.[20]

Not all Tallahassee concerts were at this level of artistic achievement. The appearance of a slave, Blind Tom, was the musical highlight of February, 1864. Blind Tom sang and played "southern songs" but the climax of his program was an original composition, "Battle of Manassas." A member of the audience described the program in this manner:

> Blind Tom is wonderful! He plays the Battle of Manassas . . . [which] begins with the booming of cannon; the rattle of musketry and above all the clear notes of the bugle. Faintly in the distance the strains of Dixie float upon the air, these strains grow louder and louder and mingle with the clashing of guns, the tramping of horses, and the sharp commands of officers. He intersperses the music with the names of the different Generals, who took the most prominent parts.[21]

The composition was even more wonderful, the participant felt, because Blind Tom was a complete imbecile.

Tableaux, or a combination fair and festival, were also popular. They were held throughout the state, but the ladies of Tallahassee raised the largest sum of money on a single night of any Florida society with a fair and festival. On May 7, 1863, they earned more than $1,450 at a combination fair and supper where they sold articles of their own manufacture.[22]

Towns where soldiers were stationed provided dances for the entertainment of both their young ladies and the soldiers. The dances were enjoyed by both groups, but the lack of suitable dresses plagued the young ladies as the war progressed into 1862. They ransacked the attics for old and discarded dresses which they restyled over and over again. Remorse sometimes overtook ladies who attended several dances, and they rededicated themselves to sewing or knitting with a new patriotic fervor; "if I can stay awake to dance and play," one such lady wrote, "I can surely keep my eyes open to knit socks for our dear soldiers . . . I must stop and knit-knit-knit."[23]

Woman's life was greatly affected by the widespread shortages. Luxuries were curtailed by the blockade and often the basic necessities of life were limited. Candles were used sparingly because of the shortage of tallow. They were lighted only on festive occasions, or when guests were entertained for dinner. Fat pine supplied light for household purposes. Most reading and knitting was done by pine firelight, but some women, especially those of the wealthier class, did not attempt to sew in that light.[24]

Clothing became scarce. New dresses were almost an unheard-of luxury because of the cost of cotton cloth. Ladies' hats early became a war casualty. Mrs. A. Rossetter of Bellview solved the hat problem, however, as she began the manufacture of bonnets from the native palmetto. They were said to compare favorably in every way with the Shaker bonnets of northern manufacture which had been the usual style in Florida before the war. Mrs. Rossetter's bonnet became popularly known as the "Dixie Bonnet" and received widespread publicity.[25] The women of Tallahassee used an adaptation of the "Dixie Bonnet" by combining the palmetto leaves with cotton cloth. These hats sold in Leon County at $5 for a man's hat and $10 for a woman's hat. The sturdiness of the combination and the reasonable price caused them to find a ready market.[26]

The lack of necessities was probably nowhere more serious than in the area of leather products. Shoes were difficult to find after the blockade became effective, and when found often sold at fantastic prices. Susan Bradford Eppes, the eighteen-year-old daughter of a wealthy Leon County family, recorded in her diary on April 7, 1864:

> Today I have no shoes to put on. . . . The very touch of my bare foot to the ground made me shiver. . . . Until the shoes for the army are finished, Mr. McDearmmid will not have time to make shoes for any one else, this is right.

McDearmmid evidently did not finish the army order soon enough because Susan platted corn shucks together and fashioned a shoe which was made comfortable by the incorporation of a velvet lining. "Everybody laughed," she recorded, "but I feel quite proud."[27]

Diet was greatly affected. Such items as mustard, black pepper, tea, imported fruits, and white sugar rapidly disappeared. Many items, including rice, molasses, and bread baked with baking soda, that had been paramount in a Floridian's diet soon became luxuries.[28] Families in the interior counties suffered less than those in the marginal areas, because they had ample supplies of chickens, eggs, syrup, and other products of rural areas. There was little diversity of diet but the food was adequate.[29]

The inhabitants of the fringe areas suffered. Julia Jackson Fisher, of Southeast Georgia near the Florida line, recorded in her diary:

> The best thing we have now is corn cake, mixed with water. Our corn is ground in a hand mill, which holds about four quarts, and is very hard to grind. The rice is beaten from the hull in a mortar made from a log and burnt out. . . . These two articles and pork have constituted our living for a year past.[30]

The fringe area of Southwest Florida fared little better.[31]

Substitutes for food and drink were sought and found. "Non-alcoholic Delights" replaced the prewar mint julep or sherry cobbler. The most palatable of these delights was a "Cream Nectar" which received much publicity in North Florida.[32] The cotton seed replaced the coffee bean in making coffee. The developer of this coffee said that he had tried all the recipes for coffee made from potatoes, rye, and grits, and that his coffee was superior to all others. Cottonseed coffee was simple to make. Wash the cottonseed to clear it of lint and soak the seed in water from twelve to twenty-four hours. Parch the wet seed slowly until the entire seed is well parched and then grind it in the coffee mill. The drink made from two-thirds parched cotton seed and one-third real coffee "cannot be told from real java, when hot milk is used." In fact, the correspondent confided, cottonseed coffee was a great boon to persons with "nervous dispositions."[33]

Shortages were especially irritating at festive seasons or special occasions. The efforts of the women to provide their children with some gaiety and festivity produced remarkable results, however. Christmas, of course, is the most meaningful season for children, and the women of Florida strove gallantly to keep the season unchanged by the war. In 1861 there were still a few toys for sale but most of the tree decorations were of home manufacture. Women took bright-hued autumn leaves, dipped them in wax and pressed them with a warm iron. These were arranged in clusters to reflect the candlelight. Long ropes of "Soddom Apples" and strings of popcorn usually completed the decorations.[34]

The slaves who had traditionally received calico cloth for Christmas received none during the war because calico, which had been 10 cents per yard in 1860, was $200 per yard by Christmas of 1861. Many of the disappointed slaves believed that Santa Claus had been killed by the Yankees when he tried to visit his southern children in defiance of the blockade. They could explain the absence of calico in no other manner. By Christmas of 1862, however, presents and decorations were even simpler. "We have had to dress old dolls anew, and make bon-bons of home-made candies, wrapped in colored paper," wrote Mrs. Long.[35]

The Christmas of 1864, after three years of shortages, taxed the inventive powers of the women to the uttermost. All presents had to be made locally and, since most women were now expert at sewing, they were homemade dolls or stuffed animals. The dolls usually represented either Confederate soldiers or nurses, while the animals were prototypes of those usually found in Africa. One animal toy which captured the fancy of an entire neighborhood was a rooster a foot high made entirely of watermelon seed.[36] Ingenuity produced a happy Christmas for the children in 1864, but the adults generally received no gifts at all.

Most Florida women bore the hardships of war without losing their high morale. Some women did aid deserters and others complained so bitterly that their husbands deserted the Confederate Army, but these constituted a small minority. Certainly no higher patriotism was displayed in the South than that of its women. The self-sacrificing devotion of Florida women to the Confederate cause "fired the heart and nerved the arm of the Southern soldier."[37] They prayed and worked constantly for a Confederate victory. Northern soldiers stationed at Jacksonville paid tribute when they declared that but for southern women the South would soon fall; the women disciplined each other with intolerance toward any slacker.[38] In fact, their zeal for the cause surpassed that of many soldiers.

The poor and illiterate, or almost illiterate, woman of the fringe areas suffered the shortages even more than the wealthy. Moreover, she was forced to do the manual labor for survival when her husband went off to war. Very little is known of her life for she wrote few letters and kept no diaries. The following touching letter probably accurately describes her life.

Orlando, Fla.
March the 27, 1864

Dear Husband I seat my Self to inform you that we are all well at this time and I hope these fiew lines will find you in good health I have no news to write much the children is all hearty And the baby grose a rite smart and he is a good boy and the Pretyest you ever saw and Alice has quit crying you wanted to no what we got to eat we got Patatoes and a little milk now we have got tenn Sucklers up I have got Some cane planted and this peas and corn hear by the house and it looks verry well And I have got all the rest of the ground that we was talking a bout planting just a bout ready to plant when I can get a horse to plant it with We haven't got any of the cows from Mizell yet And I don't no whether we ever will or not there is two of the cows that has got calvs and the other Suckles their yearling . . . the hogs that we got from Elizebeth two of the sows has got pigs But I dont no how they are doing they have hunted them some and couldnt find them the two little Jilts of the Norton Bunch has got eight pigs . . . And the rest of the bunch I dont no how they are they stay over there at Mrs. Manuals place I received a letter from you on the 18th of this month that was rote on the 8th of March and I was glad . . . to hear you was well.[39]

The majority of Florida women, rich or poor, did their utmost.

Keeping schools open was a major task. In 1861 they were operating under the school law of 1853. Under the provisions of this act the common schools were financed by a school fund which was derived from the sale of the sixteenth section of land in each township.[40] This act placed the schools under the direction of the registrar of public lands, the county commissioners, the judges of probate, and local trustees. The registrar of public lands was ex officio state superintendent of schools. He had general supervision of all common school interests. It was his duty to ascertain from the comptroller and treasurer on the first of July each year the amount of school money to be distributed among the counties on the basis of the number of white children between the ages of five and eighteen. He was also required to report annually to the governor concerning the condition of the schools. The management was entrusted to the county commissioners and the judges of probate, who respectively were made ex officio a county board of education and county superintendent of schools.[41]

This law provided for two seminaries of learning, one each in the territorial divisions separated by the Suwannee River. These soon became known as the East and West Florida Seminaries. The seminary east of the Suwannee was located at Ocala[42] and the seminary west of the river was located at Tallahassee.[43]

In 1860 there were 97 public schools with 2,032 pupils and 138 private academies and other schools with 4,486 pupils.[44] The concept of free instruction for rich and poor alike had been accepted and several counties had instituted taxation on the local level for the support of their common schools.[45] The constitution adopted in 1861 retained school legislation as it had existed before secession with the exception that the public lands now became state property.[46]

The war affected Florida schools immediately. The legislature used the funds to purchase arms for the state, and by November, 1861, $54,500 of the school fund and $48,500 of the seminary fund had been expended. The remainder of both was so small that the state treasurer did not distribute any interest from them to any school or seminary.[47] In 1862 the interest apportioned for schools amounted to $5,316.61, or to a little more than $0.235 per child.[48]

No records exist as to the actual enrollment in the common schools during the war. The law requiring annual enrollment reports from the counties became forgotten legislation with the opening of hostilities. Only seven counties made any report in 1862, and none of these was complete.[49]

Both state and local authorities attempted to keep the common schools operating. Governor Milton asked for and received legislation which provided for the issuance of state bonds to the school and seminary funds in repayment for the money used to purchase arms.[50] The legislature allowed the counties to lend at a good rate of interest any school funds not immediately necessary for their operation.[51] Legislation did not solve the problem, however. A shortage of competent teachers constantly plagued the local authorities. Several counties were authorized to fix teachers' salaries at six cents per day for each pupil taught. It was felt that this was adequate pay and would keep teachers in their school systems.[52] But pay did not solve the problem. Men volunteered for service or were later drafted, and the common schools soon were almost depleted of teachers. In most localities the schools were casualties of war by the end of 1862.

Wealthy planters who employed tutors for their children fared little better. The war and the blockade deprived them of foreign tutors, and public opinion condemned the use of physically fit young men who otherwise could be in the military service. In 1862 Mrs. David Levy Yulee wrote to her husband apologizing for the poor handwriting of their son's letter to him. She blamed it on the lack of a tutor. "You see," she wrote, "how pressing the necessity to get a tutor for . . . our precious boy. . . . We must not neglect him. It will do no harm to try [to get a tutor]. But we won't say anything of this to anybody." Their problem was not solved until 1864 when they acquired the services of a Presbyterian minister who preached on Sunday and tutored Yulee's children during the week.[53]

The war very soon affected the seminaries. Many students were old enough for military service and soon entered the army. A senior at the Ocala Seminary, Miss Jeffie Crutchfield, slated to become a primary teacher, presented a hand-sewn silk standard to the first soldiers of Marion County to enter service.[54] The final exercise of the seminary in 1861 was military and patriotic in character. The program included fourteen musical selections, eight declamations, six "compositions," a "dialogue," and three "original speeches."[55] The war spirit was manifest throughout as all portions of the program reflected enthusiasm for the Confederate cause. The exercises closed with a wild demonstration as an original song written by the principal was sung to the tune of "Dixie."[56]

Enrollment dropped at once at the East Florida Seminary after war began. Before many days had passed every boy in the senior class, a few in the lower classes, and Robert Bryce, the principal, had volunteered for Confederate service. Of these, nearly all, including Bryce, were to become war casualties.[57] The drop in enrollment was accompanied by the loss of state financial support because of the expenditure of the fund for military supplies. In an effort to reorganize and stimulate the seminaries, the legislature created a board of education for each of them. Each board was to consist of six members appointed by the governor and approved by the senate for two-year terms.[58] These boards could not run the seminaries without money, however, and the seminary at Ocala was soon almost nonexistent.[59]

The East Florida Seminary attempted to operate in 1861. William Dunbar Schull, a minister, succeeded Bryce as principal and Schull was replaced by J. H. Ringo, "about whom nothing is known except his name," in March, 1862. The seminary closed in 1863 and not until 1864 did the board of education formulate plans to reopen the institution.[60] The school meanwhile had operated as a private academy, probably using the state buildings rent free.[61] It reopened as a state school in late 1864 or early 1865. On April 20, 1865, the *Gainesville Cotton States* reported that the school was "in full operation with good patronage."

The West Florida Seminary at Tallahassee was more fortunate. West Florida had a much larger population than the area east of the Suwannee; hence, the Tallahassee seminary was able to organize into separate male and female departments.[62] The female department continued without interruption throughout the war with the exception of three weeks in the fall of 1864. The male division, however, was compelled to close for about four months in the spring of 1863 because of the lack of instructors.[63]

The two greatest problems which faced the West Florida Seminary were the familiar ones of finances and teachers. The monetary difficulties obviously came from the drop in male enrollment, the withdrawal of funds for the purchase of arms, and the inflation which plagued the state throughout the war. The seminary could do little about the men entering the service or about the state use of its funds, but it did attempt to solve the problem of inflation. It raised tuition from $60 for the academic year 1861-1862 until it reached a high of $210 for tuition and fees for the academic year 1864-1865. This three-fold rise in tuition did not keep pace with the general inflationary trend, but it aided the female department of the seminary to remain open.

The problem of securing instructors plagued all schools of the state. Some southern states did not suffer as acutely as others because their governors commissioned male intructors in the military institutes as officers in the state troops and detailed them to remain at the institution as instructors.[64] The West Florida Seminary had incorporated military drill in its regular curriculum in 1859, and the board of education petitioned Governor Milton to designate the seminary as an official Florida military school and to detail officers to the institution. The proposed legislation quickly passed both houses of the General Assembly. Governor Milton vetoed the act and returned it with the statement that he was unwilling to commission as an officer a teacher, or any other person, in order to exempt that person from military service.[65] As the manpower situation grew worse, the seminary was forced to use a rapid succession of instructors for its male department. At one time, the department was instructed solely by convalescent officers who had been invalided to Tallahassee for recovery from sickness or wounds.[66]

The board was able to stabilize the instructional staff for the academic year 1864-1865, however. Captain V. M. Johnston was employed as principal. His proposal that the board appropriate $4,500 to the male school, to be equally divided among the principal and two assistants, thus guaranteeing each a basic salary of $1,500, was accepted. From a contingent fund built up from receipts for tuition, the principal would receive an additional sum of $700 and each assistant $300, or in that proportion, the actual amounts depending on the number of boys in attendance. Captain Johnston also proposed that he become superintendent rather than principal and that he be allowed to secure his own assistants on the basis of his proposal. The board agreed and Johnston acquired the services of Robert Frazier as professor of classics and one Melton as teacher of chemistry and mathematics. Captain Johnston was instructor in military science, and the Reverend John E. DuBose taught the classes in moral science. On January 1, 1865, the board paid all teachers and early in February provided an additional instructor for the younger boys. By March 15, 1865, the board had paid all current debts and had $800 in a contingent fund.[67] The seminary had reached another milestone on March 6, 1865, when the company of cadets from the school participated in the successful defense of Tallahassee at the Battle of Natural Bridge. Within six weeks after this battle the war was over and the seminary at Tallahassee like the seminary at Ocala had to cope with the problems arising out of reconstruction.

The state legislature chartered two other seminaries soon after secession. Neither of these progressed beyond the planning stage, however, because of Union occupation of the area where they were to be built. The La Villa Institute was chartered for Duval County, near Jacksonville, and the College of St. Augustine for the city of St. Augustine.[68] Neither school was opened because the war precluded any possibility for an instruction program.

Following the capitulation of Florida, Governor William Marvin appointed a legislative committee to report on the condition of state schools. The report of January 12, 1866, gives a succinct account of the situation, saying in part:

> That the education of youth should have suffered in common with the other interests of Florida, during . . . the late war, is a painful truth, but it is rather a matter of surprise, as well as gratulation, that amid its anxieties and cares, and the suffering of its people, that efforts were made to keep alive, feeble as they were, the sacred duty of educating its children, and giving them even such occasional opportunities for instruction.[69]

This was a complimentary but factual report. Florida did not maintain its prewar level of schools, but the state never totally abandoned its education system. When possible, the schools were kept open.

Florida churches felt the impact of war as severely as did the schools. In 1860 the evangelicals dominated religion in Florida. Five of every seven church members were either Methodist or Baptist. The Presbyterians were a poor third and the Roman Catholics, Episcopalians, Lutherans, and Universalists followed in decreasing order of affiliation.[70] These churches owned 319 buildings with a combined property evaluation of $284,390, an average value for each church of $891.55. Religion in Florida in 1860 was still in a predominantly rural phase and was almost completely fundamental in doctrine.

The churches supported secession. Bishop Francis Huger Rutledge, Episcopal Bishop of Florida, as we have seen, donated $500 to the state treasury upon secession. Rutledge attended all meetings of the secession convention and offered "Secessionist" prayers at two of them.[71] The Florida Baptist Convention, meeting at Monticello on November 23, 1860, passed a resolution effectively stating the position of the Florida churches. The resolution, in part, states:

> That this convention, though assembled solely for the purpose of promoting the progress of the Redeemer's Kingdom on earth, in view of the mighty events which are now transpiring, and which . . . must affect . . . the Christian, as well as the political welfare of our whole population, and more especially of our slaves, deem it proper . . . to express their . . . hearty approbation of those who are determined to maintain the integrity of the Southern States, even by a disruption of all existing political ties.[72]

John C. Ley, a Methodist minister, reported that the Methodist conference which met during the election of delegates to the state convention of January 3, 1861, could do very little except discuss politics. When secession became a reality, he wrote, "the Church in all its operation sympathized with the excitement."[73]

Secession, the raising of state troops, and the subsequent war played havoc with individual churches. They were suddenly without deacons or vestrymen, church school teachers left for service more rapidly than they could be replaced, and the general membership itself rapidly declined in resident members.[74] The formation of local companies and regiments produced great excitement, and very often the local pastor, "as patriotic as any man," joined as chaplain. One Methodist minister, upon receiving an invitation from the men of his church to be their chaplain, answered in jest, that if they would elect him a major he would "join up." Much to his surprise, they elected him on the spot, and he had to join rather than disappoint them.[75] Another Methodist minister requested a vote of his congregation on whether he should enter service. The vote was "yes."[76]

The war not only affected local congregations but it brought changes in the structure of the Episcopal church in Florida. Some evangelicals had divided into northern and southern churches during the decade of the 1840's, but the Roman Catholic and the Episcopal churches had avoided a division because of the flexibility of their structure. The Roman Catholics were able to survive the entire crisis of secession and civil war without division, but the Episcopalians were not so fortunate. A convention of the Episcopal dioceses in the Confederate States of America met at Montgomery, Alabama, July 3, 1862. This convention and the adjourned sessions of the convention meeting at Columbia, South Carolina, created a Protestant Episcopal Church of the Confederate States. The constitution and canons of the new church were adopted by the general council, held at St. Paul's Church, Augusta, Georgia, in mid-November, 1862. The Florida diocese, of course, aided in the formation of the new church and was active throughout its short existence.[77]

The disruption of the local congregations within Florida resulted in a general laxity in organized religion. Jesse Bernard, a very devout man of Newnansville, was greatly disturbed by it in his town.

This morning [he wrote] I went to S.[unday] School as usual. There were but three regular teachers out and about sixteen scholars. Such apathy on the part of the community is really discouraging. There was no preaching and we intended on having . . . prayer meeting, but there was not even enough out for that, so after singing and prayer we broke up. Men's minds seem to be . . . engrossed with *war* . . . and spiritual matters seem to be lost sight of.

Bernard was no better pleased with his minister. "Our preacher is very derelict in his duties," he complained. The Sunday night services were largely done away with and the midweek service had entirely disappeared. Furthermore, the Sons of Temperance, of which Bernard was vice-president, had ceased to function, and Bernard feared it would not be "resusicated."[78]

Newnansville was typical of Florida towns. Organized religion ceased to exist in any degree of regularity in the fringe areas. The town of Palatka had three churches, Roman Catholic, Baptist, and Methodist, and all three were without a pastor by July, 1862. The pastors and the congregations had either joined the service or had taken refuge in another section of the state.[79] Some refugee congregations were still ministered to by their regular pastor,[80] but this was an exception to the general rule.

Religious activity did not wholly cease, however. Churches cooperated with the Confederate government in every way possible. They donated bells, iron fences, and other metal to government metal drives.[81] They aided destitute families of soldiers with food and clothing. The West Florida Association of the Baptist Church, besides donating to the needy, organized a group of Baptist farmers who were pledged to sell food to soldiers' families at a great price reduction,[82] but inflation deprived this humanitarian effort of success.

The Methodists, Presbyterians, and Episcopalians were especially interested in educating the children of soldiers. The Methodists took the lead in the project and with the cooperation of other churches formed a general agency to coordinate it. The Reverend Simon Peter Richardson, a Methodist, was appointed to head the agency; he established headquarters at his church in Madison. The agency had great hopes because of a $25,000 gift by General Bailey, owner of the Bailey Cotton Mill.[83] But again, inflation defeated a worthy cause. The Roman Catholics were more fortunate in their humanitarian efforts. Six Sisters of Mercy operated an orphanage and academy at St. Augustine throughout the war with little or no interference from Confederate or Federal authorities.[84]

Organized religion flourished in the military camps. The officers, realizing the value of the minister in instilling patriotism in their men, allowed almost unlimited activity by the chaplains and other ministers who wanted to preach to the troops. These "voices of Zion" preached to the soldiers, buried the dead, ministered to the sick and wounded, and counseled officers and men concerning their spiritual life or the lack of it. The Reverend Simon Peter Richardson, chaplain of state troops at Apalachicola, continually complained of the amount of whiskey consumed by the officers. The custom of the camp called for any officer serenaded by the band to treat the group with whiskey. Upon being informed that it was his day to treat, Richardson indignantly replied that he would not treat his beloved father if he should rise from the dead. He solved the problem by offering the band an oyster supper.[85]

The Baptists established army missions and also sent ministers into the army as chaplains. These missions were established at localities where there were concentrations of troops and were staffed by part-time chaplains. This work was financed by a special drive within the West Florida Association in 1862. The drive netted $350.50 and was adequate for the year, but currency depreciation eventually consumed the entire working capital and the program was abandoned.[86]

The records show no special work with the troops in Florida by the Roman Catholics. During the war, Florida was under the jurisdiction of Bishop Augustine Verot, Bishop of Savannah. He made two visits to the state during the war and ministered to soldiers and civilians in both Confederate and Union territory.[87]

The churches supported the Confederacy by fasting and prayer. A daily prayer service was held in Tallahassee, alternately in the Presbyterian and Methodist churches, to invoke the blessings of God upon the men in service. These services, attended chiefly by women, attracted the favorable attention of the local press. The *Sentinel,* however, reported on May 27, 1862, that it was displeased with the small number of men who attended. Surely, it said, "it is the duty of those exempt from battle to pray for those who are fighting for them!" The Florida Baptist Convention of November, 1863, petitioned the state legislature to set aside December 10 of that year as a day of fasting and prayer.[88] The legislature concurred, but decided that Christmas Eve, December 24, 1863, would be a more appropriate date.[89] Devout Floridians placed great faith in divine intervention. Mrs. David Levy Yulee, after prayer in 1864, wrote:

> But we will have all our rights in spite of the whole tribe of traitors oppressers. We have invoked the just will of God to decide between us, and as a little child I rest secure in my fathers arms.[90]

The war affected the religion of the Negroes in Florida much as it did that of the whites. The slave nearly always held membership in the same church as his master, hence most slaves were Baptist or Methodist. In 1860 the Negro members of the Methodist Church in the Tallahassee district exceeded the white members by about five hundred. The membership ratio was almost equal for the Madison and St. Johns districts, but in the Tampa district the white members were more numerous than the colored by an almost two to one ratio.[91] The First Baptist Church of Tallahassee had the largest membership of any church in the state in 1860, but its 382 members could not adequately finance it—it was a mission church with 382 Negro members.[92] The Baptist Church at Monticello had 173 members, of which only 49 were white.[93]

Internal discipline within individual churches was severe during the war. The Baptists were especially strict. The Concord Baptist Church in April, 1861, dropped two slave members, Stephen and Mahala, from the rolls after they were adjudged to be in "disorder" by a church meeting. Both slaves were defended by a "white brother of prominence." In September, 1861, the same church arraigned Tillman R. Denson and his wife, Temperence A. Denson, on the charge that they had permitted dancing in their home. They denied the charge but admitted to "joyous celebration" for men entering the service. They were acquitted.[94] The New River Baptist Church forced a slave member who ran away to recant in church, excluded Cain Strickland for use of profanity, and expelled a member who married a divorcee.[95]

Many pastors showed little toleration for the views of other churches. The Reverend Simon Peter Richardson reported that, near the end of the war, a fine looking chap came to his parsonage claiming to be a Methodist minister from Baltimore. He was allowed to give the Sunday sermon. Hearing the guest refer to his stewards as deacons, Richardson sent for "a corporal and a guard" and sent him to jail. "He asked me why, and I told him he was a Baptist . . . [and] that he had not learned the language of Zion, and therefore I would send him to jail."[96]

The record of Florida churches must also be examined in relationship to the hardships with which they were confronted. The shortage of pastors, loss of membership because of enlistment or relocation, and the loss of key personnel within the individual churches were almost disastrous. Only one Sunday school out of seventeen of the West Florida Association of the Baptist Church survived the war.[97] Contributions of the Baptist churches of the state fell from $154.89 for foreign missions in 1861[98] to $6.00 in 1862.[99] Gifts for domestic missions rose from $50.00 in 1861 to $469.60 in 1863 but inflation made the increase meaningless.[100] Gifts to the state's Baptist churches declined throughout 1864 and by the end of the war, some associations had not received a dollar from any of their member churches.[101]

The Methodists fared little better financially and found it extremely difficult to secure pastors. The Florida conference decreased annually in the number of pastors until 1864, and nearly every Methodist pastor who did remain at his church was compelled to find secular employment for a livelihood.[102] Often this employment was with some government agency. Methodist ministers held the posts of tax collector and state tax assessor in Alachua County in 1864.[103]

Few records are available to show the internal disintegration of the Presbyterian or Episcopal churches, but they probably fared no better than the others. The committee on the state of the church reported to the Episcopal State Convention in 1863 that, "Oweing to the state of the country the statistics are so imperfectly reported that the Committee find it impossible to arrive at a correct view of the state of the church . . . at present."[104]

The slave remained surprisingly loyal to his church. The figures for the loss in Negro membership during the war are available for the Methodists only, but since this was the largest denomination in the state, it serves as the best guide to the actual situation. Negro losses in membership were insignificant in 1861 and 1862. The losses for 1863 were 947; for 1864, 129; and, for 1865, 560.[105] These resulted from Union activity in Florida and from the order of the United States Secretary of War, Edwin M. Stanton, to his commanders in the South to seize the property of disloyal Methodist and Baptist churches. These disloyal churches were placed under loyal bishops and pastors and were lost to the Southern Methodists and Baptists for the remainder of the war.[106] After the war there was a formal division of the white and colored membership into separate churches.

Internal disintegration affected Florida churches much more than the trivial loss of colored members. That this disintegration was severe has been seen; it must be concluded that, as did other institutions, the churches did excellent work under very difficult circumstances. Certainly organized religion in the state cannot be condemned for its failures during the war. Rather, it must be congratulated for its effort to serve both God and humanity.

In general the home front in Florida fared no worse than that of other southern states. The fringe areas with poor transportation and communication facilities were affected more adversely than the interior counties. Even they with their history of enforced self-sufficiency were probably no worse off than isolated regions of Texas or Louisiana. This is not to say that civilians in Florida did not suffer. They did. The Florida home front suffered as much from poor transportation facilities, which prevented an adequate distribution of the available foods and supplies, as it suffered from the depredations of the Federal forces. The blockade, of course, merely compounded this suffering. The result of these hardships was a general lowering of the morale of the people. By the spring of 1865 the desire for an end to hostilities was general throughout the state.

XII

THE BATTLE OF OLUSTEE

THE MAJOR BATTLE of the Civil War fought in Florida occurred on February 20, 1864, near Olustee. The battle, involving approximately fifty-five hundred men on each side, occurred near the highway and railroad which ran between Lake City and Jacksonville. To the north of the immediate field of action was a large lake called Ocean Pond, hence many of the participants referred to the engagement as the Battle of Ocean Pond. The Battle of Olustee stopped and threw back the largest force of Union soldiers to attempt an invasion of interior Florida during the war.

The purpose of this invasion according to Major General (designate) Quincy A. Gillmore, Federal Commander of the Department of the South of which Florida was a part, was as follows:

> First. To procure an outlet for cotton, lumber, timber, turpentine, and the other products of that State [Florida].
> Second. To cut off one of the enemy's sources of commissary supplies. He now draws largely upon the herds of Florida for his beef, and is making preparations to take up a portion of the Fernandina and St. Marks railroad. . . .
> Third. To obtain recruits for my colored regiment.
> Fourth. To inaugurate measures for the speedy restoration of Florida to her allegiance, in accordance with instructions which I have received from the President by the hands of Maj. [sic] John Hay, assistant adjutant-general.[1]*

Florida had taken on a new importance for the Confederacy after July 4, 1863. On that date General John C. Pemberton, Confederate commander at Vicksburg, surrendered his entire army to General Ulysses S. Grant. Pemberton had purposely chosen to make it a

*Notes to Chapter XII begin on page 239.

"Glorious Fourth" for Grant—hoping for better terms.[2] The day was not a glorious one for the Confederacy, however, for in addition to the loss of a large army the victory gave the Union control of the Mississippi River, thus cutting off the Trans-Mississippi region from the eastern part of the Confederacy. The Confederacy east of the Mississippi was now dependent upon its own territory for the foodstuffs necessary to sustain both civilians and soldiers. Florida became the provider of much of the necessary food, especially meat, for the army during the remainder of the war.

In 1863 Major Pleasant W. White, Confederate commissary agent for Florida, received an appeal from Major J. F. Cummings, General Braxton Bragg's chief of commissary, for all the cattle that could possibly be sent to him, and sent as promptly as possible. When cattle were not immediately dispatched to Bragg, Major Cummings became more insistent. On October 5, 1863, he wrote, "All other resources are exhausted . . . we are now dependent upon your State for beef for the very large army of General Bragg." The future of the Confederate Army, he declared, rested with how well it was fed and this in turn depended largely upon the ability of the Confederacy to secure food in Florida.

The chief commissary of Georgia likewise informed Major White that cattle were urgently needed as the supply of cattle in Georgia was exhausted. Major M. B. Millen, writing from Savannah on October 10, 1863, warned Major White, "Starvation stares the Army in the face . . . I have exhausted the beef-cattle, and am now obliged to kill stock cattle." South Carolina seemed equally desperate for meat. Major H. C. Guerin, chief commissary for that state, also appealed to White in desperate tones. "We are almost entirely dependent on Florida," he wrote, "our situation is full of danger from the want of meat."

In response to these urgent requests, Major White attempted to collect food in Florida for the less fortunate areas of the Confederacy. He sent a circular containing the essence of the appeals from the commissaries to the "principal men" in the various sections of the state who were requested "to read it to . . . persons . . . you know to be true and prudent, and to begin the work contemplated immediately." The circular was not kept confidential but was nailed to posts and trees and crossroads throughout the state. The extent of the influence this had on the Union decision to invade Florida is questionable. But General Pierre G. T. Beauregard was of the opinion that the circular was "one of the main causes of the expedition to Jacksonville, and thence toward Lake City."[3]

Subsequent facts, however, tend to minimize the influence exerted by the circular. None of the correspondence of the Union commanders mentioned it, but the *New York Herald* on February 20, 1864, the day of the Battle of Olustee, said:

> Among many most extraordinary things brought to light by this invasion [of Florida] is a document emanating from the commissariat department of Quincy, Fla., in which there is startling evidence to be found of the desperate condition of the enemy.[4]

But to explain the invasion of Florida in February, 1864, on the basis of the so-called "White Circular" would be a gross oversimplification.

The reason for the sudden desire to occupy Florida in force can be found in the political situation both on the national level and within the limited area of Union control in East Florida. Of primary importance was the fact that it was a Presidential election year. With the Union at war, this fact took on added importance as the individual elected to the Presidency in 1864 would most likely, it was believed in the North, direct the war to its victorious close and dominate the reconstruction of the rebellious South. The Republican party was composed of two basic factions, Conservative and Radical, concerning the attitude toward the seceded South. Important to their national power, however, was the support given them by the Union Democrats. Because of the internal struggle within the party and the unknown factor of the extent of Democratic support, the period prior to the 1864 election seemed to all observers to be an extremely critical one for all the aspiring candidates. By the end of 1863 the two most often mentioned for the Republican nomination were the incumbent, Abraham Lincoln, and his Secretary of the Treasury, Salmon P. Chase. Chase wanted the nomination and expected military events and the support of the Radical Republicans to make it possible.[5]

Florida was one place where military and political events could be made to take place in a manner Chase thought would be advantageous both to the Union and to his personal ambitions. The principal reason for this belief was that the Union men in the occupied areas of East Florida were led by Lyman D. Stickney, a Federal Tax Commissioner. Stickney and two others, Harrison Reed, a Wisconsin editor, and John S. Sammis, a man of northern origin who had moved to Jacksonville before the war, had been appointed Federal Tax Commissioners for Florida in October, 1862.[6]

Stickney, a political opportunist, supported Chase's presidential ambitions. He also realized that without extensive Union military operations in East Florida prior to the Republican National Convention, there would be no possibility of creating a "loyal Florida" whose pro-Chase delegates would be accepted by the Convention.[7] Hence, at Stickney's urging, Major General Quincy A. Gillmore, on December 15, 1863, suggested to United States General-in-Chief Henry Wager Halleck that military operations in Florida would be profitable. Operations in East Florida, Gillmore argued, would recover the most valuable portion of the state, cut off enemy supplies, and increase the number of his colored troops. A week later Halleck replied, giving Gillmore permission to use his own discretion in the matter provided the Charleston campaign was not weakened. Gillmore advised Halleck, in return, that he planned to occupy the west bank of the St. Johns River shortly and establish small depots there preparatory to an early advance into the interior of the state.[8] Before Gillmore received a reply from Halleck, John Hay arrived at Beaufort, South Carolina, with the following letter of instructions from President Lincoln:

I understand an effort is being made by some worthy gentlemen to reconstruct a loyal State government in Florida. Florida is in your department, and it is not unlikely that you may be there in person. I have given Mr. Hay a commission of major, and sent him to you with some blank books and other blanks to aid in the reconstruction. He will explain as to the manner of using the blanks, and also my general views on the subject. It is desirable for all to cooperate; but if irreconcilable differences of opinion shall arise, you are master. I wish the thing done in the most speedy way possible, so that, when done, it lie within the range of the late proclamation on the subject. The detail labor, of course, will have to be done by others, but I shall be greatly obliged if you will give it such general supervision as you can find consistent with your more strictly military duties.[9]

General Gillmore replied immediately that there would not be "an hours delay after the Major [Hay] is ready." He assured the President that he would see that the attack in Florida was a success and that he would be there "in person to inaugurate the work."[10]

A slight complication in the plans for the Florida expedition developed on January 22, 1864. Secretary of War Edwin M. Stanton questioned the advantages of the campaign as a purely military venture, but said that if the campaign would give an outlet for cotton and aid in the enlistment of colored troops he would leave the matter to Gillmore's discretion.[11] It was in reply to this letter that Gillmore gave the formal reasons for the campaign quoted previously in this chapter. An examination shows that Gillmore incorporated ideas which would please Stanton, Chase, and Lincoln. Hence, the wisdom of the Florida campaign was not seriously questioned.

Meanwhile the politicians were busy. The books of unsigned oaths and other paraphernalia which Hay needed to begin enrolling voters arrived at Hilton Head. General Gillmore then sent him to Fernandina to enroll voters in the places occupied before the St. Johns expedition.[12] Stickney reported Hay's arrival and his purpose to Chase, but assured him that Florida would remain loyal to the Secretary of the Treasury. Of course, Stickney took the credit. He wrote:

> I have lately been occupied in organizing a Free State League, or if you please, a Chase league . . . it will work like a Charm. We receive in our organization men whom I know and on whom in trying times I can rely. Gen'l. Gillmore is very gracious, I feel sure he will do all he consistently can to help forward our Free State organization. He has given me very strong evidence that he is your friend, decided and active. Captain McGowan of the Revenue Cutter . . . is . . . a careful President man but his first officer . . . shows much zeal in our cause.[13]

Major John Hay was equally optimistic. On February 8 he wrote to the President that he had met a "most gratifying unanimity of sentiment." Those men who were at first believed to be unwilling to accept the emancipation proclamation were assuring him that they desired to "accept the accomplished events of the war." Those of more radical views, "who we have had reason to fear . . . are [also] heartily in favor of your plan."[14]

Since both political factions favored the plan, the invasion of East Florida became a reality. On February 4, 1864, Gillmore ordered Brigadier General Truman Seymour to begin embarking his troops and to leave at once for the rendezvous at the mouth of the St. Johns River.[15] On the morning of February 7, the Union transports docked at Jacksonville. No organized resistance was offered and by nightfall the city was a Union camp.

Union forces did not delay in Jacksonville. On the afternoon of February 8 a general advance to the west was begun, and that night Camp Finegan, the largest Confederate camp in the St. Johns area, was evacuated by the defending forces.[16] By sunrise on February 9, advanced Union forces had reached and occupied Baldwin, nineteen miles west of Jacksonville.[17] At Baldwin they captured, besides a few prisoners, several pieces of artillery, cotton valued at $25,000, large quantities of turpentine, resin, pitch, and tobacco, the telegraph office with complete equipment, and a train of cars. The town itself was the key to three railroad lines.[18] Leaving a small force to secure it, the Federals continued westward. Sanderson, a village thirty-three miles west of Jacksonville, was reached on the afternoon of February 10, but was not occupied in force until the next day.[19]

The Union advance was not without resistance. The Confederate forces of Brigadier General Joseph Finegan, commanding the District of East Florida, offered token opposition at several places and minor skirmishes occurred.[20] Finegan's major forces were not involved; he was willing to give ground for the time being, for the only hope of saving the state lay in securing reinforcements from the coastal areas of Georgia. Upon receipt of an appeal from Finegan, General Beauregard ordered reinforcements from around James Island and Savannah to proceed in all haste to assist in the defense of Florida. Their departure was delayed by a Federal diversionary attack on John's Island, but on February 11 reinforcements for Finegan began to move south.[21]

Floridians did not panic because of the early successes of the Union Army. Fortunately, most of the early advances were made through very sparsely populated territory, covered with scattered longleaf pines, most of which had been blazed for turpentine. The ground was covered with grass and palmetto shrubs. At intervals there were swamps, not deep, but broad and wet. One Union soldier in the advance wrote that in the entire march from Jacksonville to Olustee he did not see a total of five hundred acres of cleared land.[22]

When the Union advance became a menace to the rich planting counties of Middle Florida, demands for effective Confederate counteraction began to grow. Newspapers called for calmness on the part of the population, but at the same time called for every Floridian with firearms to prepare for the defense of his home. A grandiose guerrilla warfare was envisioned with citizens effectively fighting the Union forces in the forests and swamps of the peninsula.[23] A more realistic approach was taken by Governor Milton, who requested a sufficient number of reinforcements to protect the interior counties and demanded an immediate change of the Confederate commander. He wired Secretary of War James A. Seddon that General Finegan was no longer acceptable; he had lost the confidence of both the troops and the people. "All will be lost," Milton concluded, "without a head [general] to inspire confidence."[24] Before a change of commanders could be effected, however, the crisis occurred.

The reinforcements had been directed toward Lake City, sixty miles west of Jacksonville, and the most important town east of the Suwannee River thought to be in the path of the Union advance. The Union forces had not clearly shown their direction as diversionary raids were constantly being made, the largest of these being one against Gainesville on February 14.[25] The general line of advance, however, was along the railroad toward Lake City and then to the Suwannee River.

During the week subsequent to February 13, Finegan, who had established headquarters at Camp Beauregard near Olustee, was reinforced by several units from Georgia and South Carolina. Their arrival permitted him to organize his command into three brigades. The First Brigade, under Brigadier General Alfred H. Colquitt, contained the Sixth Florida Infantry Battalion, the Chatham Artillery (four pieces), and the Sixth, Nineteenth, Twenty-third, Twenty-seventh, and Twenty-eighth Georgia Infantry. The Second Brigade, commanded by Colonel George P. Harrison, was composed of the First Florida Battalion, Twenty-eighth Georgia Artillery Battalion, the Georgia Light Battery, and the First, Thirty-second, and Sixty-fourth Georgia Infantry. Finegan placed the cavalry, composed of the Fourth Georgia and the Second Florida, under the command of Colonel A. H. McCormick. The Florida (Leon) Light Artillery Battalion was placed in reserve. These three brigades and the reserve artillery had a total effective force of forty-six hundred infantry, less than six hundred cavalry, and twelve guns in the artillery.[26]

General Seymour had weakened his forces to some extent by leaving garrisons to the rear of his advancing front. As he neared Olustee his effective force comprised five brigades organized as follows: Colonel William B. Barton's brigade, the Forty-seventh, Forty-eighth, and One Hundred Fifteenth New York Infantry; Colonel Joseph R. Hawley's brigade, the Seventh Connecticut, Seventh New Hampshire, and the Eighth United States (colored); Colonel

James Montgomery's brigade, the First North Carolina and the Fifty-fourth Massachusetts (both colored) Infantry; Colonel Guy V. Henry's Mounted Brigade, the Fortieth Massachusetts Mounted Infantry, Independent Massachusetts Cavalry, and Battery B, First United States Artillery (Elder's Horse Battery); and the artillery commanded by Captain John Hamilton and composed of Battery E, Third United States Artillery, which included Section C of the Third Rhode Island, and Battery M, First United States Artillery which in turn included Section B of the Third Rhode Island. The entire force consisted of fifty-five hundred effectives.[27]

On the morning of February 20, General Seymour ordered his forces forward from Barber's Plantation with the intention of advancing on Lake City, and, if successful, of cutting railroad communication between East and West Florida by destroying the railroad bridge over the Suwannee River.[28] General Finegan, on the other hand, decided that the only advantageous position for the defense of the area was at Olustee, thirteen miles east of Lake City. The location was chosen because it was the only one between Lake City and the advancing Union forces which furnished in itself any natural advantages for defense. The Confederate forces were concentrated on a line running roughly north and south for almost a mile and a half. To the north of this line was Ocean Pond, a large lake, and to the south a large cypress swamp. The Florida, Atlantic, and Gulf Railroad and the Jacksonville to Lake City road along which the general Union advance was being conducted, both ran between Ocean Pond and the swamp; Finegan had good reason to believe that his defense line was well located.[29]

The Battle of Olustee began in a very unpretentious manner soon after noon on Saturday, February 20. In the morning, Finegan received intelligence of the Union advance and ordered most of his cavalry forward to skirmish with the enemy and draw them to the Confederate defense works. The cavalry contacted the Union force about four miles east of Olustee and began a slow fighting retreat toward the fixed defenses. General Finegan prepared his remaining forces for action. Apprehensive that the enemy might be too cautious to approach his fixed works, he directed Brigadier General Alfred H. Colquitt forward with three regiments and an artillery battery. The retreating cavalry joined Colquitt and were placed on the flanks of the infantry to prevent a flanking movement by the enemy. By midafternoon the battle was growing in intensity as the

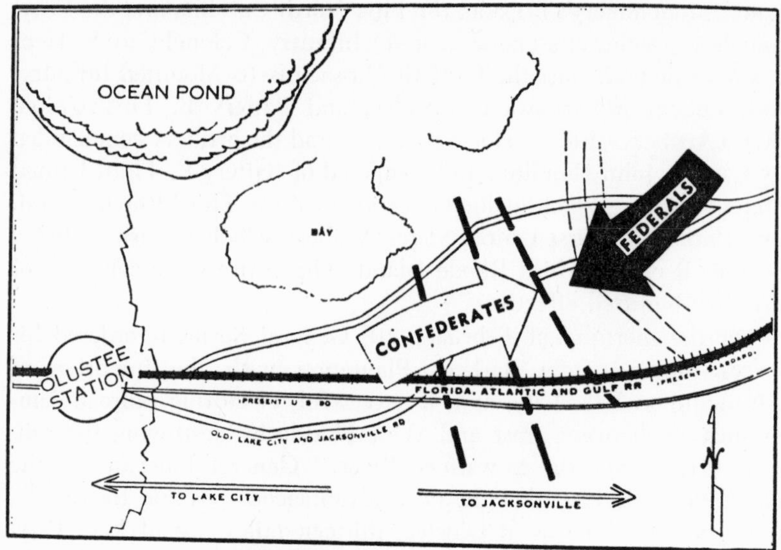

Sketch of Olustee battle site.

major forces of each army came into contact with each other roughly along Colquitt's advanced position. Thus, the Confederates were fighting forward of their fixed positions, and both armies were without the benefit of prior preparation on the site of battle.[30]

The field upon which the battle developed was a tract of firm, even ground covered with virgin pine and almost completely devoid of undergrowth. North of the railroad it had a north-south diameter of about two-thirds of a mile, being limited to the north and west by a continuous swampy bay. Small isolated bays dotted the area to the east and south. On the northern portion, a field had been cleared, and the fighting became very severe in this sector.[31]

The battle lasted until shortly past six in the evening. At this time, during a respite caused by a temporary Confederate ammunition shortage, the Union forces began a gradual withdrawal. The retreat was prevented from becoming a rout by the appearance of the Fifty-fourth Massachusetts and the First North Carolina and by the passing of dusk into darkness.[32]

The battle was a clear-cut Confederate victory. Losses were severe on both sides. The Confederates lost 93 killed, 847 wounded, and 6 missing for a total of 946 casualties.[33] Federal losses were more severe; 203 killed, 1,152 wounded, and 506 missing for a total of 1,861 casualties.[34] The exact number of prisoners taken by the Confederates is unknown. General Patton Anderson, who assumed command of Confederate forces in Florida shortly after Olustee, reported to General Hatch, the Federal commander in Jacksonville, that his command held 349 Federal wounded, of which only 7 had died.[35] Federal loss of equipment was great. Confederate forces captured 5 cannon, 1,600 small arms of various types, 400 accouterments sets, and 130,000 rounds of small arms ammunition. The ammunition had to be salvaged as the retreating Federals had thrown it into the water. The percussion caps were removed and dried to render them usable. The remaining parts of the ammunition were sent to the Confederate ordnance officer at Savannah for possible salvage.[36]

The victory produced general rejoicing throughout the Confederacy. The Confederate Congress[37] and the Florida legislature[38] voted Finegan resolutions of thanks. The greatest jubilation was naturally in Florida. One contemporary, who was at church on the morning of Sunday, February 21, wrote:

> The congregation appeared as usual, unexpecting and unmoved, when we were startled by the clergyman returning thanks for Victory. Almost every one in the building had some relative at the front [Olustee]. Some gave way to tears; others rushed out to learn the particulars.[39]

The victory produced the opposite reaction in the North. General Seymour was acidly criticized not only by the northern press but by his troops as well.[40]

While the Union Army had been advancing into the interior, Major John Hay had been busy in Jacksonville attempting to secure names in his register of persons who had taken the oath of allegiance to the United States. At first he was optimistic but this optimism changed rapidly after the defeat at Olustee. By March 1 Hay admitted that he would never get the required 10 per cent of Florida voters. He also discouraged any attempt to lower the requirements so that a state government might be established in East Florida.

Stickney carefully hid his elation over Hay's failure. He chose to remain silent while Chase's friends in the North battled for his cause. Following the indignation caused by the "Pomeroy Circular" and the subsequent rapid decline of Chase's political boom, Stickney faced reality for one brief period. On March 1 he confided to Hay that with so many states pledging themselves to Lincoln, "No power on earth can prevent his election."[41] But the next day he was once again the great "Manipulator," and wrote to Chase that he had not opposed Hay in Florida but rather had molded his "views in harmony with my own. He now works with me, and for the measure I wish to prevail."[42]

By spring of 1864 Stickney was faced with a revolt within the ranks of his political organization.[43] A convention of the "Union Men of Florida" was held on May 17 in Jacksonville to elect delegates to the Republican convention in Baltimore on June 7. Union authorities cooperated by transporting the delegations to Jacksonville from St. Augustine and Fernandina by steamboat. The Jacksonville convention was dominated entirely by enemies of Stickney. Calvin Robinson was elected chairman and the delegates chosen to represent Florida at Baltimore, Calvin Robinson, Buckingham Smith, John W. Price, John S. Sammis, Philip Fraser, and Paran Moody, were all Lincoln supporters.[44] The selection of Robinson, Sammis, and Fraser greatly disturbed Stickney; Robinson had recently been his business partner, Sammis had been fired from the original tax commission at his insistence, and Fraser was a Federal judge at St. Augustine because of Stickney's personal intervention.

The Stickney faction also nominated delegates to Baltimore. The convention voted to seat the Robinson delegation but denied any Florida delegation voting rights. Florida was granted a seat on the Republican Union National Committee and Stickney's defeat was complete when Robinson was named to the committee.[45]

Stickney's influence declined steadily during the last stages of the war. From the height of personal power before Olustee, he sustained a steadily humiliating series of defeats, culminating in the appointment of Harrison Reed, his personal enemy, to the provisional governorship of Florida. Chase and Stickney had nourished great plans for Florida but any possibility of their fulfillment died beneath the virgin pines at Olustee.

XIII

THE END OF THE WAR

FOLLOWING THEIR DEFEAT at Olustee, Union forces in Florida prepared to defend three areas of East Florida—Jacksonville, Fernandina, and St. Augustine. Of these, Jacksonville was the site of the most elaborate preparations. The fact that it was the base to which General Seymour had retreated, and its strategic position on the St. Johns River made its defense paramount. The Confederate forces pursuing Seymour took up position along McGirts Creek, twelve miles west of Jacksonville, and began to construct a series of elaborate fortifications. Reinforcements continued to arrive and by March 1, 1864, the Confederacy had over eight thousand troops in the immediate vicinity of the city.[1]* The fortifications constructed under the direction of Major General Patton Anderson, newly appointed Confederate commander for Florida, were finished by April 1, but almost immediately were rendered unnecessary by a change in Federal strategy. Brigadier General John P. Hatch of the Union Army, Commander of the Department of Florida, began the withdrawal of troops on April 8, 1864, and by the end of the month had reduced the strength of the Federal forces at Jacksonville to a minimum necessary for garrison duty. Instead of using the opportunity to seize the area, the Confederate commander also began the immediate withdrawal of troops. Both sides had decided to push operations further to the north and by mid-May, 1864, neither force was larger than one-third its size two months earlier.[2]

The problem of developing a defense for Florida arose immediately. The principal task was to cover with a small force the large area of country between the St. Marys and St. Johns rivers on the east and the Gulf Coast on the west. Fortifications were impracti-

*Notes to Chapter XIII begin on page 240.

cable because of the lack of artillery and the lack of troops to defend the fortifications already constructed. Furthermore, the enemy was on the offensive and could choose his point of attack. Another factor was that inland fortifications could be easily outflanked because of the nature of the terrain. As a result, General Beauregard, commander of all Confederate forces in South Carolina, Georgia and Florida, decided upon a mobile defense for the state.

The plan agreed upon provided for the uncontested landing of any Federal invading force of sizable numbers. The enemy advance inland was then to be contested at every opportunity with all available troops. The retreating contesting force was to destroy all supplies and communication or transportation facilities which would be of use to the Union advance. Meanwhile, reinforcements would be gathered in the interior of the state to engage the Federals in battle once they had extended their supply lines. By this plan it was hoped that Florida could be adequately defended while the major battles were being fought elsewhere.[3]

This system of defense made it imperative that an organized body of troops be available for service in the interior. Governor Milton believed that the best source for such a force was a well-organized and active state militia.[4] Confederate troops constituted the core of the defense force, but Milton desired a larger body of troops than the Confederacy was willing to commit to the state.[5] Hence, on July 30, 1864, he issued a proclamation calling upon all citizens of Florida capable of bearing arms, and regardless of age or occupation, to organize into militia companies for the defense of the state.[6]

The governor had no legislative authority for the proclamation. His constitutional authority was doubtful, but the situation demanded action and he was sustained by the citizens and later by the legislature. By November, 1864, forty-two companies had been formed with a total membership of over three thousand troops.[7] They received fifteen hundred arms from the Confederate government,[8] but it refused responsibility for their general support. Confederate commanders in Florida agreed, however, to allow troops of company strength to report to Confederate junior grade officers. This offer was generally accepted by the militia in East Florida, but those in Middle and West Florida preferred to remain independent. When the General Assembly met in November, 1864, Milton presented it with his *fait accompli* and explained that "it was necessary to depart somewhat from existing . . . laws. . . . The spirit and intention of the law . . . has . . . been carefully observed, and the spirit of the people . . . and the times did not admit of legal scruples when the safety of the State and its citizens was in hazzard."[9]

The governor then called for legislative sanction for his actions. The General Assembly quickly complied, by enacting a law that made every able-bodied white male between the ages of fifteen and fifty-five not in Confederate service a member of the state militia.[10] The defense of the state for the remainder of the war rested upon a small Confederate contingent, a small Confederate reserve force composed of officers of the Invalid Corps, all regular forces not assigned to a regular command, and the state troops.

Had the Federal government pushed a determined drive into the interior of the peninsula, the Confederate troops and state militia would have been unable to defend the state successfully. The Union, however, decided to leave Florida on the fringe of its military operations. Because of this decision, hostilities in Florida degenerated into a series of raids and counterraids which resulted in many deaths, much suffering, and great loss of property, but brought no lasting advantage to either side. Night marches, ambushes, murders, and pillaging became military procedures. Only occasionally did one of the raids take on the character of a formal battle.[11]

The largest of these Federal raids was directed against St. Marks and Tallahassee. On the afternoon of March 4, 1865, fourteen vessels landed approximately one thousand troops at the lighthouse near St. Marks, and began obvious preparation to move inland.[12] Tallahassee was immediately warned of the impending danger and frantic efforts were made to prepare a defense. Brigadier General William Miller, commander of the reserve forces in the state, left immediately for the coast with the local militia and a company of cadets from the West Florida Seminary under his command.[13] Tallahassee residents hastily began the erection of Fort Houston on the outskirts of the city where the road from the coast entered the town.[14] In the meantime, General Samuel Jones, newly appointed Confederate commander in Florida, began to rush reinforcements to the area from other sections of the state.[15]

On March 5 Federal forces began their movement inland and occupied the left bank of the St. Marks River as far inland as Newport. No crossing of the river was effected, however, and Brigadier General John Newton, commanding the invading troops, decided to cross the river at the Natural Bridge. During the night of March 5

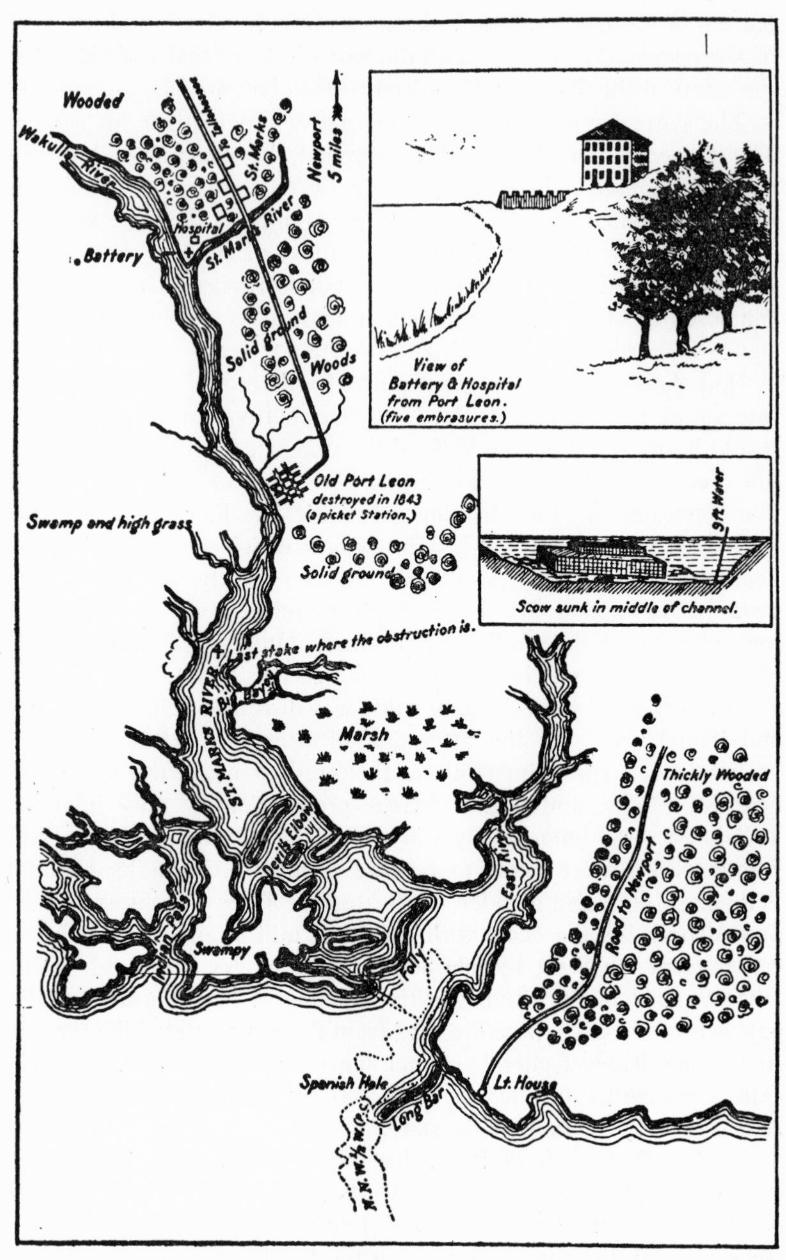

Site of the Battle of Natural Bridge, March, 1865.

both Union and Confederate forces began to move toward the Natural Bridge and early the next morning the engagement began. Two Union attempts to cross the bridge resulted in failure, and upon arrival of additional Confederate reinforcements during the afternoon, the invading troops began a slow retreat to the protection of the guns aboard their vessels. In the engagement the Confederate forces lost three killed and twenty-two wounded,[16] while Federal losses were twenty-one killed, eighty-nine wounded, and thirty-eight missing.[17] None of the cadets from the seminary was injured.[18]

The engagement, known in Florida as the Battle of Natural Bridge, caused great rejoicing throughout the state. The day following the battle a large number of curiosity seekers from Tallahassee went to the scene on a picnic and spent the day gathering souvenirs.[19] The ladies of Tallahassee prepared and served a dinner for the victorious troops on the evening of March 15 in grateful tribute for the successful defense of the city.[20] The people of Florida were in fine spirits and built the skirmish at Natural Bridge into a victory out of all proportion to its reality. "If the people of Georgia had turned out to oppose Sherman as the Floridians have in the battle fought at Natural Bridge," wrote one editor, "he never could have reached Savannah."[21]

The joy over the victory was sincere, but the distortion of its significance was a psychological reaction to the growing knowledge that the war was lost. By the spring of 1865, very few people in Florida held out any hope for ultimate Confederate victory.[22] Governor Milton certainly realized that the war was lost and as a result, on April 1, he committed suicide.[23] Upon his death, A. K. Allison became governor.

Governor Allison was no political novice in Florida. He had had a long legislative career and was president of the state senate when he succeeded to the governorship. Allison assured Jefferson Davis that he contemplated no change in state policies and that he would continue the "cordial and earnest cooperation" that had existed between Milton and Davis.[24]

This offer of cooperation was never translated into fact, for the surrender of General Robert E. Lee on April 9, 1865, for all practical purposes ended the war and the Confederacy. The news of Lee's surrender trickled into Florida. Telegraph lines were down and the news circulated to a large degree by word of mouth or through northern newspapers. "What all the world knew in full at once reached us by degrees," one contemporary recorded.[25]

General Jones, Confederate commander in Florida, attempted to clarify the situation on April 28. He informed his troops through a broadside that, while he had no official information on the subject, circumstantial evidence led him to believe that Lee had surrendered and that the Confederacy had suffered a "serious reverse." He discounted rumors of a complete Confederate collapse and reminded his soldiers that Lee had fewer men in his command than had been surrendered at Vicksburg. Jones cautioned against despondency and warned that all enemies of the Confederacy would unite to spread rumors and to destroy reports in an effort to break the morale of the army. A strong army, Jones maintained, would make it possible for the Confederate government to secure a just peace when it began negotiations with the Federal authorities. In conclusion, the general defended Lee:

> I confidently rely on the troops in this district to stand loyally . . . to their colors, and wait patiently . . . in the firm conviction that our honor has not been tarnished by General Robert E. Lee, and that our government will never accept dishonorable terms.[26]

Confusion as to the exact military situation led to confusion in many matters. The educated citizens of the state spent much time in theoretical speculation on the future. Many felt that the South was faced with three prospects: reconstruction, which was looked upon as complete subjugation; recognition of the Confederacy by the United States because of the possible confusion resulting from the assassination of Lincoln; or recognition of the Confederacy by the United States because of the direct intervention in the negotiation for peace by France. As late as April 29 many Floridians speculated on these three possibilities. Most thinking men had by then given up any serious consideration of continued warfare.[27]

Among the less educated, more direct action occurred. Many people suddenly became Union supporters, especially in the fringe areas where Confederate authority was weak or no longer existent. Some planters complained that they were not told of the possibility of an early peace and, instead of planting cotton, had planted provision crops. Most clergy and many women bitterly denounced any efforts at a negotiated peace or surrender. Some soldiers talked of emigration or continued guerrilla warfare if peace came without a Confederate victory. Others did little talking but began to plunder public warehouses and commissary stores. These speculations, threats, and lawless acts added to the confusion and by May 1, 1865, civil authority in Florida was in a precarious position.[28]

The first official information on the actual situation arrived in Florida on April 30 when General Joseph Eggleston Johnston informed Governor Allison that he had signed a convention with General William Tecumseh Sherman which terminated hostilities in North Carolina, South Carolina, Georgia, and Florida. "I made this convention to spare the blood of the gallant little army committed to me," he said, "and to avoid the crime of waging hopeless war."[29] On May 5 Johnston used similar language in an official explanation of his reasons for surrender. His action, he admitted, was a confession that all hopes of victory were gone, but he felt that he was joined in this belief by "every thinking Southern man."

Immediately upon receipt of the news of the Johnston-Sherman arrangement, Jones and the Federal commander at Jacksonville, Brigadier General Israel Vogdes, who had begun the war as a captain at Pensacola, began conferences to expedite the decisions which might be made at a higher echelon and to enforce the status quo in Florida until such decisions were known.[30] Jones agreed to use his personal influence to reduce the threat of guerrilla warfare, but emphasized that the use of white troops to occupy Tallahassee would greatly reduce the hazards of prolonged opposition to Union forces. Vogdes agreed and recommended that General Gillmore, Commander of the Department of the South, assign white troops there.[31]

General Gillmore dispatched instructions concerning the surrender of Confederate forces in Florida to Vogdes on May 8. Vogdes was to accept the surrender of all arms and public stores with the exception of the officers' side arms and horses. Jones was to make duplicate rolls of all officers and men under his command and provide the Federal commander with a copy. Each man whose name appeared on these rolls was to be paroled when he signed the parole blanks. Vogdes was to demand good behavior of all persons in Florida, and maintain strict discipline over his troops so that friction between the troops and populace would be minimized. Federal forces in Florida, Gillmore cautioned, must remember "that while we are to be humane toward surrendered enemies, these men are still rebels to whom any forgiveness is an act of grace and not of justice."[32] These instructions were forwarded to Jones on May 12, 1865.[33]

Jones and Vogdes had made elaborate plans to expedite the surrender, but events in Georgia, unknown to either man, changed the manner of the surrender of Confederate authority in Florida. Brevet Major General James H. Wilson, Commander Cavalry Corps, Military Division of the Mississippi, with headquarters at Macon, Georgia, on May 4, ordered Brigadier General Edward M. McCook to receive the surrender of the Confederate forces in the Tallahassee and St. Marks area.[34] Vogdes resented this intrusion into his command and informed McCook that Tallahassee was within the limits of the Department of the South and, therefore, under his command. "Unless you have authority from superior authority," he informed McCook, "I cannot recognize your right to receive the surrender of troops within this district."[35] Vogdes, however, was a victim of poor communications. McCook was already in Tallahassee when he wrote the letter of protest.

McCook left Macon with five staff officers, the Second Indiana Cavalry, and the Seventh Kentucky Cavalry, numbering about five hundred men on May 5. He was instructed by Wilson to accept the surrender of the forces around Tallahassee and St. Marks according to the Johnston-Sherman Convention. He was also instructed to capture nonparoled Confederates, suppress noncooperative newspapers, remove noncooperative or "sullen" officials, protect public property, and forbid public meetings "in order that excitement may be allayed and dispassionate reason may resume its way."[36] McCook's entry into Tallahassee was dramatic but unpretentious. On May 10, 1865, he and his personal staff officers left the cavalry four miles behind them and rode into town without escorting troops. As the small group of Federal officers rode into the only Confederate state capitol east of the Mississippi River which had not been captured during the war they created quite a sensation. Residents ran to see the Federal officers but watched quietly while the general was "very properly received by representative men of the city."[37] McCook and his staff received the surrender by Jones of all Confederate troops and property within Florida. The next day he went to St. Marks and there, on May 12, one of his officers received the surrender of the fort. At twelve noon, the United States flag was raised over the fort and a national salute fired. A small gunboat, the *Spray,* was also surrendered and its crew paroled.[38] McCook returned to Tallahassee and there, on May 20, the Union flag was raised over the capitol. The governor and nearly all state officials witnessed the event but there was very little ceremony attendant upon the occasion.[39] The remaining Confederate forces in the state surrendered according to a schedule arranged between McCook and Jones. All organized military units were surrendered by June 8.[40]

For all practical purposes, however, the raising of the Stars and Stripes over the capitol on May 20, 1865, marked the end of Confederate Florida. General McCook received the surrender in Florida of approximately 8,000 men, who were paroled as rapidly as possible. By June 1, 7,200 were paroled at Tallahassee alone, and as other groups throughout the state surrendered, they were immediately granted parole. Confederate property surrendered to McCook consisted of 40 cannon, 2,500 stands of small arms, 450 cavalry sabers, 1,618 bayonets, 1,200 cartridge boxes, 710 waist belts, 63,000 pounds of lead, 2,000 pounds of niter, 2,000 sets of accouterments, 10,000 rounds of artillery ammunition, 121,900 rounds of small arms ammunition, 700 pounds of musket balls, and large amounts of other ordnance stores. The quartermaster and commissary stores surrendered contained 170,000 pounds of bacon, 300 barrels of salt, 7,000 bushels of corn, 150 barrels of sugar, 100 barrels of syrup, and 1,200 head of cattle, plus 70 horses and 80 mules. Most of the horses and mules were immediately exchanged for corn and forage while those animals not exchanged were lent, subject to Union control, to needy citizens for work purposes.[41]

The arrival of Union forces in Tallahassee meant a new life for the citizens of Florida as well as the end of the Confederacy. In general they sought to accept this new situation in a peaceful and normal manner. Civilians and Federal soldiers accepted each other freely, and unpleasant incidents were unusual. Refugees returned home and began life anew. Those who returned penniless to Pensacola received a five-day food ration from the Union commander because he wished both to alleviate suffering and to encourage a return to the town.[42] The spirit manifested by the paroled prisoners was one of cooperation. On the whole, these ex-Confederate soldiers were quiet and orderly. In fact, all segments of the Florida population admitted that the Confederacy was a lost hope and that the only course left to them was submission to the laws of the United States. To most of them, however, the future was dark and uncertain. Many who had been wealthy were now penniless and their immediate problem was simplified to a matter of mere physical survival.[43]

Governor Allison realized that the political life of the state must be stabilized before other segments of life could become stable. Hence, he began the procedures necessary to establish a permanent state government. He declared himself acting governor, and issued a proclamation calling the state legislature to meet in special session, June 5, and ordered a gubernatorial election for June 7.[44] On May 12 he appointed David Levy Yulee, J. Wayles Baker, Mariano D. Papy, E. C. Lowe, and J. S. G. Baker commissioners to confer with the authorities in Washington. This commission was instructed to assure the Federal authorities that the people of Florida wished to restore immediately that relationship between the state and federal government which had existed prior to the Ordinance of Secession. The state, to this end, would take such steps and adopt such measures as the government advised.[45]

Allison informed McCook of his actions and requested that he provide the necessary passports, documents, and other papers necessary for the commission to pass through Federal lines, enter the city of Washington, and confer with the proper authorities upon arrival.[46] The general replied that he did not possess the necessary authority to grant the governor's request, but that he would telegraph for instructions. He assured Allison of his sympathy for the action, and referred to the members of the proposed commission as gentlemen who "represent a sentiment which cheerfully accepts the new order of things, and earnestly desires a restoration of the Union."[47]

The reply to McCook's inquiry came in the form of General Orders, Number 63, issued by Major General Quincy A. Gillmore. This order of May 14, 1865, declared Allison's proclamation null and void. The governor himself was proclaimed disloyal to the United States; hence, only those functions of government performed by him with the prior knowledge and consent of the Federal authorities were legal.[48] In addition to General Order, Number 63, McCook received a letter which stated that he was not to recognize "the so-called governor" or any other state officials. "Should they not desist from exercising their usurped authority," he was told, "you will arrest them and send them under guard to this place [Jacksonville]."[49] On May 19 Allison revoked the commissions of his proposed commissioners "for reasons unnecessary to detail."[50] The actual authority in Florida, civil as well as military, now rested with Federal officers.

Federal authorities now moved to consolidate their hold upon the state. On May 19 the whole peninsula was placed within the limits of the Department of the South with Israel Vogdes as commander.[51] He ordered the occupation of the entire state on May 29. This consisted primarily of occupying the important points in central and eastern Florida, its major purpose admittedly being to tighten control by occupation forces.[52] Another purpose of the occupation, not stated explicitly by Vogdes but made clear by his statement, was to impress upon the people the thoroughgoing character of the social revolution which had been wrought. For this reason both white and Negro troops were used to garrison the interior of Florida. The capstone of the assumption of control over civil affairs came on May 24, when General Vogdes declared martial law for the entire state. All proceedings at law or acts of the Confederate government, or of the state of Florida, were declared null and void. Any person who attempted to enforce any law other than martial law, if apprehended, would be arrested and tried by Federal military authorities.[53] The state was now formally under complete control of the occupation forces.

Federal forces did not institute a reign of terror under the authority of martial law. Few arrests were made for strictly political offenses. The most prominent cases in Florida were the arrest of ex-Senator David Levy Yulee, ex-Confederate Secretary of the Navy Stephen R. Mallory, and ex-Governor A. K. Allison. Of the three, Yulee received the worst treatment but even he was not grossly mistreated. In fact, there was no particular sentiment against any of the three. Their imprisonments were comparatively short and the last to be released, Yulee, was home by early spring of 1866.[54] Lawyers, practicing physicians, and ministers of the gospel, were compelled to take the oath of allegiance to the United States. Certain of the clergy objected but acquiesced "with mental reservation" when the local commander threatened to close their churches.[55] Upon leaving Florida McCook reported that he had no difficulty with any public men in the state except ministers.[56]

In addition to upholding civil law, the occupying forces adjusted, or attempted to adjust, the relationship between the ex-slave and his former owner. General Vogdes declared that the emancipation of the slave must be recognized and honored by all of the white population. The general, however, did not understand that emancipation meant idleness and ordered his troops to refuse to support idle Negroes. He also forbade any rule or regulation which would interfere with a freedman hiring himself to whomever he wished. Vogdes reminded his troops and the Negroes that the crops must be grown and harvested for "their [own] subsistence as well as that of their late masters."[57]

The Negro problem was the most vexatious of any immediate postwar problem and caused the most uneasiness. The interior of Florida had been free of raids during the last days of the war, and the planters already had their crops planted when the war ended. The planters' immediate problem became an adequate labor force because neglect of the crops at this time would result in no harvest or at best a very poor harvest. Prior to the declaration of martial law and the subsequent enforcement of emancipation, many planters throughout the state hoped to retain their slaves and follow a process of gradual emancipation after the crops had been harvested. The Federal authorities, of course, prevented this. Many planters were disappointed but only a few were disgruntled. At least, the order had the effect of settling all doubts on the matter.[58]

Some planters immediately informed their slaves of their freedom. Others delayed the announcement until Sunday, May 21, 1865. McCook's cavalry went from place to place informing the Negroes of their freedom, and by the end of May, Florida Negroes almost universally possessed the knowledge of their freedom.[59]

The Negroes' reaction was varied. Some of the more intelligent who had been treated well, and most of those who had families, almost immediately asked to stay. Nearly all who wished to remain on the plantation were allowed to do so and made satisfactory arrangements with their former owner for compensation either in money for their work or for a share of the crop.[60] Others left the plantation immediately and went either to the nearest town or Union camp.[61] The principal difficulty with Negroes came from those who had been "hired out" by their masters and had no settled home. These tended to collect in the towns and remain unemployed.[62] In general, however, no great difficulties arose between whites and Negroes.[63]

Reconstruction in Florida began with the removal of Governor Allison from the office which he had held under the constitution of Florida and the laws of the Confederacy. His removal and the subsequent rule of martial law must be considered the beginning of the process of reconstructing the state upon terms satisfactory to the dominant element in national politics. The fact that these terms of reconstruction were changed later are not a part of this story but make a restudy of reconstruction more necessary.

The Civil War had cost Florida dearly. Before secession the state voting population never exceeded 12,800 but approximately 14,000 of its men entered Confederate service.[64] It will also be remembered that more than twelve hundred white Floridians and over 800 ex-slaves served in the Federal army. Floridians fought in almost every major battle in Virginia, Tennessee, and Kentucky. The Florida First and Fifth regiments suffered such heavy losses that each surrendered with less than a company's strength at Appomattox. At least five thousand Florida soldiers died of wounds and disease during the war.[65]

The loss in Florida property and property values was enormous. Besides the incalculable loss of real and personal property caused by the depredations of Federal troops, deserters, and Union sympathizers, Floridians lost even more heavily as a result of depreciation of the value of their possessions because of defeat in the war. In 1860 the recognized debt of Florida was $221,000.[66] There was an unrecognized debt from Territorial days contracted for the establishment of banks. Of the recognized debt, all but $64,000 was contracted in the Indian wars, and Florida claimed that the United States should repay it for these expenses. The estimated contingent liabilities of the state, principally for railroad construction, were estimated at approximately $1,000,000. Thus, the state in 1860 had a debt and liabilities of only $1,221,000 and was economically sound for it averaged an annual net balance of approximately $70,000. The assessed value of property in 1860, real and personal, including slaves, was $68,929,685. The estimated value of the slaves alone was $21,610,750, which meant that real and personal property, excluding slaves, had a value of $47,318,935.

In 1865, excluding all debt which resulted from the war, and maintaining the same amount of contingent expense, the debt had risen by $149,617. The value of the railroads was so reduced that the state lost over $1,000,000 in its guarantee made before the war. The assessed value of real and personal property in 1865 was $25,000,000, a loss in property value of $43,929,685 during the war. Excluding the evaluation of slaves, this loss is reduced in terms of real and personal property to $22,318,935. This means Floridians suffered a reduction of 47 per cent in property values, excluding slaves, for the five years. The total loss in assets, property, and increase of debt, excluding slaves, was $23,058,552. Including the loss of the investment of $21,610,750 in slaves, the total loss during the war was $44,669,302.[67] The cost of the war did not stop in 1865, however, for the heartbreaks and tribulations of ten years of reconstruction were yet to come.

Florida had entered into the experiment of secession and subsequent civil war willingly. Her entry had been inevitable because Florida's domestic institutions were only replicas of the cultural, social, and economic development of the other southern states. Florida was bound especially to Georgia and South Carolina, for one-third of her population in 1860 was native to one of those states.

The triumph of the radical wing of the Democratic party in 1856 placed the political controls of the peninsula in the hands of a rabid state-rights group. These radicals, greatly aided by the violent reaction throughout Florida to John Brown's raid on Harpers Ferry, October 16, 1859, were able to consolidate their control on the state in the election of 1860. Brown's raid and the election of Abraham Lincoln as President of the United States destroyed the middle ground and forced Floridians into support of the radicals because of the belief that their social and economic institutions would be destroyed by the Republican party.

When somber reflection, amid casualty reports, replaced the first elation over secession, the radicals were replaced by men of more moderate views, who did not, however, slacken the war effort. Florida supported the Confederate government with all its resources, although these were not large, and after 1862 the most important contribution to the Confederate cause was foodstuffs, particularly beef cattle.

Neither the United States nor the Confederate States considered Florida important militarily; hence, the state never became an area of major military operations. Numerous raids and counterraids produced much hardship and suffering, but no large area was devastated by Union forces. Civilian morale was virtually destroyed, nevertheless, by the blockade, the casualty reports, and the threat of enemy invasion. By the summer of 1864, only the citizens of Middle Florida held hopes for ultimate victory over the United States. When Florida surrendered in 1865, most of her civilian population realized the completeness of the defeat and were relieved to bring the war to an end. The sparse settlement and poor communication system aided the destruction of civilian morale in the fringe areas and brought about the collapse of Confederate and state control over these areas.

Florida had not been prepared to fight a war, and as the civilian and the soldier realized this fact, he lost much of his will to continue the struggle. Confederate Florida was defeated by superior numbers and materiel, but she also had lost her will to fight.

NOTES

CHAPTER I

1. Long, *Florida Breezes,* pp. 306-8. *(See Bibliography for full information concerning works cited in notes.)*

2. During the decade of the 1850's the size of improved holdings in Florida went from 349,049 acres to 654,213 acres. Horses and cattle increased from 250,000 to 450,000 head; the cotton produced increased from 45,000 to 65,153 bales and corn from 2,000,000 to 3,000,000 bushels. See *Floridian and Journal* (Tallahassee), February 8, 1851; February 4, April 25, and July 11, 1857; May 21, 28, September 17, 1859. See also the message of Governor Madison Starke Perry on economic development, *East Floridian* (Fernandina), December 10, 1859, and January 19, 1860.

The number of slaves increased from 39,309 to 61,745 between 1850 and 1860. See *Seventh Census, 1850; Report of Superintendent . . . for December 1, 1850,* p. 160; *Eighth Census, 1860: Population,* p. 53.

Florida had only three towns with a population over 2,000. Pensacola was the largest with 2,876. Key West had 2,832 and Jacksonville had 2,118. *Eighth Census: Population,* p. 54.

3. *Seventh Census: Report of the Superintendent for December 1, 1852,* p. 46; *Eighth Census: Statistics,* p. 297.

4. *Seventh Census: Population,* p. 784; *Eighth Census: Population,* p. 56. Florida had an American-born free population of 75,370 in 1860. Of these, 39,768 had come from other states, 25,834 of them coming from Georgia and South Carolina.

5. James Daig, "Reminiscent Sketches of Gainesville's Early Days," *Gainesville Sun,* July 15, 22, 29, 1917.

6. Doherty, "The Florida Whigs," pp. 196-97.

7. Williams, "Florida in the Union, 1845-1861," p. 525.

8. Dodd, "The Secession Movement in Florida, 1850-1861," Part I, p. 17.

9. *Florida Sentinel* (Tallahassee), May 11, 1852; see also, Williams, p. 523.

10. Doherty, p. 194.

11. Williams, p. 523.

12. Cole, *The Whig Party in the South,* p. 284.

13. Williams, p. 524.

14. *Florida Sentinel,* November 28, 1854; see also, Doherty, p. 208.

15. Unidentified letter to E. L. L'Engle, April 8, 1855, Edward M. L'Engle Papers; see also, Overdyke, *The Know-Nothing Party in the South,* p. 76.

16. *Florida Republican* (Jacksonville), July 16, 1856.

17. *Ibid.,* August 6, September 24, October 1, 1856. Also see Overdyke, p. 126.

18. *Florida Republican,* November 26, 1856; *Floridian and Journal* (Tallahassee), November 29, 1856. See also, election chart in Dovell, *Florida, Historic, Dramatic, Contemporary,* I, 400-1.

19. Thompson, "David Yulee: A Study of Nineteenth Century American Thought and Enterprise," pp. 130-32; Doherty, pp. 200-1.

20. Thompson, pp. 130-32.

21. Dodd, "Secession Movement," p. 6.

22. *A Journal of the Proceedings of the Senate . . . of Florida . . . November 24, 1856,* pp. 31-33 (hereinafter cited as Florida *Senate Journal*).

23. *Ibid.,* pp. 32-35.

24. *Acts and Resolutions of the General Assembly of the State of Florida, 1845-1859,* II (1859), 9-15 (hereinafter cited as Florida *Acts*).

25. Florida *Senate Journal* (1856), p. 182.

26. *East Floridian,* November 17, 1859; January 9, February 2, 9, 16, May 17, 1860.

27. The delegates chosen were: John Milton, who was to become Florida's war governor; Charles Dyke, editor of the *Floridian* and a radical; James B. Owens; George L. Brown; Thomas Jefferson Eppes, and Benjamin F. Wardlaw.

28. For a detailed account of the happenings in the deliberations of the platform committee, see speech of James B. Owens delivered at Micanopy, May 19, 1860, in the *Florida Home Companion* (Ocala), June 5, 1860.

29. *Floridian and Journal,* May 5, 1860.

30. *East Floridian,* May 8, 19, 1860.

31. *Floridian and Journal,* June 16, 1860. Milton received his strength from the cotton counties along the Alabama and Georgia line.

32. For a full description of the Baltimore convention, see: Rhodes, *History of the United States,* II, 429-31.

33. *Ibid.,* pp. 412-29.

34. *Ibid.,* p. 410.

35. *Floridian and Journal,* April 14, 1860. See also, Thompson, "Political Nativism in Florida, 1848-1860: A Phase of Anti-Secessionism," p. 61.

36. *Floridian and Journal,* June 30, 1860.

37. *East Floridian,* July 26, 1860.

38. Milton's September speeches were in East and South Florida as follows: Volusia, Enterprise, Orlando, Ichepucksassa, Tampa, Brooksville, Sumpterville, Ocala, Palatka, Orange Creek, Micanopy, Gainesville, Starke, and Clay Court House. *Cedar Key Telegraph,* September 1, 1860.

39. *East Floridian,* July 26, 1860; Davis, "Florida Journalism During the Civil War," p. 20, contends that there were only twenty-three newspapers in Florida but agrees with the other figures given above.

40. *Florida Dispatch* (Newnansville), June 1, 1860.

41. *Key of the Gulf* (Key West), July 14, 1860.

42. September 1, 1860; see also, *Floridian and Journal,* April 21, 1860.

43. *Ibid.,* September 1, 1860.

44. *Ibid.,* November 17, 1860; December 1, 1860.

45. Williams, p. 555.

46. *Floridian and Journal,* October 26, 1860, quoted in *East Floridian,* November 10, 1860; see also, Merritt, *A Century of Medicine in Jacksonville and Duval County,* pp. 50-51.

47. November 3, 1860.
48. Madison Starke Perry Papers.
49. *East Floridian*, December 5, 19, 1860.
50. For an account of such a vigilance committee, see *St. Augustine Examiner*, November 10, 1860.
51. *Ibid.*, November 24, 1860.
52. *East Floridian*, November 28, 1860; see also, (Yonge), "Ocala Prior to 1868," pp. 85-110.
53. Florida *Senate Journal* (1860), pp. 10-14.
54. *Ibid.*, p. 15; *Floridian and Journal*, December 8, 1860.
55. Williams, p. 559; see also, Dodd, "Secession Movement," Part II, pp. 45-76.
56. Florida *Acts* (1860), pp. 15-16.
57. *Ibid.*, pp. 165-67.
58. Ferrell, "Public Opinion in Confederate Florida," p. 35.
59. *Floridian and Journal*, December 22, 1860. South Carolina had seceded on December 20, 1860, and on the same day Mississippi held its election for delegates to a convention. Elections were to be held in Alabama on December 24, 1860, and in Georgia on January 2, 1861.
60. *Journal of the . . . Convention of the People of Florida, 1861*, p. 20 [hereinafter cited as *Convention Journal*, (1861)]. Bishop Rutledge was a native of South Carolina.
61. *Floridian and Journal*, December 22, 1860.
62. Eppes, *Through Some Eventful Years*, p. 133.
63. Waddy Butler to Lucy Wood, December 14, 1860, Lucy Wood Butler Papers and Diary.
64. Eppes, pp. 136-38.
65. Ethelred Philips to James J. Philips, December 20, 1860, James J. Philips Papers.
66. Dodd, "Secession Movement," Part II, p. 59. See also, Dodd, "Edmund Ruffin's Account of the Florida Secession Convention," p. 68.
67. *Convention Journal* (1861), pp. 3-5.
68. Dodd, "Edmund Ruffin's Account," p. 68. The delegates not present were those from the four western counties of Escambia, Santa Rosa, Franklin, and Liberty, as well as several delegates from senatorial districts.
69. For a detailed discussion of this type of personality, see Dodd, "Some Florida Secession History," p. 4.
70. *Convention Journal* (1861), p. 8. The original draft of this speech is in the P. K. Yonge Library of Florida History, University of Florida.
71. *Ibid.*, pp. 11-15. The convention committees appointed were: Judiciary, Federal Relations, Foreign Relations, Commerce and Trade, Taxation and Revenue, Militia and Internal Police, Sea Coast Defense, Public Lands, Printing and Contingent Expenses, and Enrollments.
72. Brevard, *A History of Florida From the Treaty of 1763 to our own Times*, II, 47.
73. *Convention Journal* (1861), pp. 18-19. The committee consisted of the following men: Sanderson of Duval County; Allison of Gadsden County; McIntosh of Franklin County; Gettis of Hillsborough County; Tift of Monroe County; Owen of Marion County; Dawkins of Alachua County; Wright of Escambia County; Morton of Santa Rosa County; Ward of Leon County; Anderson of Jefferson County; Ladd of Wakulla County; and Boker of Calhoun County.
74. Long, pp. 303-4.

75. *Convention Journal* (1861), pp. 25-29.

76. *Ibid.*, pp. 28-30; Williams, pp. 577-78.

77. *Convention Journal* (1861), p. 32. The seven delegates who voted against immediate secession to the end were James L. G. Boker of Jackson County, W. S. Gregory of Liberty, Thomas J. Hendricks of Clay, A. L. McCaskill and John Morrison of Walton, Isaac N. Rutland of Sumter, and William Woodruff of Orange.

78. Long, p. 306.

79. *Convention Journal* (1861), pp. 39-40.

80. Long, pp. 306-7.

81. Eppes, pp. 145-46.

82. Long, p. 306.

83. Undated letter from Mrs. M. L. Vann to Caroline Mays Brevard, quoted in Brevard, p. 51.

84. Tenney, *Slavery, Secession and Success*, p. 16.

85. Ethelred Philips to James J. Philips, January 15, 1861, Philips Papers.

86. *Florida Peninsula* (Fernandina), January 26, 1861.

CHAPTER II

1. *The War of The Rebellion: A Compilation of the Official Records of the Union and Confederate Armies,* I, Series I, 348 (hereinafter cited as *Official Records*).

2. *Ibid.*, pp. 349-51. Joseph Holt, an ardent Unionist, had become Secretary of War ad interim. The information denied the Florida senators was as follows: The Apalachicola Arsenal at Chattahoochee contained a number of small arms, 5,122 pounds of powder, and 173,476 cartridges; Fort Barrancas, 44 cannon with ammunition; Barrancas Barracks, one field battery; Fort Pickens, 201 cannon and ammunition; Fort McRee, 125 sea coast and garrison cannon; Fort Taylor, 60 cannon; Key West Barracks, 4 cannon; Fort Marion, 6 field batteries and some small arms; Fort Jefferson on Tortugas and Fort Clinch on Amelia Island had incomplete fortification. Report of Captain William Maynadier, January 3, 1861, *Ibid.*, pp. 349-50.

3. *Ibid.*, pp. 442-43.

4. Dodd, "Edmund Ruffin's Account," pp. 68-69.

5. *Official Records,* I, Series I, 332-33.

6. Quoted in *New York World,* January 25, 1861; see also, Davis, *Civil War and Reconstruction in Florida,* p. 72.

7. *Official Records,* I, Series I, 333; Dodd, "Edmund Ruffin's Account," p. 76.

8. Quoted in the *New York Times,* January 10, 1861.

9. *Official Records,* LII, Part I, Series I, 3-5.

10. *Ibid.*, I, Series I, 342-47.

11. *Ibid.*, pp. 333-36.

12. Erben, "Surrender of the Navy Yard at Pensacola, Florida, January 12, 1861," p. 214.

13. *Official Records,* I, Series I, 444; LII, Part II, Series I, 5.

14. *Ibid.*, p. 334.

15. Erben, p. 214.

16. *Official Records,* I, Series I, 334-36.

17. Erben, pp. 216-17.

18. *Official Records,* LII, Part II, Series I, 5-7.

19. *Ibid.,* I, Series I, 444.

20. Perry Papers.

21. *Official Records,* LII, Part II, Series I, 7.

22. Erben, p. 218.

23. House of Representatives, *Committee Reports, 36th Congress, 2nd Session, 1860-1861,* No. 87, pp. 57-59 (hereinafter cited as *House Reports*).

24. Johnson, "William Conway, a Forgotten Camden Hero," *War Papers . . . State of Maine,* III, 6.

25. *Vendetta,* p. 6; *House Reports,* No. 87, p. 59.

26. *Official Records,* I, Series I, 336-37.

27. *Vendetta,* p. 6; *Official Records,* I, Series I, 337.

28. *Official Records,* I, Series I, 337-38.

29. *Ibid.,* pp. 445-46. The senators signing the telegram to Major Chase were Mallory, Yulee, Slidell, Benjamin, Iverson, Hemphill, Clay, Fitzpatrick, and Davis.

30. *Eighth Census: Population,* pp. 50-54. The density of the population in Florida was less than two persons per square mile. This was less than any southern state except Texas.

31. See a general discussion of this problem in the *Floridian and Journal,* June 16, 1860.

32. *Florida Peninsula* (Tampa), January 26, 1861.

33. Florida *Senate Journal,* pp. 249-53.

34. Florida *Acts* (1861), p. 62.

35. *Convention Journal* (1861), Ordinance No. 30, p. 44.

36. The state, for instance, provided for the defense of its principal port, Apalachicola, by empowering the governor to procure one field battery and one company of troops to be sent there. Also, the governor could organize a Coast Guard not to exceed sixteen men. Florida *Acts* (1861), p. 202.

37. *Ibid.,* pp. 17-23.

38. *Official Records,* I, Series IV, 117-19, 126.

39. *Ibid.,* p. 135.

40. Eppes, p. 163.

41. *Ibid.,* p. 157.

42. See *Florida Sentinel* for 1861.

43. Robertson, *Soldiers of Florida in the Seminole Indian-Civil-and-Spanish American Wars,* pp. 36-321. This contains regimental histories and company rolls with places and dates of mustering into services.

44. *Official Records,* I, Series IV, 188; see also, Robertson, p. 38.

45. *Official Records,* I, Series IV, 211, 221-22.

46. *Ibid.,* p. 412.

47. Robertson, pp. 35-135, 246-60, 296-304; see also, Davis, pp. 93-95.

48. *Convention Journal* (1862), p. 28.

49. John Milton to Jefferson Davis, October 18, 1861, John Milton Papers.

50. Milton to James A. Seddon, August 26, 1862, John Milton Letterbook.

51. Annual message of Governor John Milton, November 19, 1861, Florida *Senate Journal,* p. 10.

52. *Official Records,* I, Series IV, 352.

53. See entry for July 8, 1861, and an undated entry for October, 1861, Jesse Bernard Diary.

54. Edward L. T. Balke to J. B. Roulhac, October (n.d.), 1861, Milton Papers.

55. *Florida Sentinel,* July 7, 1863.

56. *Official Records,* VI, Series I, 308.

57. *Ibid.,* XIV, Part I, Series I, 494.

58. Report of Quartermaster General Edward Bernard, October 30, 1863, documents accompanying the governor's message, Florida *Senate Journal,* November 17, 1863, p. 32.

59. Cancelled check of June 8, 1861, and correspondence in David Levy Yulee Papers. Yulee presented a flag to the Fernandina Volunteers. The flag cost $5 and was embroidered by the ladies of Fernandina.

60. Voucher No. 5, Committee of Relief, June 27, 1861, Chandler Cox Yonge Papers.

61. Circular notice of the meeting and its decisions published in *Gainesville Cotton States,* September 28, 1861, James B. Bailey Papers. The Central Committee was composed of James B. Dawkins, James B. Bailey, and Cornelius Rain.

62. Captain B. W. Powell to Alachua Central Committee, July 16, 1861, Bailey Papers.

63. To James B. Bailey, August 6, 1861, quoted in *Gainesville Cotton States,* September 28, 1861.

64. To Bailey, August 13, 1861, quoted in *Gainesville Cotton States,* September 28, 1861.

65. August 13, 1861.

66. Report of the Central Committee, quoted in *Gainesville Cotton States,* September 28, 1861.

67. George Washington Means in Alachua Central Committee, August 27, 1861, Bailey Papers.

68. Report of the Central Committee, quoted in *Gainesville Cotton States,* September 28, 1861.

69. Bailey to Meyers, August 6, 1861, quoted in *Gainesville Cotton States,* September 28, 1861; see also, Bailey Papers.

CHAPTER III

1. House of Representatives, *Executive Documents, 36th Congress, 2nd Session, 1860-1861,* VI, *Document No. 26,* 2 [hereinafter cited as *House Documents,* (1861)]. Message from the President of the United States communicating copies of correspondence with the commissioners of South Carolina, January 9, 1861.

2. Special message on the Virginia Peace Resolution, January 28, 1861, in Moore, *The Works of James Buchanan,* XI, 118.

3. *Ibid.,* p. 66.

4. *House Documents* (1861), p. 2.

5. *Ibid.,* p. 3.

6. *Congressional Globe,* January 21, 1861, pp. 480-90.

7. *Official Records,* LII, Part II, Series I, 13.

8. Florida *Senate Journal* (1861), p. 120.

9. *Official Records,* LII, Part II, Series I, 14-15.

10. *Ibid.,* I, Series I, 445.

11. Moore, XI, 113.

12. *Official Records,* I, Series I, 352-57.

13. *Ibid.,* pp. 358, 455. Vogdes estimated 1,700 men but Bragg claimed only 1,116 as of March 31, 1861.

14. *Ibid.,* p. 448.

15. Russell, *My Diary North and South,* p. 208; see also, Davis, pp. 103-4.

16. Moore, XII, 192-210; see also, Nicolay and Hay, *Abraham Lincoln; A History,* III, 343-45.

17. Welles, "Fort Pickens. Facts in Relation to the Reinforcement of Fort Pickens, In the Spring of 1861," pp. 92-107.

18. *Official Records,* I, Series I, 360.

19. Welles, pp. 96-98.

20. The exact statement of Lieutenant Worden is in dispute. Bragg says that Worden assured him that his verbal communication was of a "pacific nature." *Official Records,* I, Series I, 36. Welles says merely that he assured Bragg the message was verbal and that he in no way perjured himself. Welles, pp. 99-101. It is almost certain, however, that perjury was committed.

21. Welles to H. A. Adams, April 14, 1861, Gideon Welles Papers.

22. *Official Records,* I, Series I, 365-66. These orders were endorsed by President Lincoln.

23. *Ibid.,* pp. 378-79.

24. *Ibid.,* Series III, p. 301.

25. *Ibid.,* Series I, p. 461.

26. News clipping dated April 11, 1861, from an unknown date of the *New York Tribune,* P. K. Yonge Library of Florida History, University of Florida.

27. Long, p. 308.

28. *Official Records,* I, Series I, 461.

29. Russell, p. 119.

30. General Order No. 2, Troops Near Pensacola, March 15, 1861, Records of the Confederate States Government, Army of Pensacola.

31. C. L. Bonney to his father, May 13, 18, June 20, August 25, September 14, 1861. Eli Whitney Bonney Papers.

32. General Order No. 16, Army of Pensacola, General Braxton Bragg, April 10, 1861, Records of the Confederate States Government.

33. *Ibid.,* No. 134, December 3, 1861; No. 137, December 13, 1861. The soldiers were Privates James Cooney and Samuel Givinn of the Tenth Mississippi Volunteers.

34. Davis, p. 117.

35. General Order No. 110, October 12, 1861, Records of the Confederate States Government.

36. Bonney to his father, June 20, 1861, Bonney Papers.

37. *Ibid.,* August 25, 1861. For the northern account of these episodes see: Morris, *The History of a Volunteer Regiment,* p. 48.

38. Russell, pp. 122-23.

39. *Official Records,* I, Series I, 410-11.

40. Bonney to his father, June 20, 1861, Bonney Papers.

41. *Official Records,* I, Series I, 413.

42. Bonney to his father, June 20, 1861, Bonney Papers.

43. William O. Fleming to his father, May 6, 1861, Fleming Papers.

44. Bonney to his father, September 14, 1861, Bonney Papers.

45. Fleming to his wife, May 21, 1861, Fleming Papers.

46. Morris, pp. 51-52. Many Confederates believed that the dock had

been burned by their own forces when the first attempt to move it failed. See Bonney to his father, September 14, 1861, Bonney Papers.

47. *Official Records,* VI, Series I, 437.
48. *Ibid.,* pp. 460-63.
49. *Ibid.,* I, Series I, 434-35.
50. Morris, pp. 34-35.
51. *Official Records,* VI, Series I, 460-63.
52. *Ibid.,* pp. 446-47, 460-63.
53. F. Moore, *The Rebellion Record, A Diary of American Events,* III, 91.
54. *Official Records,* VI, Series I, 460-63.
55. *Ibid.,* pp. 439-41.
56. Morris, p. 63.
57. *Official Records,* VI, Series I, 439-41, 460-63.
58. Pp. 160-61.
59. *Official Records,* VI, Series I, 433-44, 448-49, 469-76, 488-98.

CHAPTER IV

1. *Official Records,* VI, Series I, 267.
2. *Ibid.,* p. 276.
3. October 29, 1861, Milton Papers.
4. November 19, 1861, Milton Papers.
5. *Official Records,* VI, Series I, 286-87.
6. Milton to Stephen R. Mallory, October 2, 1861, Milton Papers.
7. Report of Franklin L. Daucy, n.d., Milton Papers.
8. C. R. P. Rodgers to Samuel F. DuPont, March 12, 1862, *Official Records of the Union and Confederate Navies In the War of the Rebellion,* XII, Series I, 595 (hereinafter cited as *Official Records, Navy*).
9. Robertson, p. 100.
10. October 2, 1861, Milton Papers.
11. Milton to Davis, November 19, 1861, Milton Papers.
12. *Official Records,* VI, Series I, 288-89, 293.
13. Milton to Davis, November 19, 1861, Milton Papers.
14. Judah P. Benjamin to Milton, November 22, 1861, Milton Papers.
15. *Official Records,* VI, Series I, 826-28.
16. *Ibid.,* p. 837.
17. *Ibid.,* pp. 848-49.
18. *Ibid.,* pp. 660-62. The property destroyed in Pensacola was a large oil factory, a quartermaster storehouse, and five small ships.
19. *Ibid.,* pp. 849-50.
20. *Ibid.,* pp. 658-59.
21. Shorey, *The Story of The Maine Fifteenth,* pp. 33-34.
22. *Official Records,* XXVI, Part I, Series I, 833-34.
23. Coley, "Civil War Reminiscences of Escambia County."
24. *Official Records,* VI, Series I, 393-94.
25. *Ibid.,* pp. 403-4.
26. Milton to Benjamin, March 5, 1862, Milton Papers.
27. *Official Records,* VI, Series I, 406.
28. Report of a Naval Planning Committee to Gideon Welles, July 5, 1861, Yulee Papers.

29. Norman Bronson to Henry Summer, August 6, 1861, Henry Summer Papers.

30. *Official Records,* XII, Series I, 573.

31. *Ibid.,* VI, Series I, 398-99.

32. *Ibid.,* pp. 93-94.

33. *Ibid.,* XII, Series I, 573-78.

34. *Official Records,* VI, Series I, 93-94.

35. Price, *History of The Ninety-Seventh Regiment, Pennsylvania Volunteer Infantry,* pp. 103-4.

36. A Committee of The Regimental Association, *The Story of One Regiment,* pp. 123-26. The April 30, 1863, issue of the *Fernandina Peninsula,* a pro-Union newspaper in the occupied city, gave the population of Fernandina as 212 white, 119 of whom were women; 1,032 colored, 951 of whom were Contrabands.

37. Tourtellotte, *A History of Company K of The Seventh Connecticut Volunteers,* pp. 79-85.

38. Michael O. Razor to his wife, March 7, 1862, Michael O. Razor Civil War Letters.

39. For a complete explanation of the reasons for the occupation of Jacksonville and St. Augustine see: *Official Records,* VI, Series I, 225-39; East, "St. Augustine During the Civil War," p. 77; Smith, "Carpetbag Imperialism In Florida, 1862-1868," pp. 99-130, 259-99.

40. *Official Records, Navy,* XII, Series I, 586-88, 599-600.

41. L. John French to L'Engle, December 22, 1861, E. M. L'Engle Papers.

42. Account of the Evacuation of Jacksonville, signed McKendree, *Florida Sentinel,* March 18, April 1, 1862.

43. *Official Records,* VI, Series I, 414.

44. Account of the Evacuation of Jacksonville.

45. *Official Records,* VI, Series I, 100, 414-15.

46. Account of the Evacuation of Jacksonville; see also, T. F. Davis, *History of Jacksonville, Florida, and Vicinity 1513 to 1924,* pp. 116-19.

47. Account of the Evacuation of Jacksonville.

48. *Florida Sentinel,* March 25, April 8, and April 25, 1862.

49. Proceedings of the Town Meeting of . . . Jacksonville, Florida, March 20, 1862, Miscellaneous Confederate Papers.

50. *Official Records,* VI, Series I, 125-28, 131-32.

51. *Florida Sentinel,* April 1, 1862.

52. *Official Records, Navy,* XII, Series I, 595-97.

53. East, pp. 601-2.

54. Mrs. Joseph L. Smith to Edmund Kirby Smith, March 12, 1862, Edmund Kirby Smith Papers.

55. *Official Records,* LIII, Series I, 221-23.

56. "Prudence," *Florida Sentinel,* March 18, 1862.

57. Tenney, p. 23; Long, pp. 363-64.

58. Entries for March and April 13, 1862, The Reverend Overton Bernard Diary.

59. Long, p. 364.

60. *Florida Sentinel,* February 18, 1862.

61. Long, p. 339.

62. *Official Records,* VI, Series I, 430.

63. *Ibid.,* XIV, Series I, 477.

64. *Ibid.,* p. 485.

65. *Ibid.,* pp. 511-12. These troops were organized as follows: Fifth Regiment Florida Volunteers, two-thirds armed, 1,500 men, at Camp Lee near Tallahassee; Sixth Regiment Florida Volunteers, fully armed, 1,100 men, stationed on Chattahoochee River; Seventh Regiment Florida Volunteers, four-fifths armed, 1,100 men, under orders for Jacksonville; First Regiment Rifles, no arms, 1,000 men; First Special Batallion, fully armed, 600 men stationed at Ricco's Bluff; three batteries of light artillery, six field pieces to each company, 450 men, one near Chattahoochee, one near Jacksonville, and one near Tallahassee; eight companies of cavalry, partly armed, 700 men, stationed in coastal areas; three companies of Six Months Missouri Volunteers, partly armed, 250 men, in Camp Lee.

66. *Ibid.,* p. 615. These troops were organized as follows: First Special Batallion Florida Infantry, 587 men; three independent companies of infantry, 261 men; three companies of Partisan Rangers, 509 men; ten companies of cavalry, 681 men; two batteries of artillery, 330 men.

67. *Ibid.,* p. 964. As of June 3, 1863, the Military District of Middle Florida had 1,520 effective troops and East Florida had only 803 effectives.

68. *Official Records, Navy,* XVII, Series I, 48.

69. Report of James H. Trapier, January 20, 1862, Milton Papers.

70. *Official Records, Navy,* XVII, Series I, 49.

71. Schellings, "Blockade Duty on The Florida Coast," entries for March 31, April 3, 1862.

72. Milton to Anderson, June 6, 1864, Milton Letterbook.

73. *Florida Sentinel,* April 1, 1862.

74. Schellings, July 27, 28, 1862.

75. *Florida Sentinel,* June 17, 1862.

76. *Ibid.,* July 15, 1862.

77. [Yonge], "Federal Raid on Tampa Bay," pp. 130-39.

78. *Official Records,* XIV, Series I, 128-32.

79. Tourtellotte, pp. 47-48.

80. *Official Records,* XIV, Series I, 128-32.

81. Higginson, "Up The St. Johns," pp. 311-25.

82. Joseph Finegan to People of Florida, March 13, 1863, *Florida Sentinel,* March 17, 1863.

83. *Florida Sentinel,* March 31, 1863.

84. *Official Records,* XIV, Series I, 232-39.

85. "Diary of Doctor Alfred Walton," *Florida Times-Union,* October 30, 1893. Doctor Walton returned the prayer book and map later.

86. Merritt, p. 56.

CHAPTER V

1. Florida *Acts* (1861), p. 93. Among the institutions were the Planters and Merchants Bank of Pensacola (February 14, 1861, pp. 93-99), the Western Bank of Florida at Apalachicola (February 14, 1861, pp. 90-100), the Commercial Bank of Lake City (February 14, 1861, pp. 100-7), the Bank of Tallahassee (February 14, 1861, p. 107), the Bank of Commerce at Fernandina (February 12, 1861, pp. 143-45), Marine and Fire Insurance Company of Pensacola (February 8, 1861, pp. 145-47), and the Hydrant Water Company of Pensacola (February 8, 1861, pp. 147-49).

2. *Ibid.,* p. 228.

3. *Ibid.*, p. 230.
4. *Ibid.*, Constitutional Amendments, No. I, p. 241.
5. *Ibid.*, pp. 67-69.
6. *Ibid.*, p. 79.
7. *Ibid.*, pp. 43-46.
8. *Ibid.*, pp. 56-57.
9. *Ibid.*, pp. 60-63.
10. *Ibid.*, p. 76.
11. L. John French to Edward L'Engle, December 22, 1861, E. M. L'Engle Papers.
12. Florida *Acts* (1862), pp. 11, 17-18. These acts related specifically to Duval County and Escambia County.
13. *Ibid.*, pp. 31-32.
14. *Ibid.*, Resolutions, No. XI, p. 67.
15. Walter Gwynn to John B. Gailbraith, April 4, 1864, Comptroller's Letterbook.
16. *Official Records,* LIII, Series I, 350-64.
17. Florida *Acts* (1862), pp. 23-24.
18. Keen, "Some Phases of Life in Leon County During the Civil War," p. 21.
19. *Gainesville Cotton States,* June 11, 1864.
20. *Florida Sentinel,* August 5, 1862.
21. Benjamin F. Allen to William Nickler, September 3, 1864, *Florida Executive Records.*
22. Allen to Robert Shields, July 21, 1864, *Florida Executive Records.*
23. Florida *Acts* (1864), Resolutions, No. I, p. 35.
24. *Ibid.*, (1862), pp. 18-19.
25. E. J. Daniels to Gwynn, April 12, 1864, Comptroller-Letters Received.
26. Gwynn to Daniels, May 27, 1864, Comptroller's Letterbook. This is the position Gwynn consistently took concerning collection of taxes.
27. Gwynn to John Lee, May 26, 1864, Comptroller's Letterbook.
28. John U. Geiger to Gwynn, April 28, 1864, Comptroller-Letters Received.
29. John L. Peterson to Gwynn, May 28, 1864, Comptroller-Letters Received.
30. John J. Addison to Gwynn, March 20, 1865, Comptroller-Letters Received.
31. Gwynn to John Budd, March 2, 1865, Comptroller's Letterbook.
32. List of Counties receiving Tax books, undated entry, Comptroller's Letterbook.
33. Estimate based on notation on unnumbered pages in back of Comptroller's Letterbook.
34. Florida *Senate Journal* (1860), p. 11.
35. Long, p. 308.
36. *Official Records,* I, Series I, 333.
37. *Ibid.*, pp. 336-37.
38. Florida *Senate Journal* (1861), pp. 249-53.
39. Milton to I. Wayles Baker, October 17, 1861, Milton Papers.
40. Milton to Davis, October 29, 1861, Milton Papers.
41. Milton to Mallory, October 2, 1861, Milton Papers.
42. Milton to Benjamin, October 28, 1861, Milton Papers.
43. Florida *Senate Journal* (1861), pp. 11-44.

NOTES TO CHAPTER V

44. Milton Family Bible, in possession of the Milton family at Marianna, Florida. John Milton's tombstone in the Episcopal Churchyard of Marianna, Florida, gives the date of birth as April 21, 1807.

45. *East Floridian,* July 27, 1860; Parker, "John Milton, Governor of Florida," pp. 346-54; Gammon, "Governor John Milton of Florida," Chapters VI and VII.

46. Milton to Mallory, October 2, 1861, Milton Papers.

47. October 29, 1861, Milton Papers.

48. See correspondence of Milton to Mallory, October 2, 1861, Milton to Davis, October 18 and 29, 1861; and Milton to Benjamin, October 28, 1861, Milton Papers.

49. Milton to Benjamin, October 28, 1861, Milton Papers.

50. Milton to Floyd, October 29, 1861, Milton Papers.

51. *Official Records,* VI, Series I, 304.

52. Milton to Floyd, November 6, 1861, Milton Papers.

53. Milton to I. Wayles Baker, October 17, 1861; Milton to Mallory, October 2, 1861; Milton to Davis, October 29, 1861, Milton Papers.

54. *Official Records,* VI, Series I, 289.

55. *Ibid.,* pp. 296-97.

56. *Ibid.,* pp. 315-18.

57. Milton to Davis, October 29, 1861, Milton Papers.

58. Benjamin to Milton, November 22, 1861, Milton Papers.

59. Robertson, p. 171.

60. *Journal of the Convention of the People of Florida . . . January 14, 1862,* pp. 4-7 [hereinafter cited as *Convention Journal* (1862)].

61. Florida *Senate Journal* (1862), pp. 28-29.

62. Gammon, p. 94.

63. L. John French to Edward L'Engle, December 22, 1861, E. M. L'Engle Papers.

64. White, "The Fate of Calhoun's Sovereign Convention in South Carolina," p. 762; Havard, "The Florida Executive Council, 1862," pp. 77-82.

65. *Convention Journal* (1862), Resolution, No. 33, p. 26.

66. *Ibid.,* pp. 4-10.

67. Gailbraith to Milton, January 30, 1862, Opinions of the Attorney General.

68. L. John French to Edward L'Engle, December 22, 1861, E. M. L'Engle Papers. The convention was to meet January 14, 1862.

69. From issues of January 7, 14, and 2, 1862, respectively.

70. January 2, 1862.

71. *Convention Journal* (1862), pp. 36 ff.

72. *Ibid.,* p. 109.

73. Florida *Senate Journal* (1862), p. 52.

74. *Convention Journal* (1862), pp. 44-45.

75. *Ibid.,* p. 57.

76. *Ibid.,* p. 63.

77. *Ibid.,* pp. 71-72.

78. *Florida Sentinel,* January 28, 1862.

79. Florida *Senate Journal* (1862), pp. 38-39.

80. Cauthen, *South Carolina Goes to War, 1860-1865,* pp. 142-44.

81. *Constitution . . . For The People of Florida, As Revised and Amended . . . on the 3rd Day of January, A. D. 1861, and . . . January 14th, A. D. 1862, Together with the Ordinances . . .* p. 31 (hereinafter cited as *Constitution and Ordinances of the Convention, 1862*).

82. *Ibid.,* p. 36. The General Assembly could repeal Ordinance 52 and Ordinance 58 because neither is listed in Ordinance 63 of the convention which lists the permanent ordinances of the convention of 1862.

83. *Ibid.,* pp. 100-02.

84. Rerick, *Memoirs of Florida,* II, 94.

85. *Constitution and Ordinances of the Convention, 1862,* p. 37.

86. *Ibid.,* p. 33.

87. February 2, 1862.

88. Gailbraith to Milton, January 30, 1862, Opinions of the Attorney General.

89. "Proceedings of the Executive Council," Florida *Senate Journal* (1862), Appendix: pp. 53-55.

90. Compare the governor's message, November 20, 1862, Florida *House Journal* (1862), pp. 20 ff, and "Proceedings of the Executive Council," Florida *Senate Journal* (1862), pp. 55-56.

91. "Proceedings of the Executive Council," pp. 55-60.

92. Exemptions were granted to the governor, members of the executive council, most state executive and judicial officials, persons exempted by the Confederacy, railroad operating personnel, and salt manufacturers.

93. "Proceedings of the Executive Council," pp. 60-63.

94. April 15, 1862.

95. "Proceedings of the Executive Council," p. 64.

96. Florida *Senate Journal* (1862), p. 46.

97. Florida *Acts* (1862), p. 33.

98. *Florida Sentinel,* October 21, 1862.

99. *Ibid.,* November 25, 1862.

100. Gailbraith to Frank Villepigue, November 17, 1862, Opinions of the Attorney General.

101. Milton to V. L. Villepigue, November 19, 1862, Milton Papers.

102. *Florida Sentinel,* October 7, 1862.

103. Ethelred Philips to James Philips, October 12, 1862, Philips Papers.

104. The Districts and the men involved were: (1) The Eighth District, David P. Hogue, elected in 1862, and P. B. Brokaw, elected in 1860; (2) Seventeenth District, E. C. Simkins, elected in 1860, and James T. Russell, elected in 1862; (3) Eighteenth District, S. St. George Rogers, elected in 1860, and John Scott, elected in 1862; Twentieth District, James Magbee, elected in 1860, and James M. Taylor elected in 1862. Florida *Senate Journal* (1862), pp. 4-5.

105. Florida *Senate Journal* (1862), p. 18.

CHAPTER VI

1. Thomas, "Florida Finance in the Civil War," p. 311.
2. Homans, "Bank Items," p. 903.
3. Florida *Senate Journal* (1860), pp. 195-97.
4. Thomas, p. 312.
5. Florida *Senate Journal* (1861), pp. 1-9.
6. *Ibid.,* (1859), pp. 102-3.
7. Florida *Acts* (1861), p. 230.
8. *Ibid.,* pp. 86-107, 140-41.

9. *Ibid.*, p. 78.
10. *Ibid.*, pp. 67-69.
11. Florida *Senate Journal* (1862), pp. 101-2.
12. Florida *Acts* (1861), p. 86.
13. *Ibid.*, pp. 43-46.
14. *Ibid.*, pp. 44-45.
15. *Ibid.*, p. 30.
16. Florida *Senate Journal* (1862), pp. 27-35.
17. Florida *Acts* (1861), pp. 8-9.
18. *Ibid.*, p. 31.
19. Florida *Senate Journal* (1862), pp. 51-52.
20. Florida *Acts* (1853), pp. 11-22.
21. *Ibid.* (1861), p. 14.
22. *Ibid.*, pp. 14-15.
23. Schwab, *The Confederate States of America, 1861-1865*, pp. 127-31.
24. Florida *Senate Journal* (1861), pp. 95-97.
25. Florida *Acts* (1861), p. 15.
26. Florida *Senate Journal* (1861), pp. 95-97.
27. Florida *Acts* (1861), pp. 26-27.
28. Homans, p. 543.
29. Thomas, pp. 311-18.
30. Coulter, *The Confederate States of America,* VII, 149-62.
31. Florida *Acts* (1861), p. 30.
32. *Ibid.*, pp. 43-46.
33. Florida *Senate Journal* (1861), p. 72.
34. Florida *Acts* (1861), p. 17.
35. *Ibid.*, p. 64.
36. *Ibid.*, p. 78.
37. *Ibid.*, pp. 28-29.
38. Moore, IV, 293-94.
39. Florida *Acts* (1862), pp. 51-52.
40. Florida *Senate Journal* (1863), p. 23.
41. Florida *Acts* (1863), p. 18.
42. *Ibid.*, p. 39.
43. Florida *House Journal* (1863), Appendix, pp. 17-18.
44. Florida *Senate Journal* (1863), Appendix, pp. 13-16.
45. Thomas, pp. 311-18.
46. *Journal of The Convention of Florida Begun . . . October 25, A.D. 1865*, p. 21.
47. Florida *Senate Journal* (1863), p. 30.
48. Florida *Acts* (1863), Resolutions, pp. 54-55.
49. *Ibid.*, pp. 71-72.
50. *Ibid.*, pp. 29-30.
51. Florida *Senate Journal* (1863), Documents, pp. 15-20.
52. Florida *Acts* (1863), Resolutions, p. 54.
53. This statement based on governors' messages, reports of the comptroller, and reports of the treasurer for the period of 1862-1865.
54. Florida *Senate Journal* (1861), pp. 170-71.
55. Schwab, pp. 285-290.
56. Florida *Acts* (1861), pp. 15-16.
57. *Ibid.* (1862), p. 14.
58. *Ibid.*, pp. 18-19.
59. Florida *House Journal* (1862), pp. 285-86.

60. Florida *Acts* (1863), pp. 24-25.
61. Florida *Senate Journal* (1864), pp. 20-21.
62. Coulter, p. 25.
63. *Ibid.*, p. 251.
64. *Ibid.*, pp. 177-80.
65. Florida *Acts* (1861), pp. 12-13.
66. *Ibid.* (1862), pp. 42-44.
67. *Ibid.*, pp. 19-22.
68. *Convention Journal* (1865), p. 17.
69. *Ibid.*, p. 21.
70. Florida *Acts* (1864), pp. 19-20.
71. Florida *Senate Journal* (1864), Documents, p. 31.

CHAPTER VII

1. October 2, 1861, Milton Letterbook.
2. Milton Letterbook.
3. *Ibid.*
4. Milton to Davis, October 29, 1861, Milton Letterbook.
5. Florida *Senate Journal* (1861), p. 71.
6. November 19, 1861, Milton Letterbook.
7. Florida *Senate Journal* (1861), pp. 28-34.
8. *Official Records,* VI, Series I, 430-32.
9. Milton to Benjamin, March 5, 1862, Milton Letterbook.
10. The river ports involved were Columbus, Georgia, and Eufaula, Alabama.
11. *Official Records,* VI, Series I, 848, 853, 862, 870.
12. *Ibid.*, p. 267.
13. Milton to Beauregard, November 6, 1863, Milton Letterbook.
14. *Official Records,* II, Series IV, 56-58.
15. *Ibid.*, pp. 94-95.
16. *Ibid.*, pp. 215-16.
17. *Ibid.*, pp. 92-93.
18. Florida *Senate Journal* (1862), pp. 34-35.
19. *Official Records,* II, Series IV, 256-57.
20. Florida *Senate Journal* (1863), pp. 8-33.
21. *Official Records,* II, Series IV, 401-2.
22. *Ibid.*, pp. 879-80.
23. *Ibid.*, III, Series IV, 851. Governor Vance of North Carolina granted the most certificates—14,675.
24. W. W. Davis, p. 190.
25. Milton to Pleasant W. White, December 12, 1863, Milton Letterbook.
26. *Official Records,* II, Series IV, 972-76.
27. To Seddon, January 26, 1864, Milton Letterbook.
28. Milton Papers.
29. Milton Letterbook.
30. *Official Records,* LIII, Series I, 349-54.
31. W. W. Davis, p. 199.
32. To G. W. Randolph, June 25, 1862, Milton Letterbook.

33. *Official Records,* I, Series IV, 1174.
34. April 14, 1864, Milton Letterbook.
35. Florida *Senate Journal* (1864), pp. 9-13.
36. *Ibid.,* p. 32.
37. *Official Records,* II, Series IV, 808-9.

CHAPTER VIII

1. Correspondence, 1855-1860, Yulee Papers.
2. Dodd, "The Manufacture of Cotton in Florida before and during the Civil War," pp. 3-4.
3. *Floridian and Journal* (Tallahassee), December 3, 1853.
4. Keen, p. 22.
5. Milton and Bailey Correspondence of June, 1864, Milton Letterbook; see also, *Official Records,* III, Series IV, 499, and Florida *Acts* (1863), p. 59.
6. Dodd, "The Manufacture of Cotton," pp. 3-4.
7. Florida *Acts* (1863), p. 59.
8. *Ibid.,* p. 52.
9. Bailey to Milton, June 15, 1864, Milton Papers.
10. Chandler Cox Yonge to George William Cunningham, July 20, 1864, Letterbook, Chandler Cox Yonge Papers.
11. *Official Records,* III, Series IV, 499.
12. Florida *Acts* (1862), Resolution No. 6, p. 65.
13. Florida *Senate Journal* (1863), Documents, pp. 52-53.
14. *Ibid.,* pp. 34-35.
15. *Florida Sentinel,* September 15, 1863.
16. Mrs. Edward Bradford to her son, September 18, 1864, Mrs. Nicholas Ware Eppes Papers.
17. For a full discussion of each method of manufacturing salt see: Lonn, *Salt as a Factor in the Confederacy,* pp. 19-34.
18. Ella Lonn estimates that one hundred thousand tons of salt a year entered the pre-war South through the port of New Orleans alone. *Ibid.,* pp. 16-18.
19. *Ibid.,* p. 30.
20. Lonn, "The Extent and Importance of Federal Naval Raids on Salt-Making in Florida, 1862-1865," pp. 167-68.
21. February 11.
22. June 3, 1862.
23. Florida *Senate Journal* (1862), p. 51.
24. Florida *Acts* (1862), Resolution No. 13, p. 68.
25. Florida *Senate Journal* (1862), p. 51.
26. *Official Records,* II, Series IV, 95.
27. Florida *Senate Journal* (1863), p. 21.
28. *Florida Sentinel,* June 3, 1862.
29. Certain saltworkers were exempted by an amendatory act in October, 1862. The Exemption Act of February 17, 1864, removed saltworkers from the exempted class, but the President and Secretary of War could detail men to work in certain industries if the need was crucial. Also by the 1864

act, state governors could exempt certain state officials and most governors included several key saltworkers in their exempted list. For a complete discussion of saltworkers and the Exemption Acts, see: Lonn, *Salt as a Factor,* pp. 61-66.

30. Florida *Acts* (1862), Resolution No. 30, p. 77.

31. *Official Records,* XIV, Series I, 753.

32. For a more detailed account of the numerous raids see: Lonn, "Federal Naval Raids," pp. 167-84.

33. A small raid was made against the salt works at New Smyrna on March 22, 1862, but was a detached event and was not part of the organized raids.

34. *Official Records, Navy,* XVII, Series I, 316-19.

35. *Ibid.,* p. 373.

36. Ethelred Philips to James Philips, undated, Philips Papers.

37. *Official Records, Navy,* XIX, Series I, 377. The Federal commanders claimed a destruction of works producing over 500 bushels per day. The water capacity of the kettles destroyed was given at 21,600 gallons per day. Under the accepted ratio of one bushel of salt to 60 gallons of water, the figure is high.

38. *Ibid.,* XVII, Series I, 467-72.

39. *Ibid.,* pp. 593-601.

40. Lonn, "Federal Naval Raids," p. 176.

41. *Official Records, Navy,* XVII, Series I, 646-49.

42. *Ibid,* p. 683.

43. *Ibid.,* pp. 707, 719.

44. *New York Herald,* December 17, 1864.

45. *Official Records, Navy,* XVII, Series I, 811-12.

46. T. F. Davis, pp. 97-103.

47. Lee, "Civil War Letters," p. 16.

48. *Eighth Census,* IV, 328. The railroads in Florida were: Florida, 154.2 miles; Florida and Alabama, 45.1 miles; Florida, Atlantic and Gulf Central, 59.3 miles; Pensacola and Georgia, 115.9 miles; Perdido and Junction, 6.0 miles; and Tallahassee, 21.0 miles. A total of $8,628,000 had been spent in constructing the 401.5 miles of road.

49. Report of James Craig to Yulee, April 1, 1861, Yulee Papers.

50. *East Floridian,* March 29, 1860.

51. Florida *Acts* (1861), p. 109. The capital stock of the company was to be $200,000.

52. *Ibid.,* pp. 112-13. The capital stock was to be $200,000.

53. *Ibid.,* pp. 116-23. The capital stock was to be $100,000.

54. *Ibid.,* pp. 123-30. The capital stock was to be $1,000,000.

55. *Ibid.,* p. 29. The capital stock was to be $300,000.

56. *Ibid.,* p. 12.

57. *Florida Sentinel,* December 12, 1862.

58. Richard Meader to Edward Dickerson, November 4, 1865, Yulee Papers.

59. *Convention Journal* (1861), pp. 48-49.

60. *Ibid.,* pp. 67-69.

61. Undated memorandum of David Levy Yulee, Yulee Papers.

62. Florida *Senate Journal* (1861), pp. 54-55.

63. *Ibid.* (1862), pp. 37-38.

64. *Ibid.* (1863), Documents, pp. 26-27.

65. Meader to Dickerson, November 4, 1865, Yulee Papers.

66. Florida *Senate Journal* (1862), pp. 60-61.
67. John Cromartie to his sister, July 13, 1862, Cromartie Papers.
68. Florida *Senate Journal* (1862), pp. 60-61.
69. *Ibid.* (1864), p. 92.
70. Perry to Noyes, March 25, 1865, A. B. Noyes Papers.
71. Memminger to Noyes, April 13, 1861, Noyes Papers.
72. Memminger to Noyes, April 26, 1861, and Chandler Cox Yonge to Noyes, August 12, 1861, Noyes Papers.
73. See correspondence between Memminger and Noyes during August and September of 1861, especially Memminger to Noyes, September 16, 1861, Noyes Papers.
74. Contract agreement, April 6, 1864, Yulee Papers.
75. For a discussion of the Florida Railroad controversy see the documents and letters sent to the Florida Senate by John Milton, Florida *Senate Journal* (1863), pp. 202-31; *Official Records, War,* LIII, Series I, 349-64; Milton Letterbook, June 9-15, 1864; Richard Meader Correspondence, November 4-12, 1865, Jason Fairbanks Correspondence, November, 1863, May, 1864, Yulee Papers.
76. Meader to Dickerson, November 4, 1865, Yulee Papers.

CHAPTER IX

1. For a description of the development of the plantation regime in Florida see: Martin, *Florida During the Territorial Days,* and Williams.
2. *Eighth Census: Agriculture,* p. 225.
3. *Ibid.,* p. 247.
4. *Ibid.,* pp. 195, 225.
5. *Ibid.,* p. 18.
6. *Ibid.,* p. 225.
7. For further discussion, see Williams, pp. 102-03.
8. April 8, 1862.
9. February 3, 1862.
10. *Ibid.,* April 1, 1862. The editor substituted the word "corn" for the word "grain."
11. Milton to Zebulon Vance, December 15, 1862, Battle Papers.
12. January 6, 1863.
13. *Florida Sentinel,* March 3, 1863.
14. March 31, 1863.
15. March 17, 1863.
16. April 13, 1863, Milton Letterbook.
17. Florida *Senate Journal* (1863), p. 21.
18. Florida *Acts* (1863), pp. 42-43.
19. *Gainesville Cotton States,* May 28, 1864.
20. *Official Records,* XXXV, Part II, Series I, 606-8.
21. May 6, 1862.
22. May 23, 1863, Milton Papers.
23. Hopley, *Life in the South,* II, 277.
24. Long, p. 364.

25. *Ibid.,* p. 331.

26. John Robinson to William H. Branch, October 1, 1863, Branch Papers.

27. The Reverend Overton Bernard Diary, April 13, 1862.

28. Charlotte L'Engle to Edward L'Engle, April 4, 1862, E. M. L'Engle Papers.

29. Florida *Acts* (1861), pp. 38-43.

30. *Ibid.* (1863), p. 30.

31. Florida *Senate Journal* (1862), pp. 57-58.

32. *Gainesville Cotton States,* May 28, 1864.

33. Florida *Acts* (1864), pp. 7-8.

34. *U. S. Statutes at Large,* XII, 319.

35. *Official Records,* LIII, Series I, 230.

36. *Ibid.,* XIV, Series I, 333-34.

37. *Ibid.,* pp. 374-76.

38. *Ibid.,* p. 341.

39. *Ibid.,* II, Series III, 42.

40. *U. S. Statutes at Large,* XII, 590-92.

41. Federal troops held Fernandina, Jacksonville, St. Augustine, Key West, and Pensacola. Only at Key West were there any "loyal" slaveholders and these had their slaves freed by Colonel Joseph Morgan on September 5, 1862, as he decreed that no employee of the Union could be forceably held in slavery. Almost all Negroes on the island were employed by the Federal government. For details see *New York Herald,* October 26, 1862.

42. For these and other jobs performed by the slaves see: Eppes, p. 163; Abby, "Documents Relating to El Destino and Chemonie Plantations, Middle Florida, 1828-1868," Part III, pp. 3-46; *Gainesville Cotton States,* June 4, 1864.

43. Florida *Acts* (1862), pp. 54-55.

44. *Florida Sentinel,* December 1, 1863.

45. Records of the Confederate States Government; Records of the Department of South Carolina, Georgia, and Florida; Special Orders, District of Florida, 1864, Special Order No. 8, March 15, 1864.

46. List of Negroes, Bailey Papers.

47. Confederate War Department, Bureau of Conscription, Circular No. 36, December 12, 1864; *Official Records, War,* III, Series IV, 933-34.

48. Francis L'Engle to Edward L'Engle, November 5, 1864, E. M. L'Engle Papers.

49. Florida *Acts* (1864), pp. 27-28.

50. This description of the steps in the impressment comes from the correspondence of J. P. Sanderson, an impressing agent, Miscellaneous Confederate Papers.

51. Lee, p. 2.

52. Undated, about March of 1862, Yulee Papers.

53. Higginson, "Up The St. Mary's," pp. 224-26.

54. *Official Records,* XIV, Series I, 374-77.

55. *Ibid.,* p. 661.

56. *Ibid.,* XIV, Series I, 226.

57. *Ibid.,* p. 850.

58. *Ibid.,* IV, Series III, 1269-70. Abstract from the official records showing the forces called for by the President of the United States, the quotas assigned, and the number furnished for the military and naval services from 1861 to 1865.

CHAPTER X

1. Ferrell, p. 35.
2. Long, p. 306.
3. Ethelred Philips to James J. Philips, January 15, 1861, Philips Papers.
4. *Official Records,* XXXV, Part II, Series I, 12, 63, 215; II, Part I, Series I, 817; III, Series IV, 1101-09. See also, undated correspondence, 1863, between Milton and Mallory and Beauregard, Milton Papers; Davis, pp. 243-47.
5. *New York Times,* March 13, 1862. Marvin became the first provisional governor of Florida after the war.
6. *Official Records,* I, Series III, 184-85.
7. *New York Herald,* January 10, 1863. See also, Report of Committee on Confederate Relations, December 9, 1861, Florida *Senate Journal* (1861), p. 161.
8. April 5, 1862.
9. "Robert Watson, His Civil War Diary," Pass-A-Grille *Gulf Beach News,* October 1, 1943.
10. Milton to John Darling, October 16, 1861, Milton Papers.
11. "Robert Watson," November 19, 1943.
12. The "wreckers" supported themselves by salvaging and selling parts of ships or cargoes which had been wrecked on the Florida Keys.
13. Florida *Senate Journal* (1861), p. 161.
14. Florida *Acts* (1861), Resolutions, p. 69.
15. June 22, 1861.
16. *Official Records,* I, Series IV, 586-92; the amended act, *ibid.,* pp. 932-39.
17. *New York Times,* April 2, 1862. This issue carries much discussion of the maltreatment of Unionists in Jacksonville by the Regulators.
18. *Official Records,* VI, Series I, 250-52; *New York Times,* April 2, 1862.
19. *New York Herald,* April 11, 1862; Moore, IV, 349.
20. *Official Records,* VI, Series I, 250.
21. *Ibid.,* pp. 124-26; Moore, IV, 82.
22. *Official Records,* LII, Part II, Series I, 372-73.
23. Unsigned manuscript letter, Confederate Letters. The dissatisfaction concerning rations and pay was often expressed in contemporary letters of civilians. See, for example, Ethelred Philips to James J. Philips, January 14, 1864, Philips Papers.
24. *Gainesville Cotton States,* April 16, 1864.
25. Petition of officials of Taylor County, Florida, to President Jefferson Davis, August 11, 1863, *Official Records,* II, Series IV, 839-40. The petition was signed by S. P. Fife, clerk, circuit court; Edward Jorday, sheriff; Robert Henderson, judge of probate; William McMillan, Neal Henry, county commissioners; Daniel C. Baker, W. J. Smart, C. F. O'Hara, justices of the peace.
26. *Ibid.,* pp. 879-80. See also, Ethelred Philips to James J. Philips, February 23, 1864, Philips Papers.
27. Milton to Beauregard, January 29, 1864, Milton Letterbook; *Gainesville Cotton States,* June 18, 1864; *Official Records,* XXXV, Part II, Series I, 444.

28. Gold, *History of Volusia County,* p. 92.
29. *Official Records,* I, Series III, 730.
30. *Ibid.,* XXVI, Part I, Series I, 780-81.
31. Brigadier General A.[lexander] Asboth to Brigadier General Charles Stone, December 27, 1863, *ibid.,* pp. 886-87.
32. General Orders, No. 82, Department of the South, Major General John G. Foster, Commanding, June 6, 1864, *ibid.,* IV, Series III, 419-20.
33. Sub-inclosure No. 1, Henry D. Capers to J. L. Cross, March 27, 1864, *Official Records,* LIII, Series I, 318-19.
34. *Florida Sentinel,* November 11, 1862; *Official Records,* I, Series III, 730; Eppes, p. 222.
35. Milton to Mallory, May 23, 1864, Milton Letterbook.
36. *Official Records,* XXXV, Part II, Series I, 444.
37. *Ibid.,* pp. 448-49, 481.
38. Milton to Mallory, May 23, 1864, Milton Letterbook.
39. McDuffie, *The Lures of Manatee,* p. 122.
40. Undated, February, 1864, account of deserter action, Edward C. F. Sanchez Papers.
41. Milton to Mallory, May 23, 1864, Milton Letterbook.
42. McKinnon, *History of Walton County,* pp. 320-21.
43. *Gainesville Cotton States,* March 19, 1864; *Florida Sentinel,* November 11, 1862.
44. Milton to Seddon, January 11, 1864, Milton Letterbook.
45. To Gwynn, February 12, 1864, Comptroller-Letters Received, 1860-1865.
46. To Gwynn, July 5, 1864, Comptroller-Letters Received, 1860-1865.
47. Telegrams, Luke Lott to Milton, February 3 and 4, 1864, Milton Letterbook.
48. Milton to Beauregard, February 4, 1864, Milton Letterbook.
49. *Gainesville Cotton States,* March 19, 1864.
50. *Florida Sentinel,* December 9, 1862.
51. *Gainesville Cotton States,* April 16, 1864.
52. Cash, "Taylor County History and Civil War Deserters," p. 48; Eppes, pp. 322-23.
53. *Official Records,* LIII, Series I, 316-20.
54. Eppes, p. 223-24.
55. Milton Letterbook.
56. Petition of twelve of the sixteen women at Camp Smith to Milton, July 7, 1864, Milton Letterbook.
57. Carraway Smith to Milton, July 19, 1864, Milton Letterbook.
58. *Official Records,* XXXV, Part II, Series I, 607.
59. Milton to Davis, September 19, 1864, Milton Letterbook.
60. *Quincy Semi-Weekly Dispatch,* March 15, 1865.
61. Quoted from *Florida Union* (Jacksonville), May 6, 1865.

CHAPTER XI

1. For a general description of women in the Confederacy, see: Simkins and Patton, *The Women of the Confederacy.*

2. Eppes, p. 162.
3. *Ibid.,* p. 179; see also, Long, p. 324.
4. Florida *Acts* (1861), p. 37.
5. Florida *Senate Journal* (1862), pp. 54-55.
6. Florida *Acts* (1863), p. 47.
7. Florida *Senate Journal* (1864), p. 36.
8. Eppes, p. 192.
9. *Florida Sentinel,* April 1, July 15, August 19, 1862; Long, p. 330.
10. Milton to Mrs. H. Louisa Guardian, April 6, 1864, Milton Letterbook; *Florida Sentinel,* November 17, 1863.
11. *Gainesville Cotton States,* May 7, June 18, 1864.
12. Long, p. 330.
13. The Confederacy maintained six hospitals with a total of 515 beds in Florida. They were located as follows: Lake City, 150; Madison, 75; Tallahassee, 100; Quincy, 126; Marianna, 50; and Camp Lay (near Madison), 14. Report of J. E. A. Davidson, February 21, 1864, J. E. A. Davidson Papers.
14. *Gainesville Cotton States,* May 7, 1864.
15. *Florida Sentinel,* January 21, 1862.
16. *Ibid.,* May 26, 1863.
17. *Ibid.,* June 9, 1863.
18. *Ibid.,* January 28, 1862.
19. *Quincy Semi-Weekly Dispatch,* March 15, 1865.
20. Eppes, p. 240.
21. *Ibid.,* p. 233.
22. *Florida Sentinel,* May 21, 1863.
23. Eppes, pp. 235-36.
24. Madeleine Saunders L'Engle to Mrs. Bradley Johnson, November 5, 1863, William Johnson L'Engle Papers.
25. *Florida Sentinel,* August 19, 1862.
26. Edmund C. Lee to his wife, April 25, 1864, Lee, p. 23.
27. Pp. 238-39.
28. Hopley, II, 277.
29. Eppes, p. 210.
30. January 6, 1864.
31. McDuffee, p. 133.
32. *Florida Sentinel,* May 6, 1862. The recipe was: Three pounds white sugar, three ounces tartaric acid, and one quart of cold water. Put in brass or copper kettle and warm. Add three egg whites, beat in three teaspoons of flour and stir until it boils for three minutes. Cool. Add one gill of essence and bottle up.
33. *Ibid.,* April 22, 1862.
34. Eppes, p. 167.
35. P. 334.
36. Eppes, pp. 253-55.
37. For an excellent account of the patriotism of southern women see, *Florida Sentinel,* July 15, 1862.
38. *Gainesville Cotton States,* May 7, 1864.
39. Martha A. Robertson to her husband, March 27, 1864, Yulee Papers.
40. Florida *Acts* (1848), pp. 12-13.
41. *Ibid.* (1853), pp. 88-92.
42. *Ibid.* (1863), pp. 87-92.
43. *Ibid.* (1857), p. 28.

44. Bush, *History of Education in Florida,* pp. 19-20.

45. Florida *Senate Journal* (1860), Appendix, pp. 8-12.

46. *Constitution of Florida as Revised and Amended . . . third day of January, 1861.*

47. Florida *House Journal* (1861), Appendix, p. 10.

48. Florida *Senate Journal* (1862), Documents, p. 21.

49. *Ibid.,* pp. 21-22.

50. Florida *Acts* (1862), pp. 97-98.

51. *Ibid.* (1861), pp. 194-96.

52. *Ibid.,* p. 212. The counties were Columbia, Suwannee, New River, Lafayette, Nassau, and Sumter.

53. Nannie Yulee to David Levy Yulee, n.d., 1862; March 28, 1864, Yulee Papers.

54. Proctor, "History of the University of Florida," pp. 47-48.

55. Program for the Exercises at East Florida Seminary, July 12, 1861, P. K. Yonge Library of Florida History, University of Florida.

56. Proctor, p. 48.

57. *Ibid.,* pp. 48-49.

58. Florida *Acts* (1862), pp. 13-14.

59. Gwynn to William Harrison, November 6, 1862, Comptroller's Letterbook.

60. Proctor, pp. 48-50

61. Rhodes, "The Legal Development of State Supported Higher Education in Florida," p. 38.

62. W. G. Dodd, *History of the West Florida Seminary,* pp. 3-19.

63. *Florida Sentinel,* May 19, 1863.

64. W. G. Dodd, pp. 16-25.

65. Florida *Senate Journal* (1863), pp. 197-98.

66. Memorial of Francis Eppes, President, to the legislature, undated 1863, Manuscripts Section, Office of the Secretary of State, Tallahassee.

67. W. G. Dodd, pp. 24-25.

68. Florida *Acts* (1861), pp. 158-61.

69. Florida *Senate Journal* (1866), p. 201.

70. *Eighth Census,* IV, 363-64. The total affiliation was as follows: Methodist, 30,360; Baptist, 20,325; Presbyterian, 9,580; Catholic, 4,350; Episcopal, 3,175; Lutheran, 600; and Universalist, 600.

71. *Convention Journal* (1861), p. 20.

72. *Journal of the Baptist Convention, 1860,* pp. 8-9.

73. *Fifty-Two Years in Florida,* p. 88.

74. G. G. Smith, *The History of Methodism in Georgia and Florida, From 1785 to 1865,* pp. 408-10.

75. Richardson, *The Lights and Shadows of Itinerant Life,* p. 173.

76. Ley, p. 88.

77. *Journal . . . of the Twenty-third Convention of the Protestant Episcopal Church, December 16, 1863,* pp. 9-20.

78. Jesse Bernard Diary, June 16, 23, and November 24, 1861.

79. John A. Cromartie to his sister, July 1, 1862, John A. Cromartie Papers.

80. *Journal of the Episcopal Church, 1863,* pp. 16-17.

81. *Florida Sentinel,* April 15, 1862.

82. Dalton, "A History of Florida Baptists," pp. 89-90.

83. Richardson, p. 178. 84. Shea, *History of the Catholic Church in the United States,* IV, 346-47.

85. Richardson, p. 174
86. Dalton, p. 90.
87. Roth, *Brief History of the Churches of the Diocese of St. Augustine Florida,* pp. 153-65.
88. Florida *Senate Journal* (1863), p. 43.
89. *Ibid.,* p. 53.
90. Nannie Yulee to Virginia C. Clay, January 24, 1864, Clay Papers.
91. *Minutes of the Annual Conferences of the Methodist Episcopal Church, South, for the Year 1860.*
92. *Journal of the Baptist Convention, 1860,* p. 8.
93. Dalton, p. 64.
94. Browning, *The Early History of Concord Missionary Baptist Church, 1841-1868,* pp. 26-28.
95. Ware, "History of New River Church, Columbia County, Florida, 1833-1912," pp. 17-18.
96. Pp. 175-76.
97. Dalton, p. 90. The figure seventeen is based on the fact that the 1860 convention journal listed seventeen churches for the association. *Journal of the Baptist Convention, 1860,* pp. 22-23.
98. *Proceedings of the Southern Baptist Convention at Its Eighth Biennial Session, May, 1861,* p. 56.
99. *Proceedings of the Ninth Biennial Session of the Southern Baptist Convention, May, 1863,* p. 32.
100. *Ibid.,* p. 41.
101. Dalton, pp. 90-91.
102. Ley, pp. 9-94.
103. *Gainesville Cotton States,* June 18, 1864.
104. *Journal of the Episcopal Church, 1863,* p. 18.
105. *Minutes of the Methodist Episcopal Church, South, 1862,* II, 549. See also, Minutes of the Conferences for 1863, 1864, and 1865, pages 549, 522, and 581, respectively.
106. Stanton to Commanding Generals, Departments of Missouri, Tennessee, and the Gulf, November 30, 1863; Stanton to Commanding Generals, Division of the Mississippi and Departments of the Gulf, South, Virginia, and North Carolina, January 14, 1864, Edwin M. Stanton Papers.

CHAPTER XII

1. *Official Records,* XXXV, Part I, Series I, 279.
2. Coulter, p. 357.
3. *Official Records,* XXXV, Part II, Series I, 392-96.
4. The *Herald,* of course, knew nothing of the Federal defeat when the article was written.
5. Randall, *The Civil War and Reconstruction,* pp. 607-10.
6. House of Representatives, *Executive Documents, 38th Congress, 2nd Session, Document No. 18,* p. 3; Smith, *"Carpetbag Imperialism,"* pp. 110-12.
7. Stickney to Chase, December 11, 1863, Salmon P. Chase Papers.
8. *Official Records,* XXXV, Part II, Series I, 276-77.
9. January 13, 1864, Robert Todd Lincoln Papers.
10. January 21, 1864, Lincoln Papers.

11. *Official Records,* XXXV, Part I, Series I, 279.
12. Stickney to Chase, January 26, 1864, Chase Papers.
13. February 5, 1864, Chase Papers.
14. Lincoln Papers.
15. *Official Records,* XXXV, Part I, 280-81.
16. *Ibid.,* p. 281.
17. *Ibid.,* p. 336.
18. Clark, *The Iron Hearted Regiment,* pp. 73-74.
19. *Official Records,* XXXV, Part I, Series I, 281.
20. *Ibid.,* pp. 281-96.
21. *Ibid.,* pp. 321-22.
22. Norton, *Army Letters 1861-1865,* p. 101.
23. Keen, p. 20.
24. *Official Records,* XXXV, Part I, Series I, 619.
25. *Ibid.,* p. 296.
26. *Ibid.,* p. 331.
27. *Ibid.,* p. 298.
28. *Ibid.,* p. 288.
29. *Ibid.,* pp. 338-39.
30. *Ibid.,* pp. 331, 352, 338, 343. The best secondary account of Olustee is Mark F. Boyd, "The Federal Campaign of 1864 in East Florida," pp. 3-37.
31. See detailed battle maps in Boyd, Appendix A.
32. *Ibid.,* p. 28; *Official Records,* XXXV, Part I, Series I, 302.
33. *Ibid.,* p. 337.
34. *Ibid.,* p. 298.
35. *Jacksonville Peninsula,* April 7, 1864.
36. *Official Records,* XXXV, Part I, Series I, 342-43.
37. *Ibid.,* p. 338.
38. Florida *Acts* (1864), Resolutions, p. 39.
39. Long, p. 365.
40. *New York Daily Tribune,* February 29, 1864; *New York Times,* March 7, 1864; *New York Herald,* February 28, 1864.
41. Tyler Dennett in Hay, *Lincoln and the Civil War in the Diaries and Letters of John Hay,* pp. 161-65.
42. Chase Papers.
43. *House Document No. 18,* p. 15; Stickney to Chase, March 16, 1864, Chase Papers.
44. *New York Daily Tribune,* June 3, 1864.
45. *New York Times,* June 9, 1864.

CHAPTER XIII

1. *Official Records,* XXXV, Part I, Series I, 368.
2. *Ibid.,* 371-72.
3. Ibid., pp. 645-46.
4. Florida *Senate Journal* (1862), p. 234.
5. *Official Records,* XIV, Series I, 846.
6. Florida *Senate Journal* (1864), pp. 15-16.

7. Milton to Davis, November 13, 1864, Milton Letterbook.
8. Seddon to Milton, October 1, 1864, Milton Letterbook.
9. Florida *Senate Journal* (1864), pp. 16-17.
10. Florida *Acts* (1864), pp. 10-13.
11. For details of these raids see *Official Records,* XXXV, Part I, Series I, 373-440, 495-98; XLVII, Part II, Series I, 166, 392; XLIX, Part I, Series I, 40-65.
12. *Official Records,* XLIX, Part I, Series I, 57.
13. *Ibid.,* Part II, Series I, 1135.
14. Keen, p. 31.
15. *Official Records,* XLIX, Part II, Series I, 1134-35.
16. *Ibid.,* pp. 1135-36.
17. *Ibid.,* Part I, Series I, 67.
18. Eppes, pp. 262-63.
19. *Ibid.,* p. 261.
20. *Lake City Columbian,* March 22, 1865.
21. Unidentified newspaper article, *Official Records,* XLIX, Part I, Series I, 64.
22. Richardson, p. 179.
23. Quoted in the *Lake City Columbian,* April 5, 1865; *Florida Union,* April 14, 1865; see also *Official Records,* VIII, Series II, 769. There are other versions of Milton's death:
(1) Cash, *The Story of Florida,* I, 458, states that Milton hung himself.
(2) Mrs. John Hardin Carter, granddaughter of Milton, in a signed and witnessed letter quoted in Gammon, says that Milton accidentally killed himself.
(3) Gammon, p. 270, says that many residents of Jackson County swear that Milton did not kill himself but fled from the state.
24. Allison to Davis, April 7, 1865, Milton Letterbook.
25. Long, p. 377.
26. Broadside by General Jones, W. M. L'Engle Papers.
27. Francis L'Engle to Edward M. L'Engle, April 29, 1865, E. M. L'Engle Papers.
28. *Official Records,* XLVII, Part III, Series I, 819.
29. *Ibid.,* p. 855.
30. *Official Records,* XLVII, Part III, Series I, 318-20.
31. *Ibid.,* p. 419
32. *Ibid.,* p. 28; *Official Records,* XXXV, Part I, Series I, 302.
33. *Ibid.,* p. 485. 34. *Ibid.,* XLIX, Part II, Series I, 601.
35. *Ibid.,* XLVII, Part III, Series I, 649. By "Superior Authority" Vogdes meant a superior to William T. Sherman. He contended that his authority came from Sherman.
36. *Ibid.,* XLIX, Part II, Series I, 602.
37. Unsigned 1866 memorandum, Yulee Papers; *Official Records,* XLIX, Part II, Series I, 943-45; Long, pp. 380-81.
38. *Official Records,* XLIX, Part II, Series I, 747, 944.
39. *Florida Union,* May 27, 1865. Mrs. Ellen Call Long gives a different version. She says only "Yankees & Negroes" watched the ceremony and that two hundred guns were fired in celebration, p. 381.
40. *Official Records,* XLIX, Part II, Series I, 984. The surrender schedule was as follows: Tampa, May 27; Bronson area, June 5; Bay Port area, June 5; Brooksville, June 8; and Lake City and the Baldwin area, about May 20.

41. *Official Records,* XLIX, Part II, Series I, 944.
42. *Ibid.,* p. 73.
43. *Florida Union,* May 27, 1865.
44. *Official Records,* XLVII, Part III, Series I, 498.
45. Allison to Yulee, May 12, 1865, Milton Letterbook.
46. *Official Records,* XLIX, Part II, Series I, 748.
47. May 12, 1865, Milton Letterbook.
48. *Official Records,* XLVII, Part III, Series I, 498-99. General Order, No. 63, May 14, 1862, also applied to Governor A. G. Magrath of South Carolina and Governor Joseph E. Brown of Georgia.
49. *Official Records,* XLVII, Part III, Series I, 538.
50. Allison to Yulee, May 19, 1865, Milton Letterbook.
51. *Official Records,* XLVII, Part III, Series I, 538.
52. *Ibid.,* p. 597.
53. *Official Records,* XLVII, Part III, Series I, 581.
54. *Official Records,* VIII, Series II, 729, 870, 895.
55. Richardson, pp. 179-83.
56. *Official Records,* XLIX, Part II, Series I, 862.
57. *Ibid.,* XLVII, Part III, Series I, 623.
58. *Florida Union,* May 27, 1865.
59. *Ibid.,* Long, p. 381.
60. *Florida Union,* May 27, 1865.
61. Long, p. 381.
62. *Florida Union,* May 27, 1865.
63. Long, p. 382.
64. Robertson, pp. 35-338. W. W. Davis, pp. 322, 324, also used Robertson as it is the only work available at the present time on the subject. My conclusion agrees with Davis, as anyone who uses Robertson must agree with the figure of 14,000 to 15,000. I believe this figure is too high by at least 1,000. However, immediately comes debate over the meaning of the terms "Confederate service," and "Militia." This author feels they are separate and distinct. Robertson lists a total of 12,792 infantry, 3,688 cavalry, and 626 artillery for a total of 17,106. Both Davis and I agree this is an exaggeration caused by duplication.
65. Robertson, pp. 79, 136.
66. See casualty columns in Robertson, pp. 35-388, and Davis, p. 323.
67. House of Representatives, *Committee Reports, 42nd Congerss, 2nd Session, 1871-1872. Report No. 22, Part I,* pp. 161-62.

BIBLIOGRAPHY

A. PRIMARY SOURCES

I. Manuscripts

William S. Allen Letter, 1862. A Civil War letter from the United States District Attorney for Florida which includes an excellent description of occupied Key West. P. K. Yonge Library of Florida History, University of Florida.

James B. Bailey Papers, 1847-1885. 200 items. Personal and business correspondence of Bailey, soldier, planter, and lawyer of Fort Clark, Florida, revealing social and economic conditions in Florida, attitudes toward Lincoln, and the problem of supplies for soldiers. The collection contains a few letters to Bailey which describe life in the army. Southern Historical Collection, University of North Carolina.

Jesse Bernard Diary, October 27, 1856-December (no date), 1861. There are also entries for September, 1883, January, 1884, and October, 1891. This diary is excellent on conditions in Florida during 1860-1861. Southern Historical Collection, University of North Carolina.

Overton Bernard Diary, 1858-1863. Written at Portsmouth, Virginia. Bernard had children in Florida and refers to them and their letters often. Good on social conditions within Florida, 1858-1863. Southern Historical Collection, University of North Carolina.

Eli Whitney Bonney Papers. 10 items. Long and interesting letters from C. L. Bonney to his father. These letters describe conditions at Ft. McRee, near Pensacola, from April until September, 1861. Manuscript Division, Duke University Library.

William H. Branch Papers, 1784-1919. 4,029 items. Folders 8-10 cover 1860-1866. Family, military, and political correspondence of William Horton Branch. They also contain papers of John Branch. Southern Historical Collection, University of North Carolina.

Theodore Washington Brevard Papers, 1821-1892. Number of items not yet compiled. 5 folders. The papers of 1861-1865 contain family news, war talk, possibility of becoming refugees, medical discharges, and general correspondence. Southern Historical Collection, University of North Carolina.

Lucy Wood Butler Papers and Diary, 1859-1863. Correspondence of Lucy Wood and Waddy Butler. Most of Butler's letters were written from Fernandina, Florida, prior to July 3, 1861. Southern Historical Collection, University of North Carolina.

Salmon P. Chase Papers, 1755-1874. Series I contains 108 volumes, 1755-1872. Series II contains 4 volumes, 1849-1873, and 20 boxes of miscellaneous papers. These papers include notes, letterbooks, diaries, journals, correspondence and newspaper clippings. Manuscripts Division, Library of Congress.

Clement Claiborne Clay Papers, 1811-1925. 8,515 items. Personal, business, and political correspondence, accounts, diaries, memoranda, college notes, scrapbooks, and newspaper clippings of Clement Claiborne Clay. Items of particular interest to Florida during the Civil War are two letters of Nannie C. Yulee to Virginia C. Clay which describe life on the Homasassa plantation of her husband, David Levy Yulee. Manuscripts Division, Duke University Library.

Comptroller's Letterbook, 1854-1867. This letterbook consists entirely of letters to and from the Comptroller of the State of Florida. 482 pages of the book are concerned with the Civil War period. Very valuable for an insight into the local governmental situation. Florida State Library, Tallahassee.

Comptroller's Letterbook-Letters Received, 1860-1865. A library letterbox of letters received by the Comptroller and divided into years 1860, 1861, 1862-1865. Approximately 350 letters on all subjects relating to Comptroller's office. Florida State Library, Tallahassee.

Confederate Letters, Florida State Library, Tallahassee.

Confederate States of America, Archives. Army. Florida. 9 items. Contains the 1864 muster rolls and payrolls of the 8th Regiment of Florida Volunteers. Manuscripts Division, Duke University Library.

Confederate States of America, Archives. Florida Hospital Reports. 13 items. Information about the hospital at Camp Simkins near New Port, Florida, for 1863-1864. Manuscripts Division, Duke University Library.

Confederate States Papers, 1861-1865. Papers of the Confederate States of America, including material relative to the Confederate State Department. The collection is composed chiefly of the "Pickett Papers" but includes items from the Confederate War, Navy, Judiciary, Treasury, Post Office and Executive departments as well as much miscellaneous material. Manuscripts Division, Library of Congress.

John A. Cromartie Papers, 1837-1865. 74 items. Cromartie wrote interesting and informative letters about his experiences in the Florida Camps of Instruction, the life of a combat soldier, and, after his capture, of his experiences as a prisoner of war. Florida State Library, Tallahassee.

Jefferson Davis Papers, 1861-1913. 40 items. These papers contain items which mostly pertain to Davis or his family after the war. There are a few unpublished letters of Davis' written during the war, but most of the contents for 1861-1865 are available in printed collections. Manuscripts Division, Library of Congress.

Jefferson Davis Papers, 1851 (1861-1865) 1890. 614 items. Personal and official correspondence of Jefferson Davis. The bulk of the material relates to the era of the Civil War. Manuscripts Division, Duke University Library.

Allen Turner Davidson Papers. 3 items. Three letters describing conditions in Fernandina, Florida, during April, 1861. Southern Historical Collection, University of North Carolina.

J. E. A. Davidson Papers. 150 items. The collection contains items of personal and official correspondence. The correspondence between Davidson, Medical Purveyor for Florida, and the Confederate States Surgeon General is especially useful. P. K. Yonge Library of Florida History, University of Florida.

Mrs. R. M. Davidson Letters. 3 items. Typed copies of three long newsy letters from the camps near Pensacola. The original letters belong to Mrs. R. M. Davidson, Quincy, Florida. P. K. Yonge Library of Florida History, University of Florida.

Charles M. Duren Letters. 17 items. Letters from a Union officer at Jacksonville in 1864. These letters deal with personal matters as well as the military activities in East Florida. P. K. Yonge Library of Florida History, University of Florida.

Nicholas Ware Eppes Papers, 1846-1887. Five family letters. Southern Historical Collection, University of North Carolina.

Julia Johnson Fisher Diary, 1864. A typed copy of a diary kept between January and August, 1864. The diary contains excellent descriptions of the hardships suffered by residents of Southeast Georgia and Northeast Florida. Southern Historical Collection, University of North Carolina.

Fleming Papers. 153 items. Collection contains correspondence concerning family and military affairs. The material is uncalendared but is arranged chronologically. Southern Historical Collection, University of North Carolina.

Hentz Diary. Typed copy of a diary kept by Doctor Hentz, a dentist, from May 3-31, 1863, while he lived at Quincy, Florida. The original diary belongs to J. D. Smith, Marianna, Florida. P. K. Yonge Library of Florida History, University of Florida.

Edward M. L'Engle Papers, 1834-1897. 5,140 items. Folders 5-7 cover the period 1859-1866. The collection consists chiefly of business, legal, and personal correspondence with members of the L'Engle family as well as many of the leading political personalities of the era. The collection is especially valuable for a description of conditions within East Florida during the war. The most valuable document in the collection is the broadside of April 28, 1865, from Samuel Jones to his troops which dealt with Lee's surrender. Southern Historical Collection, University of North Carolina.

William Johnson L'Engle Papers. Sporadic correspondence between L'Engle, a physician, and his wife, 1853 to 1863. P. K. Yonge Library of Florida History, University of Florida.

Robert Todd Lincoln Collection, 1860-1865. Number of items not yet compiled. These papers are the principal portion of the Lincoln Collection. They consist of correspondence, memoranda, and other miscellaneous materials of both an official and a personal nature. Manuscripts Division, Library of Congress.

James H. Linsley Diary. 2 volumes. Civil War diary of an officer of the 10th Connecticut Volunteers. P. K. Yonge Library of Florida History, University of Florida.

Stephen R. Mallory Diary. 2 volumes. Diary and autobiographical sketch of Stephen R. Mallory. Southern Historical Collection, University of North Carolina.

Stephen R. Mallory Letters, 1862. Ten letters to his wife during June-August, 1862. P. K. Yonge Library of Florida History, University of Florida.

Jacob E. Mickler Papers. 225 items. The collection contains material on the Second Seminole Indian War and on the Civil War. Florida State Library, Tallahassee.

John Milton Letterbook, November 27, 1863-March 21, 1865. Official letterbook of Governor John Milton of Florida. The letterbook also contains the official correspondence of Governor A. K. Allison, April 7-May 9, 1865, and a record of the Common School Fund, 1850-1852. Florida State Library, Tallahassee.

John Milton Papers, 1861-1863. These papers contain the official letterbooks of Governor John Milton, 1861-1863, and other items such as telegrams, resolutions, and other correspondence. Florida Historical Society Library, University of South Florida.

Alonzo B. Noyes Papers, 1859-1865. 250 items. These papers contain both personal and official correspondence. The accounts of Noyes as Collector of Customs at St. Marks, 1859-1865, and his vouchers as Confederate Disbursing Agent are of significant value. P. K. Yonge Library of Florida History, University of Florida.

Alonzo B. Noyes Papers, 1859-1861. Number of items not yet compiled. Official correspondence of Noyes as United States Collector of Customs at St. Marks, Florida. Southern Historical Collection, University of North Carolina.

Opinions of the Attorney General of the State of Florida, January 3, 1859-May 22, 1886. 85 pages of this bound letterbook contain the opinions of the Attorney General during the Civil War. Florida State Library, Tallahassee.

John Parkhill Papers, 1813-1891. Number of items not yet compiled. Correspondence and other papers of John Parkhill, Tallahassee banker; of his son, George Washington Parkhill, physician, legislator, and Confederate captain; of his daughter Harriet, and of his other children and grandchildren. Southern Historical Collection, University of North Carolina.

Madison Starke Perry Papers. Assorted letters, memoranda, and other items covering the years 1850-1861. P. K. Yonge Library of Florida History, University of Florida.

James J. Philips Papers, II, 1857-1870. 45 items. Letters from Ethelred Philips, physician and planter of Marianna, Florida, to his cousin. The letters are very valuable as they express Union sentiments and reactions to secession and the war. Southern Historical Collection, University of North Carolina.

Michael O. Razor Civil War Letters. Fifty letters written during the war period to his wife. P. K. Yonge Library of Florida History, University of Florida.

A. M. Reed Diary, 1848-1899. Typed copy of a diary owned by Mrs. J. Reed Pierson, 1275 Ortega Boulevard, Jacksonville, Florida. P. K. Yonge Library of Florida History, University of Florida.

Records of the Confederate States Government, 1861-1865. Number of items not yet compiled. This title covers a mass of material from all phases of the government of the Confederate States of America. Included in the collection are letterbooks, official orders, and other documents related to the conduct of a government. Of particular interest to the student of Florida during the Civil War are the Records of the Departments of South Carolina, Georgia, and Florida, Records of the Engineer Department, Records of the Army of Pensacola, and the Papers of General Sam Jones, 1861-1864. Old Army Section, National Archives.

Edward C. F. Sanchez Papers. Number of items not yet compiled. These papers contain written statements by some of the early settlers of Gainesville, Florida, and a rough draft of a history of that town from its founding through the Civil War. Also included are newspaper clippings on early Florida history and several old maps. P. K. Yonge Library of Florida History, University of Florida.

Edmund Kirby Smith Papers, 1776-1906. 2,070 items. Correspondence of Smith, United States Army officer, Confederate general, and college professor, dealing with his personal affairs, military career, flight to Mexico and Cuba in 1865, and later life at the University of Nashville and the University of the South. Of special interest are about 20 letters from his mother describing life in Union-held St. Augustine and later as a refugee inland. Southern Historical Collection, University of North Carolina.

Edwin McMasters Stanton Papers, 1831-1870. 38 volumes and 14 boxes. These papers consist chiefly of dated and undated correspondence with prominent figures predominately during the period 1861-1865. Also included are the Annual Report of 1863, the proceedings of the War Board in March, 1863, letterbooks, and other materials. Manuscripts Division, Library of Congress.

Charles Steedman Letters, 1862-1864. Civil War letters of a Union Naval Officer stationed off the coast of Florida, and, at times, Commander of the Federal gunboats on the St. Johns River. P. K. Yonge Library of Florida History, University of Florida.

Henry Summer Papers, 1861. A photostatic copy of a letter from Norman Bronson, August 6, 1861, describing life in Fernandina, Florida. A portion of the interesting letter is devoted to the blockade and blockade-running. Southern Historical Collection, University of North Carolina.

Swann Papers, 1784-1931. Number of items not yet compiled. These papers are in 13 folders, of which Numbers 6-10 are known as the Mary Martha Reid series and touch on Florida as Mrs. Reid was matron of the Florida Hospital in Richmond and corresponded with Florida officials. Southern Historical Collection, University of North Carolina.

Gideon Welles Papers, 1777-1911. 90 volumes and 25 boxes. This collection consists of correspondence, diary, record books, articles, scrapbooks, and miscellaneous items. Manuscripts Division, Library of Congress.

Chandler Cox Yonge Papers, 1860-1867. 750 items. This collection is uncalendared and nonchronological, but contains official and personal correspondence and many interesting miscellaneous items. The letterbook for 1864-1865 is of special interest for Yonge held the offices of Confederate States District Attorney and Chief Quartermaster for Florida. P. K. Yonge Library of Florida History, University of Florida.

David Levy Yulee Papers, 1830-1887. 8,000 items. These papers contain correspondence, newspaper clippings, memoranda, and miscellaneous material. Approximately 1,200 of the 8,000 items belong to the period 1860-1865. This collection is excellent for the reaction of a businessman to the internal conditions within Florida during the war. P. K. Yonge Library of Florida History, University of Florida.

II. Official Records

1. *National and State*

Acts and Resolutions of the General Assembly of the State of Florida, 1850-1865. Tallahassee: various publishers, 1850-1865.

Congressional Globe, 1860-1866. Washington: Congressional Globe Office, 1860-1866.

Constitution or Form of Government for the People of Florida, As Revised and Amended at a Convention of the People Begun and Holden at the City of Tallahassee on the Third Day of January, A.D. 1861, Together with the Ordinances Adopted by Said Convention. Tallahassee: Office of the *Floridian and Journal.* Printed by Dyke and Carlisle, 1861.

Constitution or Form of Government for the People of Florida As Revised and Amended at a Convention of the People Begun and Holden at the City of Tallahassee on the 3rd Day of January, A.D. 1861, and at a Called Session Thereof, Begun and Held January 14th, A.D. 1862, Together with the Ordinances Adopted by Said Called Session. N.p., 1862.

Eighth Census of The United States: 1860, 4 volumes. Washington: Government Printing Office, 1866.

Florida Executive Records, Office of Secretary of State, Tallahassee.

House of Representatives, *Committee Reports, 36th Congress, 2nd Session, 1860-1861.* Washington: Government Printing Office, 1861.

House of Representatives, *Committee Reports, 37th Congress, 3rd Session, Report No. 5.* Washington: Government Printing Office, 1863.

House of Representatives, *Committee Reports, 42nd Congress, 2nd Session, 1871-1872.* Washington: Government Printing Office, 1872.

House of Representatives, *Executive Documents, 36th Congress, 2nd Session, 1860-1861,* 11 volumes. Washington: Government Printing Office, 1861.

House of Representatives, *Executive Documents, 38th Congress, 2nd Session, Document No. 18.* Washington: Government Printing Office, 1865.

Journal of the Convention of Florida Begun and Held at The Capitol of the State, at Tallahassee, Wednesday, October 25, A.D. 1865. Tallahassee: Office of the *Floridian,* 1865.

Journal of the Convention of the People of Florida At a Called Session, Begun and Held at the Capitol, in the City of Tallahassee, on Tuesday, January 14, 1862. N.p., 1862.

Journal of the Proceedings of the Convention of the People of Florida, Begun and Held at the Capitol in the City of Tallahassee, on Thursday, January 3, A.D. 1861. Tallahassee: Printed at the Office of the *Floridian and Journal* by Dyke and Carlisle, 1861.

Journal of the Proceedings of the Convention of the People of Florida at a Called Session, Begun and Held at the Capitol in Tallahassee, on Tuesday, February 26th, and Thursday, April 18th, 1861. N.p., 1861.

Journal of the Proceedings of the House of Representatives of the General Assembly of the State of Florida, 1855-1865. Tallahassee: James S. Jones, Dyke and Carlisle, Dyke and Sparhawk, and other publishers, 1855-1866.

Journal of the Proceedings of the Senate of the General Assembly of the State of Florida, 1855-1865. Tallahassee: Bibley and Dyke, Hart and Barefoot, and Edwin A. Hart. 1855-1866.

Martial Law Circular, Confederate States Army at Pensacola, March 31, 1862. An original circular located at the P. K. Yonge Library of Florida History, University of Florida.

Minutes of the Proceedings of the Executive Council. Tallahassee: Florida *Sentinel* Office, 1862.

Official Records of the Union and Confederate Navies in the War of the Rebellion, 30 volumes. Washington: Government Printing Office, 1894-1927.

Senate Report 38th Congress, 1st Session, Report No. 47. Washington: Government Printing Office, 1864.

Seventh Census of the United States: 1850. Washington: Government Printing Office, 1853-55.

Sheets, William N., *Biennial Report of the Superintendent of Public Instruction of the State of Florida for the two years ending June 30, 1894.* Tallahassee: John G. Collins, State Printer, 1895.

Statutes at Large of the Confederate States of America. Richmond: R. M. Smith, 1863-1864.

The Statutes at Large of the Provisional Government of the Confederate States of America, from the Institution of The Government, February 8, 1861, to its Termination, February 18, 1862, inclusive. Richmond: R. M. Smith, 1864.

Supplemental Report of the Joint Committee on the Conduct of the War, 2 volumes. Washington: Government Printing Office, 1866.

The War of the Rebellion: A Compilation of the Official Records of the Union and Confederate Armies, 128 volumes. Washington: Government Printing Office, 1880-1901.

2. *Church*

Journal of the Baptist Convention of the State of Florida Held at Monticello, Florida, Friday, November 23rd, 1860. N.p., 1860.

Journals of the Proceedings of the Annual Conventions of the Protestant Episcopal Church in the State of Florida, 1860-1867. Various locations of publication and of publishers, 1861-1867.

Minutes of the Annual Conferences of the Methodist Episcopal Church, South, 1860-1865. Nashville: Publishing House, Methodist Episcopal Church, South, 1860-1866.

Proceedings of the Ninth Biennial Session of the Southern Baptist Convention, Held in the Green Street Baptist Church, Augusta, Georgia, May 8th, 9th, 10th, 11th, and 12th, 1863. Macon, Georgia: Printed by Burke, Boykin and Company, 1863.

Proceedings of the Southern Baptist Convention at Its Eighth Biennial Session, Held in the First Baptist Church, Savannah, Georgia, May 10th, 11th, 12th and 13th, 1861. Richmond: Macfarbane and Fergusson, 1861.

III. Newspapers and Periodicals

Cedar Key Telegraph, 1860
East Floridian (Fernandina), 1860.
Fernandina Peninsula, 1863.
Gainesville Cotton States, 1864.
Gainesville Sun, 1861.
Florida Times-Union (Jacksonville), 1893.
Florida Union (Jacksonville), 1865.
Jacksonville Herald, 1865.
Jacksonville Peninsula, 1864.
St. Johns Mirror (Jacksonville), 1861.
Jacksonville Standard, 1860.
Key of the Gulf (Key West), 1860.
Key West New Era, 1862.
Lake City Columbian, 1865.
The Nation, I-IV. New York, 1865-1867.
New York Daily Tribune, 1864.
New York Herald, 1861-1865.
New York Times, 1861-1865.
New York World, 1863.
Florida Home Companion (Ocala), 1860.
Gulf Beach News (Pass-A-Grille), 1943.
Pensacola Gazette, 1861. (Single issue.)
Quincy Semi-Weekly Dispatch, 1862-1865. (Scattered issues.)
St. Augustine Examiner, 1860-1865. (Scattered issues.)
Floridian and Journal (Tallahassee), 1860-1862. (Scattered issues.)
Florida Sentinel (Tallahassee), 1852, 1854, 1862-63.
Florida Peninsula (Tampa), 1861.

IV. Miscellaneous Contemporary Writings

Abbey, Katherine T., "Documents Relating to El Destino and Chemonie Plantations, Middle Florida, 1828-1868," Part III, *Florida Historical Quarterly,* VIII (July, 1929), 3-46.

BOYD, William K., ed., *Military Reminiscences of General Wm. R. Boggs, C.S.A.* The John Lawson Monographs of The Trinity College Historical Society, III, Durham: The Seeman Printery, 1913.

CALL, Richard Keith, *An Address To The People of Florida, From Gen. R. K. Call, December 1, 1860.* Tallahassee: N.p., 1860.

Union-Slavery-Secession. Letter from Governor R. K. Call, of Florida, To John S. Littell, of Germantown, Pennsylvania. Philadelphia: C. Sherman and Sons, 1861.

COLEY, Maggie Crary, "Civil War Reminiscences of Escambia County." A bound manuscript, P. K. Yonge Library of Florida History, University of Florida.

COX, Samuel S., *Three Decades of Federal Legislation, 1855 to 1885. Personal and Historical Memories of Events Preceding, During, and Since The American Civil War, Involving Slavery and Secession, Emancipation and Reconstruction, with Sketches of Prominent Actors During These Periods.* Providence: J. A. and R. A. Reid, Publishers, 1886.

DODD, Dorothy, ed., "Volunteers Report Destruction of Lighthouses," *Tequesta,* XIX (1954), 67-71.

______,"Edmund Ruffin's Account of The Florida Secession Convention, 1861. A Diary," *Florida Historical Quarterly,* XII (October, 1933), 67-76.

ERBEN, Henry, "Surrender of the Navy Yard at Pensacola, Florida, January 12, 1861," *Personal Recollections of The War of The Rebellion. Addresses Delivered Before The Commandry of The State of New York, Military Order of the Loyal Legion of The United States.* Edited by A. Noel Blakeman. New York: The Knickerbocker Press, 1897.

FLEMING, Francis, *Memoir of Capt. C. Seaton Fleming, of the Second Florida Infantry, C. S. A. Illustrative of the History of the Florida Troops in Virginia During the War Between The States. With Appendix of the Casualties.* Jacksonville: Times-Union Publishing House, 1884.

GORDON, George H., *A War Diary of Events In The Great Rebellion, 1863-1865.* Boston: Houghton Mifflin and Company, 1885.

GRAY, John Chipman and John Codman Ropes, *War Letters, 1862-1865.* Boston: Houghton Mifflin Company, 1927.

HAY, John, *Lincoln and the Civil War in the Diaries and Letters of John Hay; Selected and With an Introduction by Tyler Dennett.* New York: Dodd, Mead and Company, 1939.

HOPLEY, Catherine Cooper, *Life in the South; From the Commencement of the War. Being a Social History of Those Who Took Part in the Battle, From a Personal Acquaintance with Them in Their Own Homes. Spring, 1860 to August, 1862,* 2 volumes. London: Chapman and Hall, 1863.

JOHNSON, John Orville, " William Conway, A Forgotten Camden Hero." *War Papers Read Before The Commandry of The State of Maine, Military Order of The Loyal Legion of The United States,* 4 volumes. (Portland: Lefavor-Tower Company, 1908) III, 25-67.

JONES, Charles C., *The Evacuation of Battery Wagner, And the Battle of Ocean Pond. An Address Delivered Before The Confederate Survivors Association In Augusta, Georgia, on The Occasion of Its Tenth Annual Reunion on Memorial Day, April 26, 1888.* Augusta: Chronicle Publishing Company, 1888.

KELSEY, Albert Warren, *Autobiographical Notes And Memoranda.* Baltimore: Munder-Thomsen Press, 1911.

LEE, Edmund C., "Civil War Letters," Unpublished typed copy, Florida Historical Records Survey. 1937.

L'ENGLE, Gertrude Nelson, and Katherine Tracy L'Engle, eds., *Letters of William Johnson L'Engle, M.D., and Madeleine Saunders L'Engle, his Wife. 1843-1863.* N.p.: privately published, 1948.

MACFARLANE, C., *Reminiscences of An Army Surgeon.* Oswego: Lake City Print Shop, 1912.

MORGAN, James Morris, *Recollections of A Rebel Reefer.* New York: Houghton Mifflin Company, 1917.

MOORE, John Bassett, ed., *Works of James Buchanan Comprising his Speeches, State Papers, and Private Correspondence.* 12 volumes. Philadelphia: J. B. Lippincott and Company, 1908-11.

MOORE, Frank, ed., *The Rebellion Record; A Diary of American Events, With Documents, Narratives, Illustrative Incidents, Poetry, Etc; With An Introductory Address by Edward Everett,* 11 volumes. New York: G. P. Putman's Sons, 1861-1868.

NORTON, Oliver Wilcox, *Army Letters 1861-1865. Being Extracts From Private Letters To Relatives And Friends From A Soldier In The Field During The Late Civil War, With An Appendix Containing Copies of Some Official Documents, Papers, and Addresses of Later Date.* Chicago: O. L. Deming, 1903.

PORTER, David Dixon, *Incidents and Anecdotes of The Civil War.* New York: D. Appleton and Company, 1885.

RUSSELL, William Howard, *My Diary North and South.* New York: Harper and Brothers, 1863.

SCHELLINGS, William J., ed., "Blockade Duty On The Florida Coast, Excerpts From A Union Naval Officer's Diary," *Tequesta,* XV (1955), 55-72.

TENNEY, John Francis, *Slavery, Secession And Success. The Memoirs of A Florida Pioneer.* San Antonio: Southern Literary Institute, 1934.

VENDETTA, *Four Letters Addressed To His Excellency, Jefferson Davis, In Vindication of Captain Randolph, C.S.N.* N.p.: privately published, 1861.

WILLIAMS, Ben Ames, ed., Mary Boykin Chesnut, *A Diary From Dixie.* Boston: Houghton Mifflin Company, 1949.

YONGE, Julien C., ed., "The Occupation of Jacksonville, February 1864 And The Battle of Olustee. Letters of Lt. C. M. Duren, 54th Massachusetts Regiment, U.S.A.," *The Florida Historical Quarterly,* XXXII (January, 1954), 262-87.

B. SECONDARY SOURCES

I. GENERAL HISTORIES

ABBOTT, John Stevens Cabot, *The History of the Civil War in America,* 2 volumes. Norwich: Henry Bill Publishing Company, 1873.

COULTER, Ellis Merton, *The Confederate States of America* (Volume VII, Wendell Holmes Stephenson and Ellis Merton Coulter, eds., *A History of the South*). Baton Rouge: Louisiana State University Press, 1952.

DABNEY, Charles William, *Universal Education in the South, From the Beginning to 1900,* 2 volumes. Chapel Hill: The University of North Carolina Press, 1936.

LOSSING, Benson John, *Pictorial History of the Civil War in the United States of America,* 3 volumes. Hartford: Thomas Belknap, 1877.

NICOLAY, John G., and John Hay, *Abraham Lincoln; A History,* 10 volumes. New York: The Century Company, 1890.

POLLARD, Edward Albert, *Southern History of the War.* New York: Charles B. Richardson, 1866.

RANDALL, James Garfield, *The Civil War and Reconstruction.* New York: D. C. Heath and Company, 1937.

RHODES, James Ford, *History of the United States from the Compromise of 1850,* 9 volumes. New York: The Macmillan Company, 1900-1928.

SCHWAB, John Christopher, *Confederate States of America, 1861-1865; A Financial and Industrial History of the South During the Civil War.* New Haven: Yale University Press, 1913.

II. State and Local Histories

ABBEY, Kathryn Trimmer, *Florida Land of Change.* Chapel Hill: University of North Carolina Press, 1941.

BREVARD, Caroline Mays, *A History of Florida from the Treaty of 1763 to Our Own Times,* 2 volumes. Edited by James Alexander Robertson. New York: William Erwin Rudge, 1925.

BRISTOL, Lucius Moody, *Three Focal Points in the Development of Florida's State System of Higher Education.* Gainesville: Campus Shop and Bookstore, 1953.

BROWNE, Jefferson Beale, *Key West, the Old and the New.* St. Augustine: The Record Company, 1912.

BROWNING, Edwin B., *The Early History of Concord Missionary Baptist Church, 1841-1868.* Madison: Madison County Historical Society, 1946.

BUSH, George Gary, *History of Education in Florida.* Washington: Government Printing Office, 1889.

CARROLL, Mary Teresa Austin, Mother, *A Catholic History of Alabama and the Floridas,* 2 volumes. New York: P. J. Kennedy and Sons, 1908.

CASH, William Thomas, *The Story of Florida,* 4 volumes. New York: The American Historical Society, 1938.

_________, "Taylor County History and Civil War Deserters," *Florida Historical Quarterly,* XXVII (July, 1948), 28-58.

Centennial Booklet of the First Presbyterian Church, Jacksonville, Florida, 1840-1940. Jacksonville: Tutwiller Press, 1940.

Centennial of the Presbyterian Church of St. Augustine and The Coming of the Presbyterian Church to Florida. St. Augustine: The Record Company, 1927.

COCHRAN, Thomas Everett, *History of Public School Education in Florida.* Lancaster: The New Era Printing Company, 1921.

DAVIS, Thomas Frederick, *A History of Jacksonville, Florida, and Vicinity, 1513 to 1924.* St. Augustine: The Florida Historical Society, 1925.

_________, *History of Early Jacksonville, Florida; Being an Authentic Record of Events from the Earliest Times to and Including the Civil War.* Jacksonville: The H. and W. B. Drew Company, 1911.

DODD, Dorothy, *Florida Becomes a State.* Tallahassee: Florida Centennial Commission, 1945.

DODD, William George, "Early Education in Tallahassee and the West Florida Seminary now Florida State University," *Florida Historical Quarterly,* XXVII (July, 1948), 1-27; XXVII (October, 1948), 156-80.

_________, *History of the West Florida Seminary.* Tallahassee: Florida State University Press, 1952.

DOVELL, Junius Elmore, *Florida, Historic, Dramatic, Contemporary,* 4 volumes. New York: Lewis Historical Publishing Company, 1952.

EAST, Omega G., "St. Augustine During the Civil War," *Florida Historical Quarterly*, XXXI (October, 1952), 75-91.

EPPES, Susan Bradford, *Through Some Eventful Years*. Macon: The J. W. Burke Company, 1926.

FOSTER, George A., *The Methodist Church in Ocala, Florida, 1844-1953*. Ocala: *Ocala Star-Banner*, 1953.

GOLD, Pleasant Daniel, *History of Volusia County*. DeLand: E. O. Painter Printing Company, 1927.

GRISMER, Karl, *The Story of Fort Myers: The History of the Land of the Caloosahatchee and Southwest Florida*. St. Petersburg: St. Petersburg Printing Company, 1949.

HEBEL, Ianthe Bond, ed., *Centennial History of Volusia County, Florida, 1854-1954*. Daytona Beach: Volusia County Historical Commission, 1955.

HETHERINGTON, M. F., *History of Polk County Florida*. St. Augustine: The Record Company, 1928.

History of the First Methodist Episcopal Church, South [Tampa] From 1846 to 1883 and Record of Quarterly Conference from 1883 to 1937. Tampa: Historical Records Survey, Works Progress Administration, 1938.

HOSKINS, F. W., *History of Methodism in Pensacola, Florida, Its Rise and Progress*. Nashville: Publishing House, Methodist Episcopal Church, South, 1928.

KEEN, Mary W., "Some Phases of Life in Leon County During The Civil War." *Tallahassee Historical Society Annual*, IV (1939), 20-47.

LEY, John C., *Fifty-Two Years in Florida*. Nashville: Publishing House of the Methodist Episcopal Church, South, 1899.

LONG, Ellen Call, *Florida Breezes or Florida New and Old*. Jacksonville: Ashmead Bros., 1883. (Facsimile Reproduction of the 1883 Edition, Gainesville: University of Florida Press, 1962.)

MCDUFFEE, Lillie B., *The Lures of Manatee. A True Story of South Florida's Glamourous Past*. Nashville: Marshall and Bruce Company, 1933.

MCILWAIN, William, *The Early Planting of Presbyterianism in West Florida*. Pensacola: printed privately, 1926.

MCKINNON, John L., *History of Walton County*. Atlanta: The Byrd Printing Company, 1911.

MARTIN, Sidney Walter, *Florida During the Territorial Days*. Athens: University of Georgia Press, 1944.

MERRITT, Webster, *A Century of Medicine in Jacksonville and Duval County*. Gainesville: University of Florida Press, 1949.

PASCO, Samuel, "Jefferson County, Florida, 1827-1910," *Florida Historical Quarterly*, VII (October, 1928), 139-54; VII (January, 1929), 234-57.

PATRICK, Rembert Wallace, *Florida Under Five Flags*. Gainesville: University of Florida Press, 1945.

PENNINGTON, Edgar Legare, "The Episcopal Church in Florida, 1763-1892," *Historical Magazine of the Protestant Episcopal Church*, VII (March, 1938), 1-77.

PIERCE, Albert W., *From Coquina Beach to Coral Strand, a Sketch of the Progress of the Presbyterian Church, U. S. A., in Florida from 1824 to 1927*. Jacksonville: Hall Brothers, 1927.

PYBURN, Nita Katharine, *Documentary History of Education in Florida 1822-1860*. Tallahassee: Florida State University Press, 1951.

———, *The History of the Development of a Single System of Education in Florida, 1822-1903*. Tallahassee: Florida State University Press, 1954.

RERICK, Rowland H., *Memoirs of Florida, Embracing a General History of the Province, Territory and State; and Special Chapters Devoted to Finances, Banking, the Bench, and the Bar,* 2 volumes. Edited by Francis P. Fleming. Atlanta: Southern Historical Association, 1902.

ROSSER, John Leonidas, *A History of Florida Baptists.* Nashville: Broadman Press, 1949.

ROTH, Benedict, O. S. B., ed., *Brief History of the Churches of the Diocese of St. Augustine Florida.* Saint Leo: Abby Press, 1923.

SMITH, George G., Jr., *The History of Methodism in Georgia and Florida, From 1785 to 1865.* Macon: John W. Burke and Company, 1877.

STRAUB, W. L., *History of Pinellas County, Florida, Narrative and Biographical.* St. Augustine: The Record Company, 1929.

SWEET, Zeba Wilson, and J. C. Marsden, *New Smyrna, Florida, Its History and Antiquities.* DeLand: E. O. Painter Printing Company, 1925.

THRIFT, Charles Tinsley, *The Trail of the Florida Circuit Rider. An Introduction to the Rise of Methodism in Middle and East Florida.* Lakeland: Florida Southern College Press, 1944.

WARE, G. W. S., "Centenary of Providence Church on Olustee Creek, Union County, Florida." Typed copy of an original on file in the office of the Florida Baptist Convention, Florida Baptist Building, Jacksonville, Florida.

________, History of New River Church, Columbia County, Florida. Typed copy of an original whose location is unknown. P. K. Yonge Library of Florida History, University of Florida.

III. MONOGRAPHS AND SPECIAL STUDIES

BROWN, William Wells, *The Negro in the American Rebellion. His Heroism and His Fidelity.* Boston: Lee and Shepard, 1867.

CAUTHEN, Charles Edward, *South Carolina Goes to War, 1861-1865.* Chapel Hill: University of North Carolina Press, 1950.

CHASE, William H., *The Secession of the Cotton States; Its Status; Its Advantages, and Its Powers.* New York: New York Express, 1860.

CLARKE, Robert L., "Northern Plans for the Economic Invasion of Florida, 1862-1865," *Florida Historical Quarterly,* XXVIII (April, 1950), 262-70.

COLE, Arthur Charles, *The Whig Party in the South.* Baltimore: The Lord Baltimore Press, 1913.

DAVIS, William Watson, *The Civil War and Reconstruction in Florida.* New York: Columbia University Press, 1913.

DENNETT, Tyler, *Lincoln and the Civil War in the Diaries and Letters of John Hay.* New York: Dodd, Mead and Company, 1939.

DODD, Dorothy, "The Manufacture of Cotton in Florida before and during the Civil War," *Tallahassee Historical Society Annual,* II (1935), 1-8.

________, "The Secession Movement in Florida, 1850-1861," *Florida Historical Quarterly,* XII (July, 1933), 3-24; XII (October, 1933), 45-66.

________, "Some Florida Secession History," *Tallahassee Historical Society Annual,* III (1937), 1-7.

FUTCH, Ovid L., "Salmon P. Chase and Civil War Politics in Florida," *Florida Historical Quarterly,* XXXII (January, 1954), 163-88.

HARLOW, Ralph Volney, "The Rise and Fall of the Kansas Aid Movement," *The American Historical Review,* XLI (October, 1935), 1-25.

HARPER, Roland M., "Ante-Bellum Census Enumeration in Florida," *Florida Historical Quarterly,* VI (July, 1927), 41-52.

HAVARD, William C., "The Florida Executive Council, 1862," *Florida Historical Quarterly,* XXXIII (October, 1954), 77-96.

HOMANS, J. Smith, Jr., ed., "Bank Items," *The Bankers Magazine and Statistical Register,* XIII (May, 1959), 903.

LONN, Ella, *Salt as a Factor in the Confederacy.* New York: Walter Neale, 1933.

MCKEE, Thomas Hudson, *The National Convention and Platforms of All Political Parties, 1789 to 1900, Convention, Popular, and Electoral Vote.* Baltimore: The Friendenwald Company, 1900.

OVERDYKE, William Darrell, *The Know-Nothing Party in the South.* Baton Rouge: Louisiana State University Press, 1950.

PARKER, Daisy, "Governor John Milton," *Tallahassee Historical Society Annual,* III (1937), 14-21.

————, "John Milton, Governor of Florida. A Loyal Confederate," *Florida Historical Quarterly,* XX (April, 1942), 346-61.

PROCTOR, Samuel, "Early Jewish Settlements in Florida, 1764-1900." Manuscript in possession of the author, Gainesville, Florida.

RHODES, F. A., "Salt Making on the Apalachee Bay," *Tallahassee Historical Society Annual,* II (1935), 17-21.

RICHARDSON, Simon Peter, *The Lights and Shadows of Itinerant Life.* An Autobiography. Nashville: Publishing House of the Methodist Episcopal Church, South, 1900.

ROBERTSON, Fred L., compiler, *Soldiers of Florida in the Seminole Indian-Civil-and Spanish-American Wars.* Live Oak: Democrat Book and Job Print Company, 1903.

SHARP, Helen R., "Samuel A. Swann and the Development of Florida, 1855-1900," *Florida Historical Quarterly,* XX (October, 1941), 169-96.

SHEA, John Gilmary, *History of the Catholic Church in the United States,* 2 volumes. New York: John G. Shea, 1892.

SIMKINS, Francis Butler, and James Welch Patton, *The Women of the Confederacy.* Richmond: Garrett and Massie, 1936.

SMITH, George Winston, "Carpetbag Imperialism in Florida, 1862-1868," *Florida Historical Quarterly,* XXVII (October, 1948), 99-130; XXVII (January, 1949), 259-99.

THOMAS, David Y., "Florida Finance in the Civil War," *Yale Review,* XVI (November, 1907), 311.

THOMPSON, Arthur W., "Confederate Finance: A Documentary Study of a Proposal of David L. Yulee," *Florida Historical Quarterly,* XXX (October, 1951), 193-207.

————, "Political Nativism in Florida, 1848-1860: A Phase of Anti-Secessionism," *Journal of Southern History,* XV (February, 1949), 39-65.

WALKER, Norman, "The Southern Press," *The South in the Building of the Nation,* 13 volumes. Edited by Julian Alvin Carroll Chandler and Others (Richmond: The Southern Historical Publication Society, 1909), VII, 402-36.

WHITE, Laura A., "The Fate of Calhoun's Sovereign Convention in South Carolina," *American Historical Review,* XXXIV (July, 1929), 762.

(YONGE, Julian Chandler), "Ocala Prior to 1868," *Florida Historical Quarterly,* VI (October, 1927), 85-110.

YONGE, Julian Chandler, ed., "Secession in Florida, Pensacola on Its Own," *Florida Historical Quarterly,* XXVII (April, 1948), 283-99.

IV. MILITARY HISTORY

BALTZELL, George F., Colonel, U.S.A., "The Battle of Olustee," *Florida Historical Quarterly,* IX (April, 1931), 199-223.

BIBLIOGRAPHY

BORNET, Vaughn D., "A Connecticut Yankee After Olustee," *Florida Historical Quarterly,* XXVII (April, 1949), 358-403.

———, "A Connecticut Yankee Fights at Olustee," *Florida Historical Quarterly,* XXVII (July, 1949), 237-59.

BOYD, Mark F., "The Battle of Marianna," *Florida Historical Quarterly,* XXIX (April, 1951), 225-42.

———, "The Federal Campaign of 1864 in East Florida," *Florida Historical Quarterly,* XXIX (July, 1950), 3-37.

———, "The Joint Operations of the Federal Army and Navy Near St. Marks, March 1865," *Florida Historical Quarterly* XXIX (October, 1950), 96-124.

CADWELL, Charles K., *The Old Sixth Regiment* [*Connecticut Volunteers*], *Its War Record, 1861-5.* New Haven: Tuttle, Morehouse and Taylor, Printers, 1875.

CLARK, James H., *The Iron Hearted Regiment: Being an Account of The Battles, Marches and Gallant Deeds Performed by the 115th Regiment N. Y. Vols.* Albany: J. Munsell, 1865.

A Committee of the Regimental Association, *The Story of One Regiment, The Eleventh Maine Infantry Volunteers In The War of The Rebellion.* New York: J. J. Little and Company, 1896.

CROWNINSHIELD, Benjamin W., *A History of the First Regiment of Massachusetts Cavalry Volunteers.* New York: Houghton Mifflin and Company, 1891.

DAVIS, T. Frederick, Engagements at St. Johns Bluff, St. Johns River, Florida, September-October, 1862," *Florida Historical Quarterly,* XV (October, 1936), 77-84.

DICKISON, John J., "Military History of Florida," *Confederate Military History,* 12 volumes. Edited by Clement Anselm Evans. (Atlanta: Confederate Publishing Company, 1898), XI, Part 2, 1-198.

EMILIO, Luis F., *History of the Fifty-Fourth Regiment of Massachusetts Volunteer Infantry, 1863-1865.* Boston: The Boston Book Company, 1891.

FOX, Charles Barnard, *Record of The Service of The Fifty-Fifth Regiment of Massachusetts Volunteer Infantry.* Cambridge: John Wilson and Son, 1868.

HIGGINSON, Thomas Wentworth, *Army Life In A Black Regiment.* Boston: Fields, Osgood and Company, 1870.

———, "Up The St. Mary's," *Atlantic Monthly,* XV (April, 1865), 422-36.

———, "Up The St. Johns," *Atlantic Monthly,* XVI (September, 1865), 311-25.

HOLBROOK, William C., *A Narrative of The Services of The Officers and Enlisted Men of the 7th Regiment of Vermont Volunteers (Veterans), From 1862 to 1866.* New York: American Bank Note Company, 1882.

JONES, Charles C., Jr., *Historical Sketch of The Chatham Artillery During The Confederate Struggle for Independence.* Albany: Joe Munsell, 1867.

LITTLE, Henry F. W., *The Seventh Regiment, New Hampshire Volunteers In The War of The Rebellion.* Concord: Ira C. Evans, 1896.

LONN, Ella, "The Extent and Importance of Federal Naval Raids on Salt Making in Florida, 1862-1865," *Florida Historical Quarterly,* X (April, 1932), 167-84.

MCMORRIES, Edward Young, *History of The First Regiment Alabama Volunteers Infantry of The Confederate States of America.* Montgomery: Brown Printing Company, 1904.

MORRIS, Gouverneur, *The History of A Volunteer Regiment. Being A Succinct Account of The Organization, Services and Adventures of The Sixth Regiment of New York Volunteers Infantry Known as Wilson's Zouaves.* New York: Veterans Publishing Company, 1891.

NICHOLS, James M., *Perry's Saints or the Fighting Parson's Regiment In The War of The Rebellion.* Boston: D. Lathrop and Company, 1886.

PALMER, Abraham J., *The History of The Forty-Eighth Regiment New York State Volunteers In The War For The Union, 1861-1865.* Brooklyn: Veterans Association of the Regiment, 1885.

PETERS, Thelma, "Blockade-Running in the Bahamas During the Civil War," *Tequesta,* V (1945), 16-29.

PRICE, Isaiah, *History of The Ninety-Seventh Regiment, Pennsylvania Volunteer Infantry, During the War of The Rebellion, 1861-1865, With Biographical Sketches of Its Field and Staff Officers and a Complete Record of Each Officer and Enlisted Man.* Philadelphia: Isaiah Price, 1875.

PRINCE, Sigsbee C., Jr., "Edward A. Perry, Yankee General of the Florida Brigade," *Florida Historical Quarterly,* XXIX (January, 1951), 197-205.

ROE, Alfred S., *The Twenty-Fourth Regiment Massachusetts Volunteers 1861-1866.* "New England Guard Regiment." Worcester: Twenty-Fourth Veterans Association, 1907.

SHOREY, Henry A., *The Story of The Maine Fifteenth; Being A Brief Narrative of The More Important Events In The History of The Fifteenth Maine Regiment; Together With A Complete Roster of The Regiment, Embracing The Name of Every Officer And Enlisted Man Serving With It At Any Time During Its Service; And Illustrations And Brief Biographical Sketches of Nearly All The Commissioned Officers of The Regiment.* Bridgton: Press of The Bridgton News, 1890.

TOURTELLOTTE, Jerome, *A History of Company K of The Seventh Connecticut Volunteer Infantry In The Civil War.* N.p.: Privately published, 1910.

WALKLEY, Stephen, *History of The Seventh Connecticut Volunteer Infantry Hawley's Brigade, Terry's Division, Tenth Army Corps, 1861-1865.* Hartford: N.p., 1905.

WELLES, Gideon, "Fort Pickens. Facts in Relation to the Reinforcement of Fort Pickens, in the Spring of 1861," *Galaxy,* XI (January, 1871), 92-107.

WILLIAMS, Ames W., "Stronghold of the Straits. A Short History of Fort Zachary Taylor," *Tequesta,* XIV (1954), 3-25.

WILLIAMSON, Edward C., Jr., "Francis P. Fleming in the War for Southern Independence, Soldiering with the 2nd Florida Regiment," *Florida Historical Quarterly,* XXVIII (July, 1949), 38-52.

[YONGE, Julian Chandler, ed.,] "Federal Raid on Tampa Bay," *Florida Historical Quarterly,* IV (January, 1926), 130-139.

V. THESES AND DISSERTATIONS

BURTCHAELL, Peter Edward, "Economic Change and Population at Cedar Key," Master's thesis, University of Florida, 1949.

DALTON, Jack P., "A History of Florida Baptists," Ph.D. dissertation, University of Florida, 1952.

DAVIS, Horace Gibbs, Jr., "Florida Journalism During The Civil War," Master's thesis, University of Florida, 1952.

DOHERTY, Herbert J., Jr., "The Florida Whigs," Master's thesis, University of Florida, 1949.

FERRELL, Sidney Scaife, "Public Opinion in Confederate Florida." Master's thesis, University of Florida, 1950.

FUTCH, Ovid Leon, "Salmon P. Chase and Radical Politics in Florida, 1862-1865." Master's thesis, University of Florida, 1952.

GAINES, John Pendleton, Jr., "A Century in Florida Journalism." Master's thesis, University of Florida, 1949.

GAMMON, William Lamar, II, "Governor John Milton of Florida, Confederate States of America." Master's thesis, University of Florida, 1948.

HILDREATH, Charles Halsey, "A History of Gainesville, Florida." Ph.D. dissertation, University of Florida, 1954.

MICKLER, Thomas Rogers, "The Catholic Church in the Southland." Master's thesis, Georgetown University, 1923.

PROCTOR, Samuel, "History of the University of Florida." Ph.D. dissertation, University of Florida, 1956.

RHODES, Francis Arlington, "The Legal Development of State Supported Higher Education in Florida." Ph.D. dissertation, University of Florida, 1948.

SANFORD, Robert Meriwether, "The Literary Elements of the Florida Newspapers of the Civil War Period." Master's thesis, University of Florida, 1936.

THOMPSON, Arthur W., "David Yulee: A Study of Nineteenth Century Thought and Enterprise." Ph.D. dissertation, Columbia University, 1954.

WILLIAMS, Edwin L., Jr., "Florida in the Union, 1845-1861." Ph.D. dissertation, University of North Carolina, 1951.

VI. Bibliographical Aids

BARTLETT, John Russell, *The Literature of the Rebellion. A Catalogue of Books and Pamphlets Relating to the Civil War in the United States and on Subjects Growing Out of That Event Together with Works on American Slavery, and Essays from Reviews and Magazines on the Same Subjects.* Boston: Draper and Holliday, 1866.

Bibliography of State Participation in the Civil War 1861-1865. Washington: Government Printing Office, 1913.

COULTER, Ellis Merton, *Travels in the Confederate States, A Bibliography.* Norman: University of Oklahoma Press, 1948.

GREGORY, Winifred, ed., *American Newspapers 1821-1936. A Union List of Files Available in the United States and Canada.* New York: The H. W. Wilson Company, 1937.

EMIG, Elmer, "A Check List of Extant Florida Newspapers, 1845-1876," *Florida Historical Quarterly,* XI (October, 1932), 77-87.

INDEX

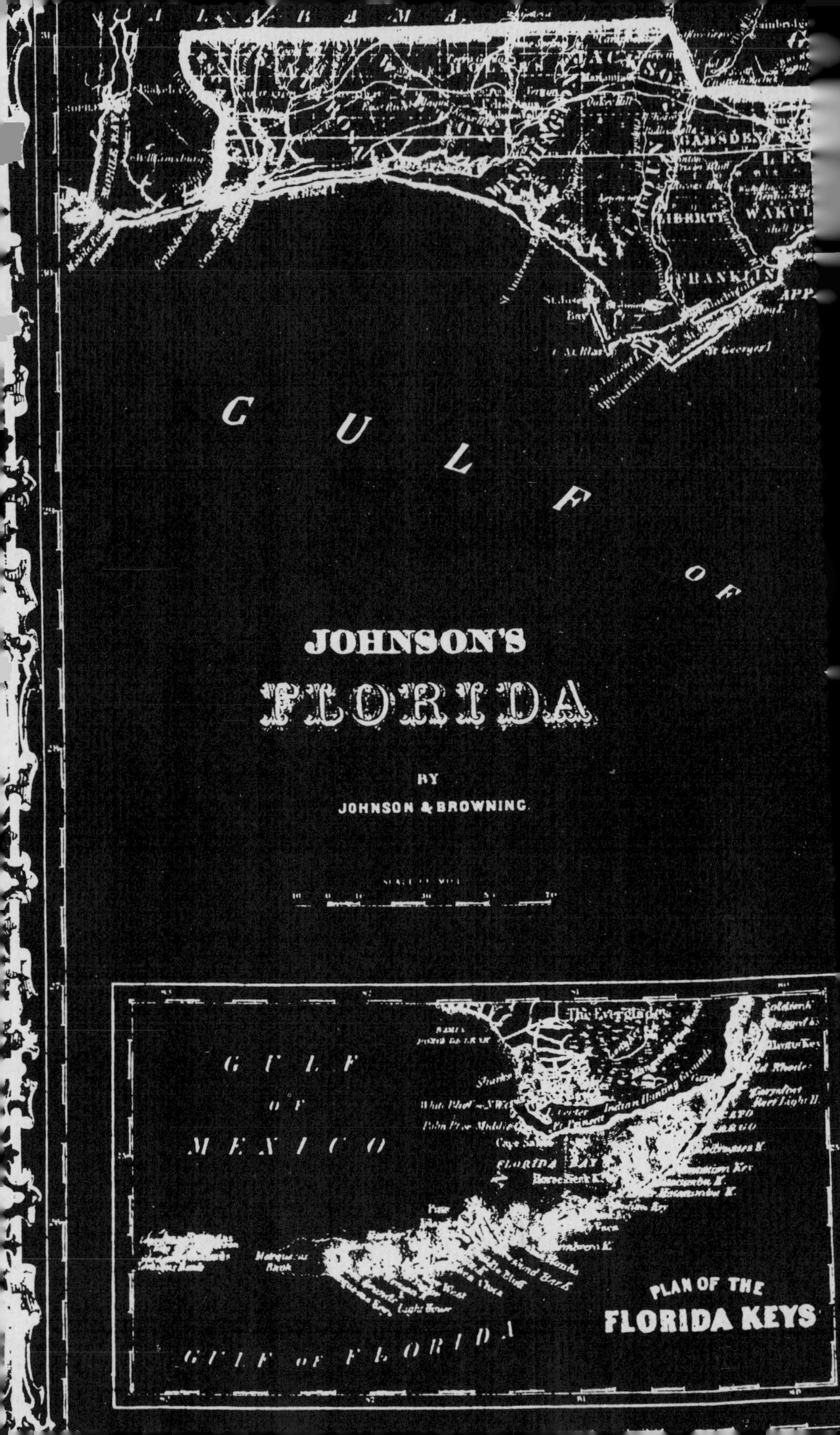

GULF OF

JOHNSON'S FLORIDA

BY

JOHNSON & BROWNING

LIBERTY

FRANKLIN

GADSDEN

WAKULLA